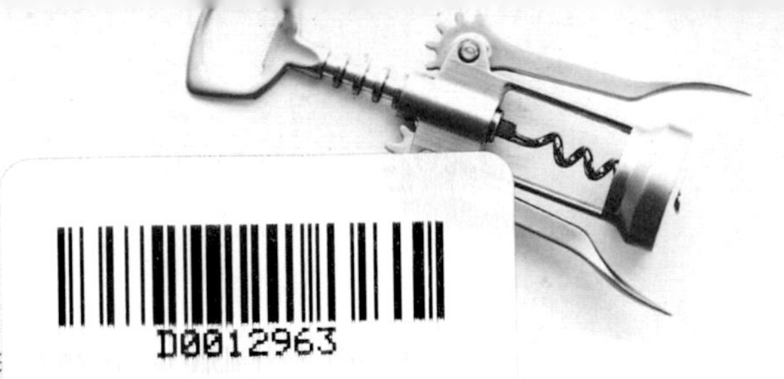

“If you ha

mysteries of wine, and the airs of people who claim to know something about it, *Cork Dork* is essential reading. Read it and you will never look at wine in quite the same way again. This is reportage of a high order.” —ROGER COHEN, author of *The Girl from Human Street*

“Reading Bianca Bosker is like sitting down with a brilliant, curious friend for an after-work drink, and suddenly finding it’s midnight and the table is littered with empty bottles. Between her hilarious exploits and thoughtful meditations on wine and life, you’ll want to stay for just one more.” —LAUREN COLLINS, author of *When in French*

“Always perceptive, curious, and entertaining . . . even those less inclined to imbibe will be intrigued by Bosker’s insights into the nature of smell and taste and the ways training and attention can increase one’s pleasure in them.”
—*Kirkus Reviews* (starred review)

PENGUIN BOOKS

Cork Dork

Bianca Bosker is an award-winning journalist who has written about food, wine, architecture, and technology for *The New Yorker* online, *The Atlantic, T: The New York Times Style Magazine, Food & Wine, The Wall Street Journal, The Guardian*, and *The New Republic*. The former executive tech editor of *The Huffington Post*, she is the author of the critically acclaimed book *Original Copies: Architectural Mimicry in Contemporary China* (University of Hawaii Press, 2013). She lives in New York City.

Cork Dork

A Wine-Fueled Adventure Among the Obsessive Sommeliers, Big Bottle Hunters, and Rogue Scientists Who Taught Me to Live for Taste

Bianca Bosker

PENGUIN BOOKS

PENGUIN BOOKS

An imprint of Penguin Random House LLC
375 Hudson Street
New York, New York 10014
penguin.com

LIBRARY OF CONGRESS CATALOGING-IN-PUBLICATION DATA
Title: Cork dork : A wine-fueled adventure among the obsessive sommeliers, big bottle hunters, and rogue scientists who taught me to live for taste/ Bianca Bosker.
Description: New York : Penguin Books, 2017. | Includes bibliographical references.
Identifiers: LCCN 2016029203 (print) | LCCN 2016031101 (ebook) | ISBN 9780143128090 | ISBN 9780698195905
Subjects: LCSH: Wine and wine making—Social aspects.
Classification: LCC TP548 .B757 2017 (print) | LCC TP548 (ebook) | DDC 641.2/2—dc23

Printed in the United States of America
1 3 5 7 9 10 8 6 4 2

Set in Baskerville MT Std • *Designed by Elke Sigal*

For Matt

CONTENTS

INTRODUCTION

The Blind Tasting

PERFUME WAS THE FIRST TO GO, BUT I'D BEEN EXPECTING THAT. Scented detergent followed, then dryer sheets. I wasn't sorry to give up raw onions or hot sauce. Not adding extra salt was rough at first, tolerable for a bit, then miserable. When I went out to eat, everything tasted like it had been doused in brine. Losing Listerine wasn't so bad; replacing it with a rinse of citric-acid solution and watered-down whiskey was. I went through a dark phase when I cut out coffee. But by that point, I was used to being a little slow in the morning. Daytime sobriety was ancient history, along with all hot liquids, the enamel on my teeth, and my Advil supply.

All this was part of the deprivation routine I cobbled together at the advice of more than two dozen sommeliers, who, over the course of a year and a half, became my mentors, tormentors, drill sergeants, bosses, and friends.

You might be wondering why I'd spend eighteen months getting coached by a bunch of pinstripe-wearing bottle pushers. After all, aren't sommeliers just glorified waiters with a fancy name (*somm-el-yay*) who intimidate diners into splurging on wine?

That was pretty much how I saw them, too, until I handed myself over to an elite clan of sommeliers for whom serving wine is less a job than a way of life, one of living for taste above all else. They enter high-stakes wine competitions (sometimes while nine months pregnant), handle millions of dollars in liquid gold, and make it their mission to convince the world that beauty in flavor belongs on the same aesthetic plane as beauty in art or music. They study weather reports to see if rain will dull their noses, and lick rocks to improve their taste buds. Toothpaste is a liability. They complain about that "new glass" smell, and sacrifice marriages in the name of palate practice. One master sommelier, whose wife divorced him over his compulsive studying, told me, "Certainly, if I had to choose between passing my exam and that relationship that I had, I would still choose passing my exam." Their job depends on detecting, analyzing, describing, and accounting for variations of flavor in a liquid that's compound-for-compound the most complicated drink on the planet. "There's hundreds and hundreds of volatiles. There's polysaccharides. There's proteins. Amino acids. Biogenic amines. Organic acids. Vitamins. Carotenoids," an enology professor explained to me. "After blood, wine is the most complex matrix there is."

With that obsessive focus on minute differences in flavor comes—actually, I wasn't sure what, exactly. At least, not when I started. I came to these sommeliers wanting to know what life was like for them, out at the extremes of taste, and how they'd gotten there. It turned into a question of whether I could get there too—if any of us could—and what would change if I did.

Some words of warning:

For you, a glass of wine might be your happy place. The thing you reach for at the end of a long day, when you switch off a part of your brain. If you want to keep it that way, then stay far, far away from the individuals in this book.

On the other hand, if you've ever wondered what all the fuss is about wine, whether there's really a discernible difference between a $20 and $200 bottle, or what would happen if you pushed your senses to their limits—well then, I have some people I'd like you to meet.

Spend enough time in the wine world, and you'll find every connoisseur has a story about *the* bottle that launched their obsession with wine. Usually, their Saul-on-the-road-to-Damascus moment arrives via, say, a 1961 Giacomo Conterno Barolo sipped in a little restaurant in Piedmont, Italy, overlooking the Langhe hills, the beech trees swaying as a gentle fog curls up from the valley floor. It's something of a formula: Europe + natural splendor + rare wine = moment of enlightenment.

My wine epiphany came slightly differently: at a computer screen. And I wasn't even drinking—I was watching others do it.

At the time, I was a technology reporter covering the Googles and Snapchats of the world for an online-only news site, and I was doing most things via screens. I'd spent half a decade on the tech beat, writing virtual articles about virtual things in virtual universes that couldn't be tasted, felt, touched, or smelled. To me, "immersive" meant websites with really big digital photos, and the words "it smells" could only ever refer to a problem—BO, a coworker's lunch, spoiled milk in the office fridge. I once made someone do a story titled "How to Take a Vacation on Google Street View," as if scrolling through blurry photos of Hawaii's Waikoloa Village could be a reasonable substitute for lounging around with a Mai Tai in the late afternoon sun.

One Sunday evening, my then-boyfriend-now-husband dragged me to a restaurant on the lower rim of Central Park. It was the type of place that prides itself on applying to food what J. P. Morgan purportedly said about yachts: If you have to ask the price, you can't afford it. I would usually have steered clear of this place for fear of bankruptcy—financial and possibly spiritual—but we were going to meet his client Dave. And Dave liked wine.

I liked wine the same way I liked Tibetan hand puppetry or theoretical particle physics, which is to say I had no idea what was going on but was content to smile and nod. It seemed like one of those things that took way more effort than it was worth to understand. Dave collected old wines from Bordeaux. I'd go so far as to say I generally preferred wines from a bottle, but I certainly wouldn't have turned up my nose at something boxed.

We'd barely taken our seats when the sommelier came over. Naturally, he was an old friend of Dave's. After offering a few platitudes about a "good year" and "elegant nose," he disappeared to fetch us a bottle, then returned to pour Dave a taste. "It's drinking really well right now," murmured the sommelier, employing the sort of nonsense phrase that's only credible to people who use "summer" as a verb. The wine, as far as I could tell, was not doing anything so much as "sitting" in the glass.

As the two men oohed and aahed over the bottle's exquisite aromas of shaved graphite and tar, I began to tune them out. But then the sommelier mentioned he was preparing for the World's Best Sommelier Competition.

Excuse me?

At first, the idea seemed ridiculous. How could serving wine possibly be a competitive sport? Open, pour, and you're done. Right?

The sommelier quickly ran through the contest's main events. Most difficult and nerve-racking of all was the blind tasting, which required him to identify the complete pedigree of some half dozen wines: the year each was made, from what species of grapes, in what small corner of the planet (think vineyard, not country), plus how long it could be aged, what to eat with it, and why.

Truth be told, it sounded like the least fun anyone's ever had with alcohol. But I love a competition, the less athletic and more gluttonous the better, so when I got home that night, I did some digging to see what this sommelier face-off was all about.

I became obsessed. I lost entire afternoons glued to my laptop watching videos of competitors uncorking, decanting, sniffing, and spitting in their quest for the title of World's Best Sommelier. It was like the Westminster Dog Show, with booze: In one event after another, well-groomed specimens with coiffured hair and buffed nails duked it out at a pursuit where success came down to inscrutable minutiae, a grim-faced panel of judges, and the grace with which candidates walked in a circle. (Sommeliers should turn clockwise, *only*, around a table.) The hopefuls chose their words as if being charged by the syllable and studied their guests (not customers—*"guests"*) for precious hints about their moods, budgets, and tastes. Seeing a desperate bid for control in the faint quiver of a hand pouring at an awkward angle, I sensed their craft was governed by stringent rules that I couldn't guess, let alone appreciate. But it was clear they were not to be broken: Véronique Rivest, the first woman ever to make it to the competition's final round, beat her fists when she forgot to offer her guests coffee or cigars. "*Merde, merde, MERDE!*" she moaned. "Shit, shit, SHIT!" There was no trace of irony. It was riveting.

I found out later that one contestant had taken dancing lessons to perfect his elegant walk across the floor. Another hired a speech coach to help him modulate his voice into a velvety baritone, plus a memory expert to strengthen his recall of vineyard names. Others consulted sports psychologists to learn how to stay cool under pressure.

If service was an art, the blind tasting looked downright magical. In one video, Véronique glided onstage, camera shutters clicking in the background, and approached a table lined with four glasses, each filled with a few ounces of wine. She reached for a white, and stuck her nose deep into the glass. I held my breath and leaned into my screen. She had just 180 seconds to zero in on the precise aromas and flavors that defined the wine, then correctly deduce what she was drinking. There are more than 50 different countries that produce wine; nearly 200 years of drinkable wines; more than 340 distinct wine appellations in France alone; and more than 5,000 types of grapes that can be blended in a virtually infinite number of ways. So, if you do the math—*multiply, add, carry the three*—you get approximately a bazillion different combinations. She was undaunted, and rattled off the profile of a 2011 Chenin Blanc from Maharashtra, India, with the ease of someone giving directions to her house.

I was captivated by these people who had honed the kind of sensory acuity I'd thus far assumed belonged exclusively to bomb-sniffing German shepherds. I felt like these sommeliers and I existed at opposite extremes: While my life was one of sensory deprivation, theirs was one of sensory cultivation. They made me wonder what I might be missing. Sitting in front of my computer screen, watching videos of people sniffing wine on repeat, I resolved to find out what that was.

I am a journalist by training and a type-A neurotic by birth, so I started my research the only way I knew how: I read everything I could get my hands on, carpet-bombed sommeliers' in-boxes, and showed up at places uninvited, just to see who I'd meet.

My first night out with a herd of New York City sommeliers did not end well. I kicked things off by crashing a blind tasting competition at a distributor's office, where I sipped a few glasses along with the judges, tasted a dozen or so wines in celebration of the winner, trailed everyone to a hotel bar for another round, then skipped dinner in favor of a bottle of Champagne that a thirsty sommelier insisted I split with him. Next, I stumbled home and immediately threw up.

Early the next morning, while I was Googling "hangover cure" with one eye open, I received a text message from the guy who'd ordered the bubbly the night before. It was a photo of six wines lined up in front of him. He was tasting. *Again.*

Lesson one: These people are relentless.

This all-hours fervor was a far cry from what I'd found when I went digging through books and magazines for clues about how I could follow in the footsteps of someone like Véronique. The literature makes a life in wine seem utterly sybaritic: a lot of fancy men (because it's traditionally been men) drinking fancy bottles in fancy places. A hard day's work was choking down a bottle of Bordeaux less than a decade old. "Casting a backward glance at my first trip to the Loire, I see a younger man who supported discomforts that sound torturous today," writes wine importer Kermit Lynch in his memoir, *Adventures on the Wine Route*. What were these torturous discomforts he endured? He "flew from San Francisco to New York, changed planes, landed in Paris, rented a car, and drove to the Loire." *Quelle horreur!*

But as I spent more time with sommeliers—eventually drinking at late hours in their apartments and being schooled in the art of spitting—I grew fascinated by a subculture I didn't see reflected in anything I'd read about wine. For a field that's ostensibly all about pleasure, the current generation of sommeliers, or "somms," puts themselves through an astonishing amount of pain. They work long hours on their feet late into the night, wake up early to cram facts from wine encyclopedias, rehearse decanting in the afternoons, devote days off to competitions, and dedicate the few remaining minutes to sleep—or, more likely, to mooning over a rare bottle of Riesling. It is, in the words of one sommelier, "like some blood sport with corkscrews." Another called what they feel for wine a "sickness." They were the most masochistic hedonists I'd ever met.

Nothing I watched or read captured all the idiosyncrasies of the trade. Many decades ago, sommeliers were often failed chefs. They were booted from kitchens, then conscripted to a job they performed with all the charm of the beasts of burden for which they're named. (The word "sommelier" comes from *sommier*, Middle French for packhorse.) They had a reputation for stalking the floors of stuffy French restaurants wearing dark suits and scowls, like judgy undertakers. But the latest up-and-coming somms have left fancy schools to eagerly pursue what they consider a calling. They are, like me, in their late twenties, childless, worried about rent, and still trying to convince their parents they haven't ruined their lives by not going to law school.

Armed with master's degrees in philosophy or Stanford engineering degrees, these self-proclaimed "white-collar refugees" espouse lofty theories about service and ambitious ideas about wine's potential to move the soul. And they've brought both youth and XX chromosomes to an industry that's long resembled a good-ol'-boys fraternity.

Initially, my interest was largely journalistic. All my life, I've been obsessed with other people's obsessions. I've never stood in line for hours to scream my head off at a teenage heartthrob or decided to "date" a character in a video game, but I've spent years writing about—and trying to figure out—the sort of people who do. So naturally, the somms' passion instantly sucked me in. I became fixated on understanding what drove them. Why were they consumed by wine? And how had this "sickness" upended their lives?

Yet as I dug deeper into their world, something unexpected happened: I started to feel uncomfortable. Not with the sommeliers—who, aside from a tendency to overserve me, were perfectly charming—but with my own attitude and assumptions. The truth is, the strongest emotion I'd ever felt for wine was something like shame-infused guilt. More than any other edible thing on this planet, wine is celebrated as part and parcel of a civilized life. Robert Louis Stevenson called wine "bottled poetry," and Benjamin Franklin declared it "constant proof that God loves us"—things no one's ever said about, say, lamb chops or lasagna, delicious as they might be. The somms spoke of bottles that sent their spirits soaring like a Rachmaninoff symphony. "They make you feel small," one gushed. I didn't have a clue what they were talking about, and frankly, it sounded farfetched. Were they full of shit, or was I somehow deficient in my ability to appreciate one of life's ultimate pleasures? I wanted to know what these oenophiles meant, and why otherwise rational people devote mind-boggling amounts of money and time to chasing down a few ephemeral seconds of flavor. To put it more bluntly, I wanted to know: What's the big deal about wine?

When I drank a glass of wine, it was as if my taste buds were firing off a message written in code. My brain could only decipher a few words. "Blahblahblahblah wine! You're drinking wine!"

But to connoisseurs, that garbled message can be a story about the iconoclast in Tuscany who said *Vaffanculo!* to Italy's wine rules and planted French Cabernet Sauvignon vines, or the madman vintner who dodged shell fire and tanks to make vintage after vintage all through Lebanon's fifteen-year civil war. That same mouthful can tell a tale about a nation's evolving laws, or the lazy cellar dweller who botched his task of cleaning the winery's barrels. These drinkers' senses offer them access to a fuller world, where histories, aspirations, and ecosystems emerge from tastes and smells.

My obliviousness to such nuances started to drive me crazy. Now as I listened to my friends swear off Starbucks for $4 cold-brew coffee or rave about single-origin chocolate bars, I began to notice a paradox in our foodie culture. We obsess over finding or making food and drink that tastes better—planning travel itineraries, splurging on tasting menus, buying exotic ingredients, lusting after the freshest produce. Yet we do nothing to teach ourselves to be better tasters. "We are as a nation taste-blind," wrote M. F. K. Fisher, a criticism that, from everything I'd observed, remains as true today as it was in 1937.

A more personal and profound concern quickly overshadowed my journalistic curiosity. I'd lately had flashes of frustration with my tech-centric existence, the textures of stories and life all flattened by the glossy sameness of screens. The more I learned, the more confined and incomplete my own tiny corner of experience appeared. Merely writing about the sommeliers suddenly seemed inadequate. What I wanted, instead, was to become like them.

I began to ask myself: What would it take for me to uncover the same things in wine that they did? Did these pros get where they are through practice alone? Or were they genetically blessed mutants born with an innate sensitivity to smell?

I'd always assumed that super sensers were born, not made, the way Novak Djokovic was endowed with the wingspan to crush all comers. Turns out, that's no excuse. As I began supplementing my YouTube binges with a healthy diet of scientific studies, I found that training our noses and tongues depends first and foremost on training our brains.

Only, most of us haven't bothered to do so. Biased by thinkers as far back as Plato who dismissed taste and smell as the "minor" faculties, most of us don't know the basic truths about these two senses (which we actually have a tendency to confuse with each other). We mix up where we register different tastes (hint: not only in your mouth). We're not even sure how many tastes there are (almost certainly more than the five you've heard of). And we're convinced that humans evolved to be the animal kingdom's worst smellers (even though recent research suggests that's a myth). In essence, we all but ignore two of the five senses that we've been given to take in and interpret the world.

I was impatient to make a change and discover what I was neglecting, both in wine and in life. The somms I met described how their training had helped them do everything from finding fresh pleasure in their everyday routines, to staying true to sensory perception, fending off interference from extraneous noise about price or brand. It seemed possible for any of us to relish richer experiences by tuning into the sensory information we overlook. And I was thirsty to give it a go.

This book traces the year I spent among flavor freaks, sensory scientists, big-bottle hunters, smell masterminds, tipsy hedonists, rule-breaking winemakers, and the world's most ambitious sommeliers. It is not a wine buyer's guide, or a credulous celebration of all wine-drinking traditions. In fact, it explores the ways in which the industry is—in the words of one Princeton University wine economist—"intrinsically bullshit-prone." But clear aside the bullshit, and what remains are insights that have relevance far outside the realm of food and drink.

Less a journey from grape to glass (though there will be glimpses at how wine is made), this is an adventure from glass to gullet—into the wild world of wine obsession and appreciation in all its forms and with all its flaws. It's an investigation of how we relate to a 7,000-year-old liquid that has charmed Egyptian monarchs, destitute farmers, Russian tsars, Wall Street moguls, suburban parents, and Chinese college kids. Prepare to go behind the scenes in Michelin-star dining rooms, into orgiastic bacchanals for the 0.1 percent, back in time to the first restaurants, and into fMRI machines and research labs. Along the way, you'll meet the madman who hazed me, the cork dork who coached me, the Burgundy collector who tried to seduce me, and the scientist who studied me.

The relationship between taste and appreciating life runs through our language. We say variety is the "spice" of life. In Spanish, the verb *gustar*—to like or to please—comes from the Latin *gustare*, meaning "to taste," the same root for our English word "gustatory"—concerned with tasting. So, in Spanish, when you say that you like something—clothes, democracy, artwork, can openers—you are, in an ancient sense, saying that it tastes good to you. In English, when we apply ourselves with passion and enthusiasm, we say we've done something with "gusto," which stems from the same Latin root. A person who likes the right things is said to have good taste—no matter if those things, like music, cannot be tasted at all.

Taste is not just our default metaphor for savoring life. It is so firmly embedded in the structure of our thought that it has ceased to be a metaphor at all. For the sommeliers, sensory scholars, winemakers, connoisseurs, and collectors I met, to taste better is to live better, and to know ourselves more deeply. And I saw that tasting better had to begin with the most complex edible of all: wine.

Cork Dork

CHAPTER ONE

The Rat

WHEN YOU INFORM YOUR FRIENDS AND RELATIVES THAT YOU HAVE left your stable job as a journalist to stay home and taste wines, you will begin to get concerned phone calls. You say: I'm going to hone my senses and find out what the big deal is about wine. They hear: I'm quitting my job to drink all day and improve my chances of ending up homeless.

I told them there was nothing to worry about. I was going to get a job in the wine industry. It's a real profession. I would be able to pay the rent. The problem was that it had been nearly two months and there was no job yet, not even the prospect of one. And I *was* drinking more. Going to wine events, meeting with anyone who would talk to me, cracking open two or three bottles of Pinot Noir at a time. The hand towels in my bathroom were stained purple from the red wine that clung to my lips. When my husband went out without me, friends asked him, "Where's Bianca?" and then, in a hushed voice: *"Is she drinking?"*

Wine people love to talk about wine, I'd assured myself. Show up, demonstrate interest, and ride the Grand Cru Express from there. When I quit my job, it wasn't like I had *no* plan. I had a tentative three-step program sketched out with all the cringeworthy confidence of a pushy reporter. First, I would get a new job. The only way

I could understand the sommelier experience was to join their ranks, I reasoned. Modestly, I figured I would shoot for assistant sommelier at a restaurant with two Michelin stars (I could work my way up to three stars). Second, I would find a mentor, a wise Obi-Wan Kenobi type who would recognize that the Force was strong within me and teach me the secrets of the palate and the nose. Third, I would pass the Court of Master Sommeliers' Certified Sommelier Exam, a daylong test for wine pros, so I could ascend to higher echelons of the industry.

That was before I knew that somms had a name for people like me: I was a "civilian"—an outsider, a customer, an amateur, who didn't know what it was like to count thousands of bottles of wine over the better part of a day in the chill of a cellar, or placate the restaurant owner's fussy friend who sent back a $2,100 bottle of 1988 Guigal "La Landonne" for being "too weak" (which is like claiming a rocket launcher is "not explosive enough"). Civilians, even wine-collecting connoisseurs, do not *really* know what it means to live for—and rearrange your whole life around—a few fleeting chemical reactions on your tongue and in your nasal passages. Civilians enjoy wine; sommeliers surrender themselves to it, blinded by the kind of inflamed passion that leads to irrational, even self-destructive, life choices. Civilians are humored because, technically, sommeliers exist to serve them and the system requires that someone pay the check at the end of the meal. But they are kept at arm's length and there is a line they cannot cross. These uninitiated amateurs, a class to which I indisputably belonged, are not worthy of admission into the sanctum sanctorum of sommeliers' cellars, tasting groups, and restaurant floors.

In short, my initial confidence was completely misguided. While I spoke to many people in the wine world during those first couple of months, the only skill I can say I truly mastered was picking which wine pairs best with a generous serving of humble pie. (Answer: any wine.)

That's approximately where my life stood when I met Joe Campanale.

In a restaurant scene notorious for being stingy with praise, everyone I talked to considered Joe a superstar. Barely thirty years old, Joe had already opened four successful restaurants in downtown Manhattan as a partner and beverage director. His track record was all the more remarkable because New York is to restaurant failure roughly what Saudi Arabia is to oil production. Restaurateurs kept telling me the same joke: How do you make a small fortune in the restaurant business? Start with a large fortune.

Every job I had tried to finagle my way into so far wanted the one thing I didn't have: experience. But the only way to get experience was through a job. To wrangle a meeting so I could float the idea of being hired, my latest strategy had been to go as far as my journalistic integrity would allow in hinting I'd like to write a glowing profile of all the exciting things going on at [insert restaurant name here]. Then I'd casually drop my interest in becoming a sommelier. It had not been going well.

I felt like a hapless fisherman wearily casting out my line one last time before returning to shore empty-handed yet again. But with Joe, something funny happened.

A bite.

"Our cellar hand—actually, she just got injured and she won't be able to do the necessary . . ." Joe let his gaze stray to my biceps. "Well, it's a little bit of a physical job," he explained. "Can you lift boxes?"

Not really, no, but of course that's not what I told Joe. I wanted to hear more about this cellar-hand business. It sounded anachronistic, a little like a chimney sweep or town crier. I quickly learned that cellar hand was the polite title. Around the restaurant, it was called cellar *rat.* It didn't have quite the ring of my previous title, "Executive Technology Editor." Never mind that. I was desperate. Desperate to break into the industry, desperate to prove to all those who loved me that I was not on the fast track to rehab, and certainly desperate enough to ignore all the warning signs.

I accepted on the spot. I would be working at L'Apicio, the newest and largest restaurant in Joe's growing empire. The interview had been suspiciously quick, and I had only a dim idea of what the job entailed. It paid $10 an hour, but the real reward came from the access I'd get to Joe's expertise and his wine.

During my months of unemployment, I had been collecting career advice from sommeliers and wine-industry veterans. They laid out a picture of a traditional system of apprenticeship and patronage that seemed more like something out of Renaissance Florence than twenty-first-century New York. A sommelier is not like a lawyer. There are no years of formal schooling you must go through and no government licenses you must secure. In theory, anyone can waltz into a restaurant and *call* herself a sommelier. In practice, this will get you nowhere. Especially in a world-class food city like New York, it would be like me pulling on a pair of baggy pants under a striped shirt and trying to walk into Yankees Spring Training. If your goal is to be a sommelier at one of the planet's top restaurants, the process of getting there makes law school look like a comparatively short, cheap walk in the park.

In the unofficial apprenticeship system, a novice might begin stocking bottles as a cellar rat, graduate to back-waiter or wine-store clerk, eventually advance to server, then to sommelier, and, one day, maybe, to head sommelier or beverage director, the person who oversees all things liquid, from espresso to Zinfandel. That might lead to a job as a general manager or off the floor to serve as a wine director for a restaurant group. An earlier generation of sommeliers established their reputation by word of mouth, parlaying their mentor's good name into plum jobs. But competition has intensified, and now up-and-coming wine pros are combining the old-fashioned approach with the imprimatur of diplomas, pins, and certificates from august-sounding organizations like the Wine & Spirit Education Trust, or the Court of Master Sommeliers. It can take years to get a spot in the best restaurants, and even then you need the perfect combination of hard skills, charisma, and that je ne sais quoi that can't be taught.

The cellar-rat job was not sexy, but it fit perfectly in my (revised) plan. Joe promised that it would give me an excellent view into the wine program—what sells, when, to whom, how, for how much—and that I'd familiarize myself with wine regions just by handling his bottles. Plus, the quid pro quo of the wine trade ensured that in exchange for my labor I'd have ample opportunity to taste. I'd have carte blanche each Thursday to sample wines with Joe, who welcomed a rotating lineup of distributors eager to audition bottles for his lists. On top of *that*, I'd get a free pass to sample as much wine as I could stomach at the near-daily tastings hosted by local distributors, all-you-can-drink wine buffets meant to showcase new inventory to the city's somms.

In a sense, entry-level jobs in the wine world pay not in cash but in tastes. Especially for young sommeliers, the most coveted positions present the chance to sample a wide variety of bottles. I met a sommelier who'd abandoned the top post as wine director at a hip Napa Valley restaurant—along with a girlfriend, house, car, and dog—for a far less prestigious job in New York, with the sole aim of improving his palate. "I can taste more wines in a night in New York than in a year in California," he explained.

As cellar rat, I would go from trying three to four (cheap) wines a week on my own to trying dozens if not hundreds of wines a week from every imaginable region and at every price point. This is why it is almost impossible to become a master taster without either working in the wine business or being very, very rich. There would be weeks when I'd be able to try thousands of dollars' worth of wine without paying a cent. For a neophyte like me looking to build her mental library of tastes from scratch, it was a dream come true.

What Joe conveniently failed to mention was that my dream job had a track record of ending in disaster.

At one o'clock on a Wednesday, I presented myself to L'Apicio's assistant beverage director Lara Lowenhar, a Long Island native in her thirties with pencil-thin eyebrows, round cheeks, and dark maroon lipstick the color of her perfect, polished nails. She walked me through the checkered history of past cellar rats.

The first was most memorable for all the huffing and puffing she did lugging wine boxes up stairs and a face that got "really red." She didn't last long. Her successor spent a lot of time crying in the cellar. "It was too much for her," said Lara in a throaty voice, the legacy, I guessed, of the decade or so she'd spent shouting over packed dining rooms. "When I say manual labor, I am not kidding. It was just *too much* for her." Her replacement wound up getting sick on the job—something about low blood sugar—and the replacement's replacement, the one who'd gotten hurt, had been a problem practically from the start. "I forget her name, that's how insignificant she was," Lara said with a sigh. "She was actually the one that tried my patience the most because I couldn't understand what was wrong. She taught me how not to yell. . . . She was really frustrating." And now, Lara had me.

"I'm very patient," Lara informed me. It came out sounding more like a warning, one of those hollow assurances, like "dolphin-safe," that produces doubt by even having to be uttered.

Lara started my tour of L'Apicio by the service entrance, which I was to use from now on. Housed on the Lower East Side next to a boiler repair service and two artisanal juice shops, L'Apicio had unmarred double doors that opened from East First Street directly into the hive of the kitchen. It was noisy and active, and I was instantly in somebody's way. I did a spastic jig to dodge two pans of roasted vegetables and jerked into a tray of candleholders. Lara, correctly surmising that I was a danger to myself and others, launched into a spiel on the decorum of the floor. "When you're walking in a restaurant and you're going to be behind somebody, you either put your hand on their back while you're walking past or you say 'behind' so that they know not to turn around," she instructed patiently. We sidestepped a man in Crocs hurling flattened cardboard boxes onto an already full dumpster, then past someone—BEHIIIIIIND!—carrying soup pots to a sink. People were polishing glasses, hacking at mushrooms, measuring out grated Parmesan, and humming along to Shakira. Just beyond, at a grid of white prep counters, the real action was under way. A blur of bodies hoisted copper pots and skipped knives across bundles of green. Lara didn't even attempt to steer me through.

None of this would involve me. I was there to lock myself, alone, into a small, dark, freezing closet that Lara generously introduced as the wine cellar. It was narrow enough that the two of us couldn't stand shoulder to shoulder; long enough to fit forty bottles of wine stacked side by side, neck to neck; and tall enough that I couldn't see to the upper shelves without scrambling up a stilctto-thin metal ladder.

"This is the Bible," Lara said, thrusting a clipboard with wrinkled sheets of white paper into my hands. "This is the most important thing in your life."

The most important thing in my life appeared to be written in code. I stared blankly at one line: "DETTORI MOSCADEDDU 2010 L12 DE."

"This is our cellar map. It runs in alphabetical order by producer, with producer, fantasy name, vintage, and then the locations," said Lara.

"L12 DE" referred to bottles that were on the left-hand shelf, in row 12, columns D through E. "Dettori" was short for Tenute Dettori, the producer. "Moscadeddu" was the *nome di fantasia*, or fantasy name, an optional nickname that winemakers may give a certain line of their wines to set them apart, or, I was getting the impression, to torture cellar rats like me. Lara tried to help me get my bearings. Generally speaking, she explained, a bottle's label lists some combination of producer name, fantasy name, and vintage (the year the grapes were harvested). It might also specify the grape variety used ("Pinot Gris," "Fiano," "Aglianico") or the appellation, the region in which the vines were grown ("Sonoma Valley," "Soave," "Chianti"). But often, it won't list both. Especially for European wines, producers assumed the name of the appellation was all a drinker needed to glean what kind of grape had been used for the wine. Only a feeble-minded philistine wouldn't know that, by law, a Chianti has to be made with at least 70 percent Sangiovese grapes if it carries the quality assurance of a DOCG certification (short for Denominazione di Origine Controllata e Garantita). Ditto for, say, a DOCG Barolo, which must be 100 percent Nebbiolo.

I picked up a bottle in L15 J and studied the label trying to find its producer, just to see if I could hack it on my own. "Coenobium" was written in huge letters across the top. That had to be the producer.

"Um, koh-no-bee-yum?" I guessed.

That was the fantasy name, and it was pronounced "*Sen*-no-bee-yum." I tried again. "Lazio?" That was the name of the town. Lara ran her finger down a long paragraph in Italian, past the fine print about alcohol level and bottle number and sulfite content and some government identification code. She stopped next to a microscopic line of text at the bottom edge of the label. "Monastero Suore Cistercensi" it read. The producer. Of course.

I was in charge of cellaring all new wine when it arrived. If there wasn't room in the cellar, I should make room in the cellar. I had to unpack the bottles, put each one into a slot, and label its slot in the Bible.

"I don't care where anything is," Lara said. She paused and corrected herself. "But yeah, you definitely want the higher frequency items, like this, here." She considered that statement. "And this"—she pointed at a bottle of red that looked indistinguishable from all the others—"shouldn't be all the way down here." Lara also definitely *did* care about how I placed the wine on the rack, since the cellar was visible from the L'Apicio dining room. "When you pull the front bottle out, pull the back bottle up"—they were two-deep per slot—"because it makes the cellar look full." Oh, and don't mess up, or someone could order a bottle and no one will be able to find it. "And that just sucks for our life."

I attempted to scribble notes as Lara plowed ahead in what seemed like a foreign language. "If something says BTG, then it's BTG, unless we're eighty-six on it." "Your p-mix now lives on the bin map board." This was crucial because I had to religiously check the p-mix (wait, what?) on the bin map (where?) to do something I didn't catch. I'd also need the POs (come again?) that Lara promised to email me before each delivery. New whites had to go into the lowboy, where Lara needed . . . was it two of each? Three? *Shit.* She led me out of the cellar, which I was to keep at vampire-safe darkness to avoid warming the sleeping bottles, and we stopped in front of the lowboys—waist-high fridges behind the bar. I took advantage of a pause in machine-gun-fire instructions to clarify: *BTG* was a wine served "by the glass," *eighty-six* meant "there's no more," *PO* stood for "purchase order," *p-mix* was short for "product mix," and the large metal bowls of hot-sauce-slathered chicken and rice I'd been eyeing in the corner were "family meal" for the staff.

"We call each other a family," said Lara, "because we see each other more than we see our families."

For the next phase of our tour, she ushered me into the coat closet, where Lara raised her arm to pull down a ladder that unfolded from a trapdoor in the ceiling. The rickety ladder resembled the sort of tall thing painters might use, only steeper, suspended from the air, and a few years past its prime. It led up into the attic, which, from the looks of it, was a very dark, very cramped, very uninviting space filled with cardboard boxes and piles of laundry—uniforms, napkins, rags. It was the overflow cellar. Rent in New York being what it is, Lara had to risk less-than-ideal storage conditions and shove excess bottles into the ceiling.

Lara nudged me to climb up the "terrible ladder"—her words—to a so-called landing at the top that consisted of a foot-wide frame around the side of the trapdoor. It was supposed to fit both me and a box of wine. It looked too tiny for either. I was expected to carry twelve-bottle cases of wine—about forty pounds, or nearly a third of my body weight—into and out of the attic on this "terrible ladder."

"I'm scared of it and I've been climbing up and down it for two years," Lara said. I tottered my way up into the crawl space, then watched Lara demonstrate the least risky way to descend. Apparently, my best bet was to get down on my butt, shimmy myself and a box of wine toward the steps a few inches at a time, stand on the upper rungs, and then hoist all twelve bottles to my chest while not tumbling forward onto the concrete floor below. "I've seen a couple of people take a dive, and it doesn't look fun," Lara volunteered.

I am not someone who spends a great deal of time visualizing her own death. But I knew enough to know that dying while ferrying bottles of Pinot Grigio to entitled yuppies was (a) not how I wanted to go out and (b) now a distinct possibility.

I couldn't help but envy the chefs. They got food—colorful, obvious, familiar, recognizable food. I got 1,800 cold bottles with names I had no clue how to pronounce, made in places and with grapes I'd never even heard of. The chefs danced around the kitchen together as a team. I was on my own. They also got to stand on solid ground. I was in over my head.

In my previous job as a journalist, I'd maintained more or less the same routine for five years: Wake up, take the subway to Eighth Street, and arrive at the office by nine thirty a.m. in time for the editorial meeting. Per my Joe-given right as cellar rat, I began visiting free tastings hosted by wine distributors, the middlemen who sell to stores and restaurants a selection of bottles they either import themselves or first buy from importers. Under my new regimen as an official member of New York's wine army, I was nursing my first glass of wine around the same hour I'd usually be running through the morning's headlines. Most days, I was drunk by noon, hungover by two p.m., and, around four in the afternoon, deeply regretting the burger I'd devoured for lunch.

New York was a much, much drunker city than I'd ever imagined. At any time of the day, any day of the week, I could join men in suits to stagger around, purple-toothed and a little buzzed, sampling New York's newest wines. I took the advice of a young sommelier who'd also had to learn to taste on a budget, and used the tastings to feel out the distinct flavor profile of each of the "noble grape" varieties, so called because they're some of the world's most planted grapes. One week, I'd drink nothing but Sauvignon Blanc—from Sancerre in France, Marlborough in New Zealand, Santa Ynez Valley in the United States, and Margaret River in Australia—until my nose and mouth had a handle on all its grassy, limeade permutations. The next week would be exclusively Gewürztraminer. Then Tempranillo, and so on through the biggest celebrity grapes. By keeping the grape variety consistent, I was trying to wrap my tongue around each one's character—Merlot's plumminess, say—and how the grape changed as it crossed climates and countries.

Each Thursday, I'd stumble over to L'Apicio from the distributor free-for-alls for another round of tasting with Joe. For three hours at a stretch, sales reps stopped by with bottles. And I tried them all. Knowing that Joe likes wines with a story to them, the distributors played up the eccentric origins of whatever wild-card winery they'd added to their portfolio. "It was founded five generations ago and revived by his great-granddaughter. . . . There are Roman ruins all along these vineyards and this big hill was Julius Caesar's vacation home. . . . The winery owns a therapy donkey. . . . There was a made-for-TV movie about the producer's time in a forced-labor prison. . . ."

But that still wasn't enough drinking. Blind tasting groups, where somms drill one another on their flavor-deducing skills, would be critical to my success in becoming a better taster. I could get feedback on my tasting technique and learn the ropes from people who knew the art of "blinding," while splitting the costs of opening some eight to twelve wines. So far, I'd weaseled my way into two groups. Fridays I met with other beginners. Wednesdays I gathered with advanced sommeliers. They preferred to taste early in the day, believing their senses to be more alert in the morning than after a day of stimulation, and most of the group worked nights, so at ten a.m. every Wednesday, we'd show up to a somm's apartment in Queens lugging bottles, their labels hidden under crumpled aluminum foil or tall knee socks. Our host lived in a one-bedroom she'd decorated in a style best described as Vinous Chic. There was a waist-high bottle of corks in the corner, a floor-to-ceiling wine fridge, wine encyclopedias in place of coffee-table books, and framed wine labels hanging on walls painted the deep color of Syrah. Our sessions usually started with someone gossiping about the poor form of the guy who'd decanted her wine the night before. By the end, all of us, starving from having skipped breakfast, were debating what wines paired best with stale Doritos.

After my first blind tasting with the pros, they assigned me homework. I had shown up wanting to learn how to taste. That, apparently, was far beyond my level. "First, you need to learn to spit," a no-nonsense somm named Meghan informed me after watching me struggle through a glass. There was an art to expectoration, and it didn't in any way resemble my tactic of positioning my mouth directly over the frothy contents of the spit bucket and dumping out wine with a slack-jawed "blah." They introduced me to "spitting with confidence"—pursing my lips to shoot out a forceful, steady stream—and the "double-spit"— spitting twice per sip, to be extra sure I didn't swallow alcohol and absorbed only a minimal amount through my mouth's mucous membrane. The first time I tried their fancy way of spitting, droplets from the communal spit bucket splashed up onto my cheeks and forehead. "I had a hard time spitting with confidence at first," Meghan assured me. "It just takes practice."

In between my liquid training, I was sniffing at quinces, munching different apple varieties, and seeing how long I could smell the herbs at my local Fairway supermarket before arousing the suspicions of the security guard. I was trying to heed the advice I'd received to develop my sense memory, implanting the impression of animals, vegetables, and minerals in my mind so I'd be able to recognize these odors in a wine. I'd been clinging for years to the fantasy that gluttony would make me a better person, so I was thrilled to hear that my top priority should be to eat and drink copious amounts. "First things first, program your brain with a lot of information," advised Ian Cauble, a Master Sommelier from California. "Eat a lot of food, taste a lot of fruits. You have to taste all different citruses. You have to try the peel, the pit, the juice from ripe oranges, under-ripe oranges, over-ripe oranges, navel oranges, a Meyer lemon, an under-ripe green lemon, a lime . . ." So it wasn't oysters and caviar. But if chewing grapefruit skin would make me a better taster, I was game.

Then another pro talked me into adding a little dirt to my diet.

"Lick rocks when you're walking around outside," suggested this sommelier, who obviously did not live in Manhattan, where this pastime will either get you poisoned or committed. "I lick rocks all the time."

"What kind of rocks?" I asked, more out of polite curiosity than a desire to emulate him.

"Any rocks that I haven't licked before," he told me. "It's fun to taste the difference between red slate and blue slate. Red slate has more iron in it—it has more of a bloody meat flavor. Blue slate has more of a wet, river-stone taste to it."

Over the course of these powwows, my unofficial wine advisers made me see that at least one aspect of my original three-part plan had been spot-on: taking the Court of Master Sommeliers' Certified Sommelier Exam.

Since 1977, the aristocratic-sounding "Court" has entrusted itself with the solemn duty of ensuring no one takes the "sommelier" name in vain. As the chief examining body for professional sommeliers, the Court sets the standards for every aspect of somm behavior. (See, for example, its guidelines on thanking customers for a compliment.) A credential from the Court isn't mandatory. But like an MBA or a Grand Cru label for humans, a Court diploma serves as a seal of approval that can help sommeliers earn more money, advance more quickly, and provide concrete proof of their competence. (There are four levels of qualifications that progress from Introductory Sommelier to Master.) A growing number of restaurants require their somms to have Court diplomas, and thousands sit for the tests each year, despite twelve-month waiting lists for certain exams. Those who stick it out—and make the cut—are welcomed into a family of powerful wine pros who look out for their own. One aspiring Master Sommelier compared passing his test to getting made in the mob. If that was the case, I was ready to prick my finger and say my vows. Ever since I'd decided to embark on this journey, I'd suspected that I couldn't fully comprehend sommeliers' sensory existence and wine fanaticism unless I threw myself into their routines and became one of them. Since I didn't have years to work my way up through the usual channels, getting the Court's Certified credential was my best shot at getting promoted from cellar rat to a spot on the floor.

To prove themselves worthy of the Certified title, aspiring somms must demonstrate their knowledge of wine theory (What's the most widely cultivated grape in Madeira?), their skill at serving wine (Have they executed the seventeen steps required to properly pour a glass of red?), and their blind tasting prowess (Can they deduce an anonymous wine's aromas, flavors, acidity, alcohol intensity, tannin level, sweetness, region of origin, grape variety, and vintage?). These three areas reflect the fundamental skills needed to perform the sommelier's duties, but merely completing these tasks is not enough. Hopefuls must show they can maintain elegance and poise, even in the face of nightmare dinner guests or dining-room disasters. The exam is a test of mental fortitude, confidence, and grace under pressure. And everyone I spoke to about it had a horror story.

"You show any sign of weakness and it will be exposed in a brutal way," Master Sommelier Steven Poe told me when I asked him for advice. "Before I did my service exam, I turned to the rearview mirror in my car and I was like, 'THOSE *MOTHERFUCKERS*! THEY'RE GOING TO TRY TO FUCK YOU UP! THEY'RE GOING TO *FAIL*! YOU'RE GOING TO *SUCCEED*! GO IN THERE AND TAKE THEM FUCKING PRISONER AND KICK THE FUCKING *SHIT* OUT OF THEM.' And I took this much scotch"—he held up an invisible shot glass with two fingers and knocked it into his mouth—"and I crushed it."

There was no class I could take to pass the Certified. Instead, what the Court provides is a two-page reading list consisting of eleven books and three wine encyclopedias. Everything I needed to know I'd essentially have to learn on my own. Just to take a shot at the Certified, I'd first have to pass a qualifying exam, which itself bore the warning that a minimum of three years in the wine and service industry was "strongly recommended." I was giving myself a year to do it all.

As you might imagine, the response to my idea of going from cellar rat to Certified to somm in that period of time was less than encouraging.

"They're cracking down on people now. And they'll be especially hard on you because you're a journalist," warned one of the sommeliers I tasted with every Wednesday. The recent documentary *Somm* and TV series *Uncorked* had boosted interest in the Court's exams, so rumor was, the test had gotten more difficult in an effort to weed out the weak. Weak civilians, especially.

A Master Sommelier, who'd proctored many exams himself, tried to boost my spirits, but only succeeded in making me feel worse.

"They just want to make sure you can handle service and won't freak out and start crying and run out of the room," he told me.

I was concerned to hear that was even a possibility.

"Does that happen often?" I asked.

"*Alllllll* the time." But it could get so, *so* much worse, he added. While attempting to decant over an open flame, more than a few examinees had lit themselves on fire.

When I explained all this to my husband, Matt, he delivered the most realistic and unvarnished prognosis of all.

"Have you thought about asking for your old job back?"

I could see why he might be pessimistic.

My performance as a cellar rat had reached a new low one afternoon while preparing for a wine dinner Joe was hosting for a small group of connoisseurs.

I was just finishing up my shift when Joe asked me to take down the "seven-fifties" that he and Lara put aside on one of the upper shelves of the cellar (a standard bottle of wine is 750 milliliters). Lara had assured me I didn't have to baby the wines when I was cellaring them, so to show Joe what an old hand I was, the wines got it rough. I descended the ladder with bottles sticking out of the crook of my elbows, turned upside down, jutting out at all angles from my chest.

It was only when I bounced them down on a table that I realized what precious cargo I'd been carrying. These were gems from iconic Italian producers, including Antinori's "Tignanello," the first in what became a movement of Super Tuscan wines that blazed trails by combining Sangiovese grapes with French varieties. It would probably take me a month of cellar ratting to afford a seat at this meal. Joe came over and glanced over the loot.

"These have been standing up in the cellar since yesterday to help the sediment gather at the bottom," he said. "It's important we don't jostle these wines."

I said nothing.

Joe took a corkscrew from his pocket and began to remove the metal foil covering the cork. He placed the corkscrew's inch-long blade under the ledge at the top of the bottle and circled the neck, making two neat cuts—clockwise halfway around, then counterclockwise the other way. Then, with his thumb propped up on the edge of the bottle's lip, he used the knife to flip the metal capsule away from the bottle. It came off so naturally it looked like the wine was tipping its hat. Joe twisted in the corkscrew's spiral metal worm and with a flick of his wrist, it appeared as though the Tignanello had voluntarily surrendered its cork. The bottle hadn't moved an inch from where I'd first set it down.

I watched him repeat the drill, then asked if I could have a go. I began to saw at the neck of the bottle. This was clearly painful for Joe to watch.

"You don't have to move the bottle so much," he said.

I sawed more gently.

His face looked scrunched, like he'd just tasted some corked Chianti. "Really, try to keep the bottle still."

I stopped sawing, positioned the blade under the lip of the bottle, as he'd done, and swiped up, jamming the knife deep into the flesh of my thumb. Pinpricks of blood appeared.

Joe was more concerned about what was happening to the wine. "You *don't* have to move the bottle," he tried again, as if I might have misheard him the first few times and thought shaking the wine was the proper maneuver. He took the wine key from my mangled hand. I didn't want to even attempt inserting the corkscrew, and he didn't volunteer the chance.

I was now supposed to decant the wines, something I'd never done before in my life.

"Do you know how to decant a wine?" Joe asked.

"Oh yes," I lied.

About twelve people were showing up for this dinner and we had only a single bottle of certain wines to go around, barely enough to pour a couple ounces for each guest. To ensure not a drop would go to waste, Joe, evidently less than confident in my abilities, gave me a "refresher" on decanting. He held the glass decanter at a slight angle in his left hand, and, with his right, tipped the open bottle so its neck was parallel to the table, suspended over a lit candle, as its contents flowed into the decanter. He watched the flame through the shoulder of the bottle. If and when the flame was obscured by small black particles, he would stop pouring to avoid getting the sediment—deposits of tannins and tartrate crystals—into the decanter. Decanting was meant to remove the sediment that can form in a bottle as it ages, and also aerate the wine, exposing it to oxygen, which helps coax out its flavor, Joe explained. He disappeared and left me to finish the remaining bottles.

I repeated the steps: decanter in left hand, bottle in right, wine in the—dammit. Wine on the table. Dripping everywhere. I steadied the bottle. Easy does it. If I watched the bottle's neck to be sure I was pouring into the decanter, then I couldn't keep an eye on the bottle's shoulders to be sure dark splotches of sediment weren't floating by. But if I watched the bottle's shoulders, then I couldn't keep track of where I was pouring, and wine leaked down the sides of the decanter's narrow funnel. And of course I wanted to keep one eye on Joe, in the kitchen, to be sure he didn't see what was going on. I darted my eyes back and forth and struggled to settle into the glug-glug-glug rhythm of the bottle. Then there was a flood.

Wine sloshed onto the table, drenching my hands and the flickering candle. It looked like the white wax was melting into blood. Come to think of it—I glanced at my thumb—that might be blood. I grabbed a stack of white cocktail napkins and tried to mop up the spill before Joe would notice it. I could see him finishing up a conversation in the kitchen. There was no longer wine on the table. Just a small mountain of crumpled white napkins stained red. I stuffed them into my pockets, picked up another bottle, and started pouring it into the next decanter. Another flood.

Wine dribbled down the decanter and soaked the candle again.

Joe was walking toward me and only a few feet away now. I dabbed at the candle with a napkin, only slightly burning myself. Joe was now at my elbow. He looked at the candle, oozing Sangiovese. He looked at the bulge of napkins in my pocket. He didn't say anything. He didn't have to.

"There's something I want to ask your help with," he said. "Can you go and buy stickers?"

I was unintentionally living up to the cellar-rat name. Like an oversized rodent infiltrating an otherwise reputable establishment, I steadily wreaked havoc on order and civility. I lost bottles, dropped bottles, hid bottles, and made entire cases of wine disappear.

I spent a full month trying to track down a bottle, on the upper end of L'Apicio's offerings at $192, that I'd misplaced somewhere in the cellar. Lara made me check every single one of our almost two thousand wines, three times over, before finally admitting defeat. Then a bottle of the Ceritas went missing. This hip, organic winery sold very selectively to restaurants, and having its name on the list was a badge of honor that Lara had to earn: She was allocated only a handful of Ceritas wines each year—the distributor's way of rewarding Lara for ordering lots of other bottles from his portfolio on a regular basis. She'd spent a year pushing the Lioco Chardonnay, a good but less impressive Californian wine, in exchange for the privilege of buying about three bottles of the Ceritas. And I'd just made one of them vanish.

The very patient Lara managed to be civil about all these mishaps at first. Four weeks into my tenure as cellar rat, she sent a friendly reminder asking me to cross off old cellar locations when restocking wine. She followed up shortly after that to ask why she could never find my tally of the wines that were running low. Ah, yes, that. I'd entirely forgotten about that. Her notes got curter and more frequent as the weeks went on. Where was the Graci "Arcuria"? We'd been delivered four cases of the La Ghiga Barbaresco, so why did the cellar map only list storage for one?

Over the course of one Friday, I received five emails from Lara, each with an itemized list of grievances. A white wine came in and I hadn't stocked it in the lowboy. She was *still* finding bottles in the front of the cellar that didn't match the ones behind them. *Another* white didn't get put into the lowboy. I really, really needed to stop writing in the margins of the bin map. Could I not tell the difference between a red and a white wine? I'd put the whites from Occhipinti together with the reds. The Gruet wasn't ours, and neither was the Primaterra. They were meant for our sister restaurant—hadn't I read Lara's email?

I registered the emotional toll my work was taking on Lara the following week during inventory. Once a month, we had to record, in tenths of a bottle, the fullness of every container of liquid on the premises so Lara could track her profits and costs. She was standing with her laptop open on the surface of the bar and I was crouching on the floor reading out the name and quantity of wine in the lowboys. I'd only recently remembered that I was supposed to be checking the fridges each day to be sure we had two bottles—no less, no more—of each wine.

"Forlorn Hope Trousseau Gris, three!" I yelled.

"Three," she confirmed.

"Graci 'Arcuria,' three!"

"Three?" she asked.

"Failla, three!"

It was a wine I'd told her we were sold out of three weeks before.

Lara got very quiet and closed her eyes. She pinched the bridge of her nose like she had a headache and spoke. Extremely. Slowly.

"I have a system for a reason," she said. "We have a system to follow. People aren't following the system. They're not. Following. The. System." She crumpled on the floor next to me with her back against the lowboy. She didn't look at me. She stared straight ahead. "This is what I go to therapy for."

I gradually fell into the rhythm of the restaurant, and with it, the cadence of the city's hedonists. We sold the most expensive wines on Tuesdays, Wednesdays, and Thursdays, the nights that native New Yorkers came out to play. They were "true Manhattan diners," Lara said with obvious admiration, epicures who didn't care to bother with the weekend hoi polloi. Friday and Saturday were slow for wine and big for booze. "Bridge and Tunnel" was the explanation—visitors from New Jersey and the boroughs. The high rollers weren't excused from ridicule. I asked who was going all out on the pricey Gaja that Lara asked me to set aside one Tuesday. "Oh, a birthday party for some rich guy," jeered one of the chefs. Another night's dinner was for "someone with too much money on his hands."

The hidden language of wine lists was also starting to reveal itself. I now understood that restaurants would generally charge me as much for a glass of wine as they'd paid wholesale for the bottle, and I'd be charged about four times *that* to buy the bottle from them. (Four glasses of wine per bottle . . . you do the math.) At L'Apicio, wines with odd-numbered prices sold best, and nothing was less than ten bucks a glass. "We are trying to bring in a nice clientele," said Lara.

By-the-glass wines were big moneymakers for everyone. Winemakers and distributors craved a BTG spot since it meant rapid turnover and regular orders. At more upscale restaurants, BTG prices were calculated with a specific motive in mind: "rape, pillage," as one somm put it. Savvy beverage directors levied a "gimme tax" on glasses of brand-name grapes like Chardonnay and Malbec. They could charge more because most drinkers see a familiar grape, go on autopilot, and think, *Give it to me; I don't care what it costs.* Those wines were status symbols and safe standbys. When I went out to eat, I started steering clear of the classic crowd pleasers. "Cabernet" was somm-speak for "easy money," so for a shot at drinking great wine for good value, I stuck to whatever looked unfamiliar and vaguely intimidating—say, a Mondeuse Noire from the Savoie in France. Thanks to the golden rule—"You can't make margin on shit people don't know"—some somms would offer their favorite obscure wines at a lower markup, then make up the difference with the gimmes. Love of fine flavors, I was learning, could trump the push for profit.

At the same time, I began to feel out the hierarchy of the city's wine corps. The people who were day drinking with me belonged to the three-tier system—consisting of winemakers, distributors, and sommeliers (or store retailers)—that wine, like all alcohol, must pass through before it reaches our tables. The process is deliberately complicated. Following the repeal of Prohibition, lawmakers introduced the middlemen—distributors—hoping they'd prevent the rise of a Big Booze lobby, make it more expensive and less efficient to buy alcohol, and thus save us from becoming a nation of cirrhosis-afflicted binge drinkers.

Winemakers, obviously, make the wine. They are occasionally trotted out during the busiest buying season (September, May) to charm customers with their syrupy French accents.

Distributors sell the wine. The best of the best are industry-wide celebrities, whose reputation for finding gems is so established that their endorsement may be all somms need to buy a bottle. Many are former sommeliers who got sick of the nightly grind working the floor, and almost all know they have to suck up to their former colleagues. They have expense accounts to treat somms and beverage directors to lavish meals, or fly them around the globe to tour the wineries in their portfolios. At tastings, the somms I bumped into were almost always gearing up to travel somewhere with a distributor on a winery's or trade bureau's dime—Corsica, Australia, Chile. It didn't seem like a conflict of interest to anyone except me. Might not sommeliers sell wines just because they'd had a nice trip, not because the bottles were any good? "It's the way it is," a rotund distributor in his fifties informed me. "They go, they have a good experience, they express their thanks by putting something on their list." At L'Apicio, business was personal, and Joe and Lara played favorites with friends. "There will usually always be a Turley on our list by the glass," Lara told me, referring to California winemaker Larry Turley. "We happen to be really good friends with him and his daughter, and so we just kind of give that to them."

Sommeliers, in the most literal sense, are the people who buy wines for a restaurant, then sell and serve them to guests. They choose the theme for their list, what quantities to buy, ways to pitch customers, how they'll articulate a winemaker's vision, and ultimately control the financial health of the restaurant. At L'Apicio, wine and spirits accounted for around a third of everything that we sold on a given night. Since bottles had a higher markup than steak, the liquid kept L'Apicio liquid. "If I'm not doing something right, the restaurant really suffers. It *really* suffers," said Lara. Sommeliers might seem like mere messengers by comparison with chefs or bartenders, who make the things they serve. Yet the most talented somms are also creators in their own right, using wine, language, setting, psychology, and the senses to craft a singular experience, through liquid in a glass, for the person who tastes it. "Wine," declared the nineteenth-century novelist Alexandre Dumas, "is the intellectual part of the meal."

Almost as long as humans have been making wine—around seven millennia—drinkers have demanded a dedicated person to serve it. Even as the responsibilities evolved, one aspect of the job has stayed consistent, and could account for somms' stuck-up reputation: The lucky individual charged with serving wine has enjoyed a privileged position relative to other servants and staff. Wine is special—the ancients believed it had divine origins—and by extension, so are the people who handle it.

One of the earliest references to a "sommelier" (the word hadn't yet been invented) appears in the Book of Genesis. Cupbearers, who poured and served wine, were the confidants and counselors of Egyptian kings, and in a biblical story, Pharaoh calls on his wine steward for help making sense of a dream. The vision, which the cupbearer has the bright idea of calling on Joseph to decipher, turns out to presage a drought, and the country prepares by stockpiling grain. (It was an auspicious start: It's essentially history's first sommelier who, indirectly, helps avert the disaster of a seven-year famine.) The job wasn't always so depressing. Ramses the Great, who expanded Egypt's vineyards during the thirteenth century BCE, counted on his own team of "sommeliers" to steer him between wines that were *nfr* (good) or *nfr-nfr* (very good).

A few hundred miles to the north, the ancient Romans staged blowout feasts lubricated by special servers in charge of pouring wine. These attendants, unlike the regular help, dressed regally in ornate tunics embellished with purple and gold embroideries. Roman party-goers knew to scrutinize the men who poured their wine as closely as the wine itself, since hosts paired the most respected guests with the most attractive young male servers. As the first-century philosopher Seneca recounts, these attendants were expected to satisfy more carnal appetites than banqueters' thirst for wine: Though the wine steward "has already acquired a soldier's figure," he is "kept beardless by having his hair smoothed away or plucked out by the roots, and he must remain awake throughout the night, dividing his time between his master's drunkenness and his lust."

The history of the modern sommelier begins several millennia later. Though freed from their erotic duties and tweezing, the cup-bearers of the Middle Ages continued to function as status symbols that European kings and princes paraded at parties. Young nobles vied for spots pouring royals' wine, and lesser aristocrats aped the trend, ornamenting dining rooms with their own stewards. The job of "sommelier" became official in 1318 under a decree by France's

King Philip the Tall, though for a few hundred years, it required managing the pack animals, *bêtes de somme*, that transported things between households. By the seventeenth century, somms had been promoted: A *grand seigneur* would have a *bouteiller* to stock and store his wines, a *sommelier* to select and set them out for the table, and an *échanson* to serve them.

Working in private households, these early sommeliers, who predated restaurants, had responsibilities far exceeding anything the Court of Master Sommelier Exam would cover. According to *A Perfect School of Instructions for the Officers of the Mouth*, a French seventeenth-century service manual, sommeliers were in charge of: cutting fruit into whimsical shapes, washing and pressing linens, polishing silver, setting the table, as well as when mealtime rolled around, fetching, presenting, and tasting the wine. A wealthy family's "wine butler" was part server, part winemaker, and part alchemist who drew on elaborate recipes to rescue fake, faulty, ropy, pricked, and adulterated bottles. Oysters could fix a sour wine, and a servant handbook from 1826 even includes instructions for faking French classics. (For knock-off Bordeaux, fill a bottle with equal parts Devonshire cider and port, age for one month, and serve—"the best judge will not be able to distinguish them from good Bordeaux.") In the hierarchy of household help, these cellar dwellers were considered a cut above the rest, and they acted accordingly. "At Welbeck the upper servants adopted an arrogant attitude towards the under servants," fumes the Duke of Portland's former footman in his memoir of service in Edwardian England. "Mr. Clancy, the wine butler, was the haughtiest and most pompous of them all."

The first restaurants unleashed sommeliers on the public in the years leading up to the French Revolution. They initially appeared in Parisian haunts like La Maison Dorée, a see-and-be-seen favorite of Dumas and Balzac that boasted a two-story cellar with around eighty thousand bottles, about fifty times L'Apicio's stockpile. At long last, anyone, regardless of class, could be advised and served by sommeliers, who wielded their influence to upgrade wine's reputation. For much of its life, wine had been a humble thirst quencher that people drank all day, every day, largely because the non-booze options, like bacteria-ridden water, might kill them. ("When the water of a place is bad, it is safest to drink none that has not been filtered through either the berry of a grape, or else a tub of malt," advised Victorian author Samuel Butler.) But as sommeliers became a fixture in dining rooms lobbying on behalf of wine, they elevated it into a cultural pursuit with an air of sophistication. Food pairings followed. In the nineteenth century, as the menu of nonlethal beverages and their respective venues expanded (coffee was sipped at cafés, whiskey at bars), wine forged a connection with the table. For a time, chefs like Charles Ranhofer of Delmonico's, then the crème de la crème of Manhattan restaurants, counseled pairing wines with diners' personalities: Tastes "are formed on temperament," Ranhofer writes, such that those with a "bilious nature" will enjoy "a stimulating wine such as Bordeaux," while "gloomy dispositions" might fancy an "aphrodisiacal" like Burgundy. That was one way to match diners and bottles, but today, most sommeliers use another metric: taste. Just how their fastidious focus on flavor helped them select the right bottle for a customer, who might have an entirely different idea of what a "good" wine was, remained a mysterious process—one I was dead set on seeing in action.

After a few months at L'Apicio, I had (mostly) stopped misplacing bottles. I had mastered the pull, the cellar read, inventory, and the producer names for 99 percent of the wines in the cellar. I was writing the BTG tasting notes for L'Apicio's servers, and had conquered the "terrible ladder." I felt like I had a grip on not only the *what* but the *why* of what went on in the restaurant.

Perhaps the most important thing I learned, though, was that L'Apicio could take me only so far. Joe and Lara treated their jobs like, well, jobs. It was a means of sustaining life. It was not life itself. They were normal, well-adjusted people. But I hadn't quit my job to hang around normal, well-adjusted people any longer than I had to.

As I made my rounds through the city, I kept coming across a different breed of sommeliers for whom the work is not just a job, or even a lifestyle. It is a religion. And not a go-to-church-on-holidays religion. We're talking Martin-Luther-ninety-five-theses-nailed-to-a-door-level fervor. "You can call it a cult if you want," one of their kind told me.

Their workday does not begin when they clock in on the floor. They spend their mornings in tasting groups refining their palates, review flash cards for seven hours at a stretch, and sniff slate for fun. "Vacation" means gathering intelligence at vineyards in California or Spain. They rearrange their lives around the nose and tongue—both theirs *and* yours. And they are of significant value. A somm at a Midtown restaurant told me she sold $3 million of wine a year. Actually, I'd misunderstood: $3 million was what *one diner* had bought in the course of a year, she later corrected me. The somms' affectionate nickname for one another: "cork dork."

These were the people I wanted to meet, but they weren't at L'Apicio. They occupy a more intense, insular, and elite stratum. By and large, they work at the restaurants that make the *New York Times* critic feel lucky to have a job—the places that count oligarchs and tech billionaires among their clientele, where you've long since given up hope of getting (or affording) a reservation. These somms serve $6,000 wines with regularity to people as obsessed with flavor as they are. They are committed to tasting for tasting's sake. And they, like me, were preparing for a Court exam—the Master Sommelier Exam, in their case.

There was one aspiring Master Sommelier in particular whose name came up again and again in my conversations with somms, distributors, and wine collectors. A few called him Rain Man, after the autistic savant played by Dustin Hoffman. "A lot of the other somms are a little weirded out by him," someone told me. "But you know, he knows it all."

I was no longer a civilian, but far from a somm. I was still on the hunt for a mentor, my very own Obi-Wan Kenobi, who would be wise, kind, old, and mysterious. What I found in Morgan Harris was something very different.

CHAPTER TWO

The Secret Society

My initial interactions with Morgan were, admittedly, strange.

We first bumped into each other at a wine festival, the Wine Bar War, where Morgan skipped the pleasantries to recite an ode to the virtues of his wine fridge. His station was the only one serving red wine cooled to cellar temperature in a blistering Brooklyn warehouse, and he took immense pride in this bit of forethought. I admire that level of obsessive-compulsive hedonism, plus I'd heard some intriguing things about Morgan, so I emailed him to ask if he'd be free to chat about how and why he became a sommelier.

"I have done a lot of thinking and writing about this for myself, to work out why what I do is actually of cultural and social importance, rather than just being an intermediary in moving widgets through a distribution channel," he replied, by way of "yes." He suggested drinks at Terroir, a snug wine bar in the East Village that blasts Iggy Pop and the Who and keeps its wine list in graffiti-covered binders. He called it one of his "'spiritual homes' in the wine world."

Morgan arrived on his bike in a hipster uniform of jeans, a vintage T-shirt, a gray beanie, and battered Saucony sneakers, which he'd lifted from his dad's closet. He'd rather drink his money than wear it, he explained, folding his long legs under the narrow bar counter. He yanked off his hat, shaking loose a single curl that dangled and danced on his forehead like a fuzzy exclamation point. Morgan was bike messenger from the neck down and Hugh Grant from the chin up: lazily, rascally handsome, with blue eyes, a well-defined jaw, and poofy waves of dramatic hair.

Before I could express a preference, he summoned two glasses of sherry for us to share. "Sherry is one of the most complicated things," he began. He launched into a lecture, delivered at a speed usually reserved for reciting drug side effects on TV commercials, about the biological and oxidative aging process for Amontillado sherry; the nuances of Fino, Manzanilla, Amontillado, and Oloroso sherries; the killer pairing of an Oloroso with olives and eighteen-month-old *jamón*; the "umami-type flavors that are more of that oxidation"; the widespread confusion of dryness and tannin; and wine trends of the 1800s. He soon had both feet propped up on the legs of my stool and was pounding the counter under my chin for emphasis, his curl bouncing along excitedly. Did I know about Thomas Jefferson's love for Madeira? That Barolo wasn't dry until 1870? The stomach-churning richness of nineteenth-century meals? "You look at those historic menus from the 1880s from, like, Delmonico's, it's, like, hol-ee *shit*!" He threw his head back and waved both hands in the air for emphasis, or maybe he just couldn't control himself. "These people were just trying not to *die*!" He wanted me to know that the most expensive wines on the *Titanic* had all been German Rieslings. He declared tasting notes "fundamentally evil." He admitted to lusting after a $1,400 bottle of Champagne—"a steal!"—that would be "a borderline religious experience." He rattled off the strengths and weaknesses of his palate with the ease of a basketball star ticking off stats for a recruiter: rotundone-deaf, mixes up Nebbiolo and Sangiovese, suspected supertaster status. He was working on his own oeuvre about wine—"more manifesto or religious tract than it is a wine book"—that was meant to "occasion a sea change to adjust

America's metanarrative about how they see themselves relative to wine."

"The greatest lie that's been sold to the American populace is that they're not in control of their own tastes," he preached, curl quivering as if in agreement.

This was typical Morgan: borderline professorial, a tad hyperbolic, and extremely long-winded. "There's a propensity towards my confidence and my comfort with certain things shortchanging me actually listening to people," he told me later, far past the point at which I'd figured that out.

Morgan ordered us another two glasses of wine, and plowed through his personal history. He was twenty-nine, had studied theater at Emerson (a small liberal arts college that appropriately started as a "school of oratory"), and had abandoned acting to pursue sommelierdom. (You might remember Morgan's knuckles from *21*, the movie about card counters in Vegas casinos. Morgan played a hand double.) In seven years, he had worked his way up from serving just-okay wine at a red-sauce joint in Boston to helping powerful men with large expense accounts pick out bottles at Aureole, Chef Charlie Palmer's Michelin-starred restaurant on the edge of Times Square. Morgan joined Aureole after being fired from Jean-Georges, the crown jewel of French chef Jean-Georges Vongerichten's international empire. Morgan, never one to deny himself liquid pleasure, had helped himself to a margarita one evening while reviewing order forms in the back office. And that was the end of that.

He was in his second year of trying to pass the Master Sommelier Exam, the highest rank restaurant wine pros can reach. In terms of difficulty and prestige, attaining it is the dining-room equivalent of being made a Navy SEAL. But while there are 2,450 active SEALs, only 230 people have ever become Master Sommeliers. To put that in perspective, 200 people sit for the exam annually. Ninety-five percent of them fail. On average, in the years leading up to the test, Master candidates will taste more than 20,000 wines, study for 10,000 hours, make more than 4,000 flash cards, and affix 25 laminated maps to the walls of their shower stalls. The theory section of the test is often used to weed people out. (What's the altitude of the Fiano di Avellino appellation? Didn't think so.) Morgan had nailed theory on his first try, which left the tasting and service portions for him to pass. He would be attempting both sections in the late spring, around the same time I aimed to take my own Certified exam. I felt a tug of kinship for this guy who was also turning his life upside down for one of the Court's tests, would be prepping on the same time line as me, and maybe—possibly, hopefully—would let me join him in his training regimen.

I could also relate to him because I too am an exceptionally nerdy person. I am so hopeless when it comes to physical activity and so content being bathed in the LED glow of the computer screen that my husband introduces me to his friends as an "indoor kid." I mean, I was the *technology* editor for a website. My job was to commune with fellow nerds. And I met them, in every shape and size, by the dozens—programmers, hackers, futurists, roboticists, you name it. But even I, surely one of the world's foremost connoisseurs of geekery, was awestruck by Morgan. He had accomplished a remarkable feat: He'd gone so far in the direction of nerdy that he came back around to cool, or something like it that I found even more compelling. The air around him practically vibrated with the intensity of his passion for wine. His enthusiasm was magnetic.

Our first evening together lasted almost three hours. Unable to squeeze a word in edgewise, I had to wait until Morgan had disappeared into the bathroom to request the check. I was running half an hour late for dinner with a friend.

"Whatever you want to parse out of the experience, just let me know because I'm there to help you process it," Morgan said as we parted.

I knew just what to ask him—and Plato would never have approved.

Our collective distaste for taste (and smell) begins with Plato. To the great Greek philosopher, these were the no-good degenerates of the five senses. While Plato argued that hearing and sight could bring aesthetic pleasure, the experiences of the nose and mouth were fleeting, intellectually bankrupt stimulations. At best, they merely tickled the body. At worst, they turned men into savages. As Plato saw it, our appetite-fueling flavor apparatus—the "part of the soul which desires meats and drinks"—was no better than "a wild animal which was chained up with man." Left to its own devices, this inner beast could provoke such frenzies of gluttony as to make "the whole race an enemy to philosophy and music." Coming from a philosopher, this was an especially heinous crime.

This mind-set was perpetuated by generations of thinkers, who likewise turned up their noses at, well, their noses (and tongues). These were the untrustworthy sensory organs, corrupting gateways to gluttony and vice, all wrapped up with the ugly needs of the flesh. It is "clearly impossible," wrote Thomas Aquinas, "that human happiness consists in pleasures of the body, the chief of which are pleasures of the table and of sex." René Descartes considered sight "the noblest and most comprehensive of the senses." Immanuel Kant, who agreed vision was "noblest," scorned taste and smell as "nothing but senses of organic sensation." (He singled out smell as the "most ungrateful" and "most dispensable" sense, which "it does not pay to cultivate.") This snobbery toward the senses leaked into fields far beyond philosophy. Even scientists declined to research these primitive, obsolete faculties. In a book on odors, Jacques Le Magnen, a groundbreaking twentieth-century researcher focused on taste and olfaction, felt it necessary to justify his interest in what he dubs one of the "minor senses."

I'd heard whispers about a group of aspiring Master Sommeliers who flouted these anti-sense sensibilities at their weekly meetings at the restaurant Eleven Madison Park (EMP, for those in the know).

Theirs was rumored to be the Holy Grail of New York blind tasting groups, the highest-level in the city. One sommelier warned me there was a waiting list to join "because it's so cutthroat." (She'd been shunned.) I'd heard stories of people who were blacklisted for bringing the wrong wine or missing a week without notice. There weren't auditions, applications, or interviews to get in. Instead, like country clubs or Skull and Bones, your best bet was to befriend the right people, work at the right places, and look for occasions, such as competitions, to show you knew your Meursault (a Chardonnay grown in Burgundy's Meursault village) from your Marsannay (a Chardonnay grown about twenty miles over in Burgundy's Marsannay village). I asked Victoria James, a wine prodigy who'd recently earned a spot in the group, whether I might be allowed in. "It's very serious," she said, then repeated that two more times. "It's very serious. It's just *very serious.*" She spoke of fights erupting over the typicity of bottles of Chablis. "Like, 'How could you bring this Chablis because 2013 was a warm vintage and obviously it's not showing typically?' "

Blind tasting groups usually segregate along experience level, so I had no business tasting with Master Sommelier candidates. But that's exactly what I intended to do. "Blinding" with strong tasters enhances the feedback you receive, hence groups' pickiness about admitting new members. I met a woman who'd taken a second job, with a two-hour commute, to work for a Master Sommelier—just so she could taste regularly in his presence. Many others fly themselves around the country to do the same. A good coach can tell you if your acid calls are off base, how to distinguish a Sangiovese made in Montalcino from one made in Chianti, and which floral scents are missing from your sense memory.

Although I'd been promised introductions to whoever ran the EMP group, weeks had passed, and despite much nagging, nothing had materialized. Morgan was a member. I emailed him almost immediately after we left Terroir. Could I come?

He was noncommittal at first. I pushed, prodded, and pleaded until, finally, there came a concession. On a frigid day, when most of the group's twelve or so members were swamped with work emergencies, Morgan relented. I'd have to agree to a compromise, however: I could observe and I could taste the wines. But given my level, I couldn't speak.

For the sommeliers in Morgan's blind tasting group, showing up at ten o'clock each Tuesday morning to taste at EMP had all the glamour of a date with the StairMaster. They'd been doing this every week for years. It was their tongue cardio.

But I was not jaded and I was not experienced, and I did not play it cool. I hauled open EMP's large brass doors feeling very impressed, both with the somms with whom I was about to taste, and with myself for having been initiated into this secret wine society, hiding in plain sight in one of the city's most visible restaurants. My grandiose mood was only compounded by the sumptuousness of EMP's formal dining room. It was like getting a hug from someone's extremely rich great-aunt. I parted heavy velvet drapes to reveal an Art Deco masterpiece of a room. Enormous gridded windows looked out over a park, and the double-height ceilings were caked in layers of molding with pink scalloped trim. Morgan waved me over to a linen-covered table in the back, and I sidestepped a florist arranging bouquets of dogwood and amaryllis that would have had trouble fitting into my studio apartment. My boots echoed loudly on the floor, like footsteps in an empty church. And in the food world, there is something approaching holy about EMP. The restaurant has racked up serious accolades, including a spot at number four on the San Pellegrino list of best restaurants in the world. EMP spends ten months training its staff to pour water and employs people with the title of "dreamweaver," whose job it is to enhance the meal through miniature miracles, like delivering a sled to a guest who, over the third course, mentions wanting to play in the snow. Dinner for one begins at $295, takes three and a half hours, and, the theory goes, makes an impression that lasts a lifetime—which is conveniently the amount of time you might need to pay off your credit card bill, if you order some of the top bottles on offer.

Four guys out of the group's twelve or so members had shown up. They'd been tasting together for nearly four years. Dana Gaiser was a sommelier-turned-distributor who'd graduated from Stanford with a degree in mechanical engineering. He was in his midthirties, had frenetic Edward Scissorhands hair, and exuded this-month's-*GQ* cool in a tight suit and a pink shirt. Jon Ross, who was just a few years younger, had on a rumpled sweatshirt and looked exhausted—no surprise for someone who puts in the punishing seventy-hour workweek that's standard for a sommelier at EMP. "They own you. Like not even vaguely," Morgan told me. Yannick Benjamin was a sommelier at the University Club, a members-only club favored by the city's bankers, lawyers, doctors, and trust funders. A car accident in 2003 had left Yannick wheelchair-bound, but that didn't stop him from following a long line of Benjamin men into the restaurant business. Morgan was Morgan. All four tasters were prepping for the Master Sommelier Exam. Yannick was attempting it for the ninth time.

Dana, Jon, and Yannick were sullen and sleepy. Morgan chattered like he'd just blown a few lines back in the kitchen. "Has anyone told you the dirty sommelier mnemonic for remembering bottle sizes?" he said, pouring his wines into decanters so that all details about the bottle, including its shape, would be disguised. "'Michael Jackson Really Makes Small Boys Nervous.' So Michael is Magnum; Jackson is Jeroboam; really, Rehobaum; makes, Methuselah; small, Salamanzar; boys, Balthazar; nervous, Nebuchadnezzar." (With slight variations depending on the region, a magnum contains the equivalent of two standard bottles; a Jeroboam holds four; a Rehobaum, six; a Methuselah, eight; and from there the volume increases by four bottles per size up through the Nebuchadnezzar, which holds twenty standard bottles and guarantees a good time.)

I apologized for not having brought wine and offered to bring some next time.

"No, it's okay. If you did, we'd most likely just whine and yell at you about it like little bitches," said Jon.

It wasn't an empty threat. Blind tasting practice works best when sommeliers train with classic examples of wines. The bottles should exemplify the typical style of a Malbec from Mendoza, Argentina, or a Grenache blend from Châteauneuf-du-Pape in France, for instance. "Like, if you bring seven-year-old Chilean Cabernet and an unoaked $16 bottle of Mâcon Chardonnay, you're wasting my fucking time," snapped Morgan. Another no-go was repeatedly showing up with niche grape varietals that were not among the fifty or so believed to be fair game for the Master exam. (Though the Court doesn't reveal what wines are eligible for the test, examinees have spent years trying to reverse engineer what the judges might throw at them, so they have a pretty good idea.)

"Everything still tastes like toothpaste," Jon complained, as we arranged ourselves around a table in the employees' dining room. "Usually brushing my teeth doesn't affect me, but I used a different toothpaste than normal. So I will not be using that one again."

I hoped no one would get close enough to smell the minty freshness of the Listerine I'd gargled before leaving home. Brushing my teeth was also beginning to feel like a bad idea.

We had eight wines to go through. Jon had put out plastic spit buckets, and because service never stops, the choice of sparkling or flat water. Today we'd be "round-tabling": Each person would taste one wine at a time and, per the format of the Master Sommelier Exam, recite their analysis out loud. The others would listen and critique.

"Okay, I'm counting the 'ums'!" Morgan announced. With his theater background, he appreciated the need for polished delivery. Plus, the Master Sommelier blind tasting test allows twenty-five minutes to get through six wines—three white, three red—so with just fourish minutes per glass, each "uhhh" and "hmmm" could eat up valuable time.

Whites were first, and Dana was up.

"He can do a flight on the nose alone," Morgan boasted. Dana didn't correct him.

I picked up my glass and stuck my nose into it. Dana was still inspecting the color, so I took my nose out and examined the liquid. On the spectrum of red or white, this was a white wine. So far, so confident, I thought. Wrong.

"Pale gold, with some rim variation at the meniscus, flecks of gold and green. It's star bright, no signs of gas or sediment, and viscosity is moderate-plus," Dana said in a low monotone, speaking as quickly as he could. So "white" wasn't quite what they were going for.

I sniffed. It smelled, I hated to say it, like wine. *You're a writer, you can do better than that*, I chided myself. I sniffed harder and lifted the glass closer to my face. Wine dribbled into my nostrils, down my chin, and onto my lap. I dabbed at my face with a page from my notebook. I sniffed again—maybe one could say apple. Something sweet? Yes. Apple and sweet, I decided. A flicker of doubt: Could sweetness be smelled?

Dana was already racing ahead. "Ripe peaches and peach candy. Apricot. Meyer lemon. Candied grapefruit. Some very liqueur-like fruits, slightly candied. Tangerine. Candied tangerine and candied orange peel. Getting a slightly Grand Marnier thing going on. Honeysuckle. Um"—Morgan made a check mark—"Lily. Heavy cream. Yogurt. Butter. Butterscotch. Slight hint of tarragon and basil. There's uh"—check—"vanilla and baking spice indicating new oak *barrique*."

He hadn't even tasted it yet.

I alternated between skepticism and awe. Candied tangerine? Grand Marnier? Really? I rushed to take a sip. I liked the wine, I knew that. The apple flavor was there again . . . right? I mostly tasted Listerine.

Dana took a sip and gargled the wine. He picked up an herb garden and spring bouquet on the palate. Sweet basil, dried lilac, honeysuckle. "There's lilies, Easter lilies, all the types of lilies." He called it dry, with moderate-plus acidity, and moderate-plus alcohol.

Dana paused and took a deep breath, crescendoing to his final conclusion: "I'm going to call this 2010—no, 2011 Viognier. France. Rhône Valley, Northern Rhône, Condrieu."

Morgan pulled out the bottle and read off the label. It was indeed a Viognier, a floral, richly perfumed grape. It was from France, from the Northern Rhône. Within the Northern Rhône, it was from Condrieu, an appellation five hundred acres in size that is about half as big as Central Park. And it was a 2012.

My mouth dropped open. I wanted to applaud. Instead, I adopted the stony façade of the others, who looked unimpressed. Morgan pointed out that Dana had gone ten seconds over his allotted time. Jon quibbled with Dana's acid call.

"I think there's a saltiness in this wine that makes you think the acid is higher," said Jon.

Morgan sniffed at the wine. "It smells like hot dogs."

"Orange Tic Tacs," Jon corrected. "Or rubber chicken."

Dana shook his head. "Rubber chicken is more like . . . Clare Valley. Aussie Riesling."

Morgan, Jon, and Yannick each took a turn blind tasting a white, and after critiquing one another's notes, started in on the reds. Relegated to silence, I listened to their analysis and tried to work out what each wine might be while desperately struggling to detect whiffs of the improbable things they claimed to smell. More than an hour passed in a blur of adjectives spoken into the echoing cavity of a wineglass. "Wet asphalt," "surgical glove," "dried pomegranate," "asparagus pee," "pyrazines," "terpenes," "Dana's taint." A few of these aromas were familiar, some I'd never smelled before, and others referred to chemicals in the wine that I was hearing about for the first time. The guys spent awhile arguing about how to best describe the smell of an oxidized Chenin Blanc. Dana suggested dried cardboard, Jon countered with cereal box or Apple Jacks. Morgan voted Cheerios.

I joined Morgan for lunch afterward at a greasy diner around the corner. We tore into the food, our stomachs frantic after being teased by all the sniffing and tasting with no swallowing. The blind tasting part of Morgan's brain stayed in overdrive. I was getting the sense it never switched off. He described a comparative bacon tasting he'd organized with his roommates the other weekend. He dissected how I could spot Chablis by its "oyster-shell kelp yogurt"–ness. He deconstructed what made my burger delicious. "The whole reason this dish is excellent is the contrast between this sweet-and-sour thing and this salty-fatty thing," he explained through mouthfuls of an egg-salad sandwich. "You can't deny that there's an umami-ness. Why do you put a tomato and some lettuce on it? Tomatoes have a ton of acid. That's why the experience is enjoyable. Because there's the contrast of flavors. The sweetness of the ketchup with the salty-fatty. And yeah, there's a *ton* of vinegar in ketchup."

It wasn't a romantic way to think about a meal. But I appreciated Morgan's deconstruction. It gave me a new way of wallowing around in the pleasure of each bite. Morgan prattled on about what he'd pair with foie gras. I focused on the sugar and acid of the ketchup, and how it played off the fattiness of the fries.

I was allowed to taste with the EMP group the following Tuesday, and every Tuesday after that. My lunches with Morgan became a regular routine and I picked up more about his life story over plates of grilled cheese and pastrami. He'd grown up in Seattle, "solidly middle class," the son of two general internists and the oldest of three kids. His parents drank wine every now and then, usually a half bottle of Kendall-Jackson Chardonnay—the approachable mass-market rom-com of the wine world.

Morgan has always blazed through his passions like a forest fire, consuming everything in his path. "My brain has a tendency to want to organize small differentiating units into systems," he told me. "Part of it is my desire to complete. To know a thing in its entirety, or as close to it as you can." When he was a little kid, he'd sic himself on LEGOs. His mom would buy the most elaborate sets she could find, and he'd assemble them in an afternoon, then never touch them again. He graduated to trading cards. In elementary school, Morgan memorized every Magic: The Gathering card (its mana cost, expansion symbol, supertype, number) in a collection so huge that even now he couldn't lift it if he wanted to. Video games came next. He'd power up a new one and think, "I want to do every single subquest, I want to fight every single monster, I want to solve every single puzzle, because then you've seen it all. You can put it in a box, zip it up, and say, 'Well, that was that world.'" Obviously, when Morgan discovered rock 'n' roll, he was incapable of just enjoying the music. "As soon as I started learning about classic rock, it was like, 'Okay, well, here's Led Zeppelin, now, let's buy every single album, let's listen to every single song and figure out how they all fit together.' Like, 'I'm going to learn everything about these bands. I'm going to learn this fucking music. I'm going to learn everything about all their weird B-sides. I'm going to learn whose girlfriends they fucked.'" And now, wine. At last, Morgan had found a topic with an infinite number of expansion packs.

During his first three years in New York, Morgan balanced acting aspirations with jobs at wine bars around the city, but he soon felt a stronger tug toward wine. He loved talking with people. He even loved being on his feet, a physical aspect of the job that others find exhausting. "I would rather impale myself on a spit than go do temp work," he told me. He abandoned his auditioning after a fall spent working the harvest at a winery in Washington state, where he bunked with a blowtorch-wielding rodeo clown who made sculptures from horseshoes in his spare time. When Morgan returned to the city that winter, in 2011, it was with a singular focus on wine and honing his craft. He got a job managing Corkbuzz, a downtown wine bar for über-oenophiles owned by a Master Sommelier. Then he went to Jean-Georges, then Aureole. Morgan being Morgan, he couldn't be in wine without taking it to its illogical extreme. All the while, he threw himself into books, competitions, classes, and tastings. This wasn't just about selling good bottles. He believed that wine could reshape someone's life. That's why he preferred buying bottles to splurging on sweaters. Sweaters were things. Bottles of wine, said Morgan, "are ways that my humanity will be changed."

Despite his lofty pronouncements, Morgan, as well as many of the other somms I would come to know, was not without a sense of irony. He knew how ridiculous his job could appear to a casual observer—a glorified, overpaid waiter with a drinking problem. Or, even less charitably, a sycophant sponging off the rich and powerful, hawking wines for their price as much as their quality. Morgan was aware that what he was doing was not exactly saving the planet or rescuing orphans. But he had pushed through the self-awareness to the other side. It was *only* wine the same way that a Picasso is *only* paint on canvas and Mozart is *only* vibrations in the air.

Our weekly routine evolved into a semiweekly routine. Morgan finagled me a spot in his other blind tasting group. This one met Saturday mornings at the headquarters of Danny Meyer's Union Square Hospitality Group, the force behind more than a dozen New York restaurants that are each landmarks in their own right. Eventually, I was even allowed to speak. I was blind tasting, out loud and for all to judge.

Tuesdays we would pair up with partners and take turns going through two different flights of six wines. Saturdays we round-tabled. Whoever was captain that week chose a problem area to drill down on, then bought specific wines around that theme (say, tannic reds or oaked whites from warm climates). The bottles we tasted averaged around $25 each, which was expensive enough to ensure they'd be classic expressions of whatever style they represented, and also cheap enough to keep us from bankruptcy. Still, the costs added up. During his most intense study periods, ahead of big exams, Morgan would drop $250 per week on practice wines. Add that to the cost of flying to be coached by Master Sommeliers, or traveling to the tests themselves, and he was spending about $15,000 each year prepping for the Master Sommelier Exam, a solid chunk of the approximately $72,000 he made annually at Aureole. Morgan shrugged off the expense when I asked about it. "It's still a lot cheaper than a college degree or grad school," he said. Plus it left plenty to splurge on fun wines. Not long after we met, Morgan treated himself to three cases of wine worth $1,200—almost double his monthly rent.

Correctly identifying a wine in a blind tasting feels so impossibly difficult that the first time I did so, only one thought came to mind: I am a genius. I realized, in that moment, that I must be a sensory savant. My taste buds—probably unprecedented in history—were poised to be unleashed on the world. Famous winemakers would beg me to taste their best bottles. I'd field six-figure offers from wine magazines desperate to make me their star critic. Maybe seven-figure.

This fantasy lasted all of thirty-seven seconds, which is exactly the time it took me to start in on the next wine. From the first sip I was lost. Two weeks went by before I correctly called another wine.

Facing down a flight of six wines was like being caught on a booze treadmill set to Usain Bolt mode. The first wine would go okay. By the third I'd be in a full-blown panic. Tannins would be piling up in my mouth. I'd be picking up and putting down glasses, trying to shock my nose into smelling something. *Oak? Pepper? Some pepper somewhere, please?* I'd commit the ultimate blind tasting sin, and try to cheat by grasping for some external logic, beyond the glass, that could provide me with a pattern or clues. *Glass One was Grenache, so would Daniel really bring us a second Grenache?* (Answer: It wasn't, and why not?) Paranoia would set in. *Were all the red wines actually the same thing? Had I lost my sense of smell?* When the timer went off, I didn't stop—I dropped.

Even so, I thought my tasting skills were improving. That was until I received an email from one of the sommeliers I'd partnered with on a recent Tuesday. We'd met that week at Del Frisco's, a Midtown steakhouse that had paintings of naked women hung above its decommissioned cigar lockers. While my partner blinded the wines, I'd done what I saw everyone around me doing: I took notes on what he said, then read them back to him, pointing out the attributes he'd skipped over. Huge. Mistake. Sure, I might have progressed. But I had a long way to go before I was anywhere close to respectable. This was their world, and I'd have to prove myself if I wanted to live in it.

This was made explicitly clear when my partner emailed me a few days later. "I wanted to apologize for being a total dick when we tasted together at Del Frisco's," the guy's email to me began. "Tasting is this sacred thing we do. It is like wings for paratroopers. If you don't have them you're not part of the troop and you'll never understand why. When you began to give me feedback, I thought to myself, 'Who the fuck does this girl think she is?' "

Morgan, who seemed to like having me as his captive audience, volunteered to tutor me in the fundamentals of tasting and suggested I join him at a distributor event. Besides coaching me, he'd be going to rehearse grape varieties he missed during blind tastings and to pick up ideas for winemakers to recommend to guests (or judges, during exams and competitions).

I arrived to find him doing triage on the catalog of wines on offer. There were about ninety-five different producers, each pouring between two and ten bottles each. We had a long day ahead. We would need to be focused and systematic, Morgan warned.

"First, this is a social event unto itself. People are here as much to network as to drink," he said, weaving us through a crowded aisle of tables. "Second, do not swallow or you will be dead."

He paused in front of a row of Champagnes and volunteered our glasses for pours. His eyes bugged out after he took a sip.

"This wine is fascinating!" Morgan yelped. He said this a lot, and it was requiring me to rethink the meaning of the word "fascinating." To Morgan, "fascinating" could apply to: Germany's *Flurbereinigung* land reform in the 1970s owing to the drawbacks of old cadastral maps; something about the nuance of *cru* versus *crû* that may have led to confusion about the actual meaning of Grand Cru; Bolivian *eau de vie*; and the Champagne we were drinking made without *dosage*, a mixture of sugar and wine often added to bottles of sparkling wine, sometimes called the *liqueur d'expédition*. (A quick warning: oenophiles use an unnecessary number of French words in daily life. Towel is *serviette*, bubbles are *pétillance*, and table settings are the *mise-en-place*. Pretentious? *Oui*.)

We stopped by each of the producers that Morgan had staked out in advance. The way he talked about the wines immediately made me curious to smell whatever he'd just tried. "Salami farts," he'd proclaim. We tasted a red from Burgundy he pronounced the "Sophia Loren of wine," a Chablis he called "the crack cocaine of Chardonnay," and a Riesling he christened "the face that launched a thousand ships." An excellent Pinot Noir was a "fuck-you-sideways wine," a big California Cabernet was a "fuck-you wine"—aka a "purple bazooka," aka "solid juice," aka "purple oak juice." He deemed one Sauvignon Blanc "asparagus fart water with extra grapefruit."

Morgan plunged into the five key attributes that make up the "structure" of a wine: sugar, acid, alcohol, tannins, and texture, also referred to as "body." These contribute to our overall impression of a wine, and are in certain ways the Esperanto of wine-speak. Morgan and Jon could spend all day—and probably have—debating whether Viognier smells more like hot dog or rubber chicken. But qualities like the acidity or alcohol in a wine are measurable, objective, and immediately understood.

So how do you distinguish these traits?

Imagine you've got a glass in front of you. Step one: Look at it. Even before involving your nose or tongue, you can pick up clues about structure and flavor. Pinch the stem of the glass with your fingers, then rotate your wrist in a few swift circles, swirling the wine so that it coats the sides of the goblet. Watch the speed and width of the droplets, or "tears," that roll down after you've stilled your hand. Thick, slow tears with clear definition suggest the wine has higher alcohol levels, where thin, quick tears, or wine that falls in sheets, hint at lower alcohol levels.

Next: Smell. Always. And not just in one spot. Hold up the glass so it's nearly parallel to the floor—that way more of the wine's surface area is exposed to the air—and sniff while making the sign of the cross over the liquid with your nostrils, just to be sure you've hit the aromas from every angle. Some people swear by opening their mouths while they sniff, so they pant like a dog. So much for wine being "civilized."

Now you can sip. Swish the wine around your mouth, then purse your lips like you're about to say "oh no" and—*oh no* is right—suck in air over the wine so it feels like it's bubbling on your tongue. "Aerating" the wine, the official term for wine snobs' slurping, helps release its odor molecules, which combine with taste to form flavor. You'll look ridiculous and probably lose friends, but you'll get more from your wine.

Next, spit it out or swallow. Place the tip of your tongue against the roof of your mouth, and pay attention to how much you salivate. A lot or a little? Swimming pool or sprinkler? If you're not sure, tip your head forward so your eyes are facing the floor. If you opened your mouth right now, would you drool? If so, you're tasting a higher-acid wine. If not, it's likely a lower-acid wine. (The former tends to hail from cooler growing regions, and the latter from warmer areas.) To be sure you know what you're looking for, think of a lemon. A sour lemon that you cut in half. A sour, yellow lemon wedge that you squeeze over an empty glass. Now, take that sour lemon juice and raise it to your lips for a drink. Not to get too personal, but how much saliva is in your mouth? You should feel drool pooling on your tongue. That's how our mouths react to sour tastes (or even the thought of sour tastes): We produce saliva, which acts as a buffer to neutralize the harshness of the acid.

Prepare yourself for another sip when you're ready to gauge the alcohol. Table wines generally range from 9 percent to 16 percent alcohol (tequila is around 40 percent, by comparison). A precise sense for alcohol is key: A 1 percent variance could make the difference in whether a blind taster guesses a Riesling is from France or Australia. Alcohol can tip you off to where a bottle's grapes were grown (and much more, like the temperature during a growing season). If you're wondering why, keep in mind that every wine begins its life as a sweet stew of grape juice, called the must, that's all mashed up with grape skins, seeds, stems, and pulp. (Contrary to tasting notes, nothing like honeysuckle, peach, or orange Tic Tacs is added to the wine to flavor it, though some stray spiders, rats, mice, and snakes scooped up from the vineyard can accidentally get mixed in.) Fermentation of the must is kicked off by yeast—whether naturally occurring or added for desired effect—that then converts all or some of the grapes' sugar into alcohol. Warmer climates lead to riper grapes with a higher concentration of sugar, which, by the laws of fermentation, will produce wines with higher alcohol. Grapes from cooler climates generally have lower concentrations of sugar, yielding wines with lower alcohol. So which is it—high or low? Swallow a mouthful of wine and exhale, as if you were trying to check whether your breath stinks. (Spitting will rob you of the full effect.) Take note of how far into your mouth and throat you can feel the burning heat of the alcohol. The back of your tongue? It's probably lower alcohol—around 12 percent for reds. The back of your throat, near your jaw? Medium, closer to 13, edging on 14 percent. Are you warm all the way down by your sternum? Could be 14 plus—high. Alcohol is a feeling more than a taste. Try to remember to your last tequila shot, which set fire to your tongue, throat, esophagus, and belly. The more a drink burns, the more alcohol it contains.

Take a sip again. Feeling good yet? On to tannins. These are natural compounds—polyphenols, if you want to get technical—that can come from the skins, stems, or seeds of grapes, as well as the wood barrels in which a wine may have been aged. (The latter is more often responsible for the tannins in white wines, which usually spend less time than reds soaking in skins and seeds.) Tannins are more a texture than a taste, and therefore distinct from whether the wine is "dry," which refers to the absence of sweetness. And yet, confusingly, tannins leave your mouth feeling dried-out and grippy—more like sandpaper for tannic wines (like young Nebbiolo), or like silk for low-tannin wines (say, Pinot Noir). Some tasters swear they can differentiate between tannins that come from grapes, which make their tongues and the roof of their mouths feel rough, and tannins from oak barrels, which dry out the spot between their lips and gums.

The so-called body of a wine, also more touch than taste, derives from its alcohol and sugar content. Think of the difference in viscosity between skim milk, whole milk, and heavy cream. Better yet, hold each in your mouth. That's along the lines of what makes a light-, medium-, or full-bodied wine.

Go ahead and have another sip. Finally, sweetness. Like the other attributes that make up structure, sweetness exists along a spectrum. But instead of "high" on one end and "none" on the other, which would be altogether too reasonable, an early wine-loving sadist decided to label the scale from "sweet" to "dry" with terms like "semi-sweet" and "off-dry" in between. That's right, the erudite wine connoisseur must describe a wet liquid as "dry." Think back to that messy grape sludge, the must: In a "dry" wine, all the sugar was fermented into alcohol. But winemakers will sometimes opt to halt fermentation, so there's sweetness, or "residual sugar," in the final product.

Sweetness should be easy to recognize, since we've all had sugar.

Here's where it gets interesting: If the acid in a wine is high enough, we can be fooled into perceiving much less sugar than there really is, or even that there's none at all. Go back to that imaginary lemon juice you squeezed into a glass. Now pretend you've got a second glass with sugar water. Taste the sugar water alone. Ugh, sweet. Try the lemon juice alone. Blech, too sour. Combine equal parts lemon juice and sugar water. Delicious. A touch of acid can transform a saccharine mouthful into a delightful drink, and vice versa. This is Coca-Cola's secret. The ten cubes of sugar contained in a can of Coke would be foul if drunk with tap water. But they become delectable in soda, which pairs the sugar with phosphoric acid in levels that give Coke a pH on par with some animals' stomach acid. A similar logic gives white wines high in acid *and* sugar, like certain Rieslings, the invigorating tension in their tastes that makes them so delightful. An "enlivening energy," Morgan declared when he tasted one such wine, like "balancing a thousand-pound barbell on a tight rope." So how do you tease the two tastes apart? The drool test can alert you to high levels of acid, so you're aware you might be underestimating the sweetness. And since residual sugar can make wines more viscous, you can also sense sweetness by feeling out the weighty thickness or pillowy softness of a wine.

Morgan was taking only two sips of the wines we tasted for every four gulps that I did, and I realized later that professional tasters know to budget their sips and sniffs. "Tasting the same samples many times in succession is useless, such repeated attempts simply result in a total loss of sensitivity," states the famed enologist Émile Peynaud in his handbook, *The Taste of Wine*. Prolonged exposure to a scent makes our noses temporarily "blind" to that odor, a process known as olfactory fatigue. By the third or fourth whiff of a wine, your nose might be saturated with its perfume, so you're no longer sensitive to its smell. This is annoying when you're fighting the clock to guess White Wine Number 3. It's a blessing when you're assigned the middle seat next to a guy who hasn't discovered deodorant. "So long as they have been carefully registered, first impressions are the best," insists Peynaud. (He also frowns on drinking water while tasting wine—it throws off our palates—and I resolved to save hydration for before or after tasting only.)

Morgan and I hadn't even made it halfway around the floor of the distributor tasting. But I'd repeated my analysis of structure—sniff, swish, drool, exhale, spit—so many times, with so many wines, I'd lost count. I was spitting, double-spitting. And yet the alcohol still seeped in through the surface of my mouth. I was feeling ill and a little green.

We bumped into Morgan's friend Jerusha, a young woman our age who worked the floor at a restaurant in Soho. I asked her for any tips on recovering from these marathon tastings, and she suggested detox tea to defend against the alcohol.

Morgan scoffed at us both. He was still going strong. "Being relentless is my defense," he said.

The best tasters train their tongues and noses long before they ever tackle a flight of wines. How I treated my body in the days, hours, and minutes before sitting down to a glass would determine my tasting and smelling success. Put simply: My life needed some drastic rearranging.

Each sommelier has his own routine designed to keep his palate alert and wine-ready. Michael gave up coffee. Kristie insisted on diluting hers with milk. Yannick drank his cold. A different Michael believed ice water was all he needed to jolt his taste buds into action. Paolo Basso, one-time champion and three-time runner-up in the World's Best Sommelier Competition, swore by staying just a bit hungry at all times. Like the mightiest hunters of the animal kingdom, he insisted it made him like "a famished beast who smells his prey."

I surveyed sommeliers for their palate-enhancing techniques. The first step was self-knowledge, they said. I needed to monitor my tongue for its recovery time, which meant how long it took to get rid of the aftertaste of whatever I'd most recently ingested. Through trial and error, I determined my tongue needed around two hours to fully neutralize, which became my cutoff for eating, drinking, or teeth brushing before tasting. This had the added benefit of ensuring I'd always go in hungry, primed to sniff out flavors. Like Morgan, the other wine pros I spoke to had amassed a detailed profile of their noses and tongues' temperaments. "I notice that when I live closer to the water, my palate is better," said Craig Sindelar, a Chicago-based sommelier. Conrad Reddick, Craig's former colleague at the modernist restaurant Alinea, suggested tracking my palate performance against the biodynamic calendar, a chart more often used to guide farmers who harvest their vineyards biodynamically, following principles that meld the nature-conscious values of the organic movement with the good-vibes mysticism of crystal healers. (For example, biodynamic winemakers keen on "helping spirit to penetrate matter" are advised to bury a deer bladder stuffed with yarrow weed in their fields.) Conrad had found bottles' flavor changed depending on whether the biodynamic calendar dubbed it, say, a "fruit day" (better) or "root day" (worse). According to some oenophiles, barometric pressure could also flatter or mute a wine. I started a log of how external factors, like the dry air from my apartment's heater or rainy mornings, seemed to meddle with my sensing.

Next came self-deprivation. There could be no gustatory or olfactory noise to interfere with the signal. Morgan didn't brush his teeth before tastings, believing the mint tainted his taste buds for the morning. Afraid of burning their tongues, the somms Devon Broglie and Craig Collins refused to drink any liquids above a tepid temperature for the entire year and a half before their Master Sommelier Exam. Coffee, soup, tea—they took it all cold. Yannick stuck to iced coffee for the same reason. Cool foods only: check. Others tailored their diets to avoid heavy foods the day before a tasting. I swore off raw onion, garlic, and boozy cocktails, which have a tendency to cling to my tongue like houseguests who've overstayed their welcome. Cigarettes were an obvious liability, but I don't smoke. Andrew Bell, the president of the American Sommelier Association, advised students taking his blind tasting course, in which I'd enrolled, to avoid extreme flavors so they can sensitize their tongues to lower doses of taste stimuli. Having difficulty gauging the alcohol in wines? "Cut out the fucking spirits for a month," he instructed a classmate. Stiff cocktails could make wine, with its lower alcohol level, go down like water. Andrew had even stopped adding extra salt to his food—anything beyond what it was served with—and, at one point, had ditched coffee, calling it "a palate killer." I found this hard to believe, given how many sommeliers enjoyed an espresso-heavy diet. "Everything changes," Andrew insisted. "It obscures your palate." Since I was already trying to make up for lost time, I was willing to try anything that might speed up my improvement. What the hell, I figured: I added coffee to my no-fly list, and figured I'd put down the saltshaker too. As an extra precaution, I gave up superspicy foods after hearing that a friend's father, a renowned French chef, banned his kitchen staff from touching the fiery stuff out of concern that blunted tongues would lead to overseasoned dishes. It *is* possible: Daily exposure to spicy foods can desensitize the tongue's nerve endings to heat, so a dash of Sriracha could escalate to drowning everything in hot sauce. We also seem to adapt to the saltiness of our saliva, which can be affected by the amount of salt we consume. (It's worth noting that spiciness is a temperature sensation that activates pain receptors, not a taste that acts on taste buds.)

And then there was consistency. Sticking to a routine—at tastings and before them—was essential. It ensured you could limit all confounding variables and get down to what was in the wine. Craig Sindelar used a neti pot before tastings to flush out nasal debris. One of the guys in my tasting group traveled with his own granola, so when he tasted on the road, his gustatory baseline wouldn't change. A friend of his, a sommelier in California, knew he performed best when he tasted at ten o'clock in the morning, so when he found out he'd have to take his Advanced Sommelier Exam at eight o'clock Texas time (six in the morning, Pacific time), he reset his internal clock to ensure that come exam day, eight a.m. Texas time would feel like ten a.m. California time, his golden hour. Every day, for three weeks before the test, his wife woke up at four o'clock in the morning to pour him a flight of wines. I was with Morgan at our Saturday blind tasting group when I heard this story. My reaction was "That's insane." Everyone else's was "How far in advance do you know your tasting time?" At several sommeliers' recommendation, I stocked up on my brand of Crest toothpaste to be sure I'd never have to switch. And because consistency means controlling for how everything around you smells, I went ahead and stockpiled my preferred brands of deodorant, shampoo, conditioner, and body wash, and switched to scent-free laundry detergent. I'd long ago retired my perfume, because only an ignoramus wears perfume to a wine tasting.

I began to worry more about issues of technique. I'd been following sommeliers' instructions to build sense memory by smelling plants and foods at every opportunity. But as I did so, I grew concerned I might not be smelling in the right way. Should I sniff in short, quick inhalations or long, deep ones? What should I be thinking about to make the impression stick? Waving stuff in front of my nose wasn't enough.

I went to see Jean Claude Delville, a French perfumer who, coincidentally, had created the fragrance I'd stopped wearing, along with numerous classics like Clinique's "Happy." He'd memorized more than 15,000 aromas in his quest to become a "nose"—industry lingo for perfumer—and offered to help me tackle my smell training more systematically. I met him at his office, a gleaming Tribeca loft with high ceilings and white columns, and he whisked me down to his lab, which was wallpapered in brown glass vials. He dipped two thin pieces of white paper into a container marked "Pamplewood," and held one out for me to smell. Apparently, even teaching me to spit had been premature. "What is important is to learn to breathe," Jean Claude said, instructing me to follow his lead. He brought the essence to his nose and drew in a single, long breath, so deep I saw his chest swell. He held it—*one Mississippi*—then exhaled. "You exhale through your nose because the molecule gets stuck in your nose otherwise," he coached. In his student days, he'd take samples of the odors he wanted to master and lock himself in a dark room, then sniff one at a time while trying to associate the smell with places, people, moments, or forms. "For me, patchouli: It's brown, it's red, it's earthy, it's mystic. And the shape for me is weird. A triangle, because it's aggressive a little bit," he said. "You have to believe something in order to remember it, good or bad." Another perfumer, also French, assured me I'd get nowhere unless I started assigning words to smells. "It is better if you do it aloud," he said. "Do it in the shower. At breakfast. Lunch. Herbs, spices, meat, everything. Even in the street. The car, the diesel, the air. When you have time, just a few seconds, you can put words to it. Little by little, you will become better." That night I stood over the kitchen sink flipping open spice jars and inhaling their fragrances one by one. Riding the subway became an exercise in classifying human bodily functions: sweat, urine, faint residual tinge of vomit. I tried to muster the same enthusiasm for these odors as Jean Claude, who delighted in the olfactory tableau of public transportation. He made a point of relishing it each morning. "I inhale and then I hold my breath. And I exhale—wow! It's rich, it's so simple."

The rituals the sommeliers stuck to and the sacrifices they made could often be more superstitious than scientific. But for the people who followed them, they worked. More than that, the stakes were high enough that they were willing to give it a shot.

It surprised me to learn that Morgan did not deny himself much.

His approach to tasting was firmly psychological. It started with a mind-set rather than an eating regimen. One of his favorite guides in the matter was *Zen in the Art of Archery*, a German philosopher's account of the six years he spent studying archery with a Zen master in Japan. Morgan emailed me a quote from the book, with the subject line "This Speaks to Me." It read:

> The right shot at the right moment does not come because you do not let go of yourself. You . . . brace yourself for failure. So long as that is so, you have no choice but to call forth something yourself that ought to happen independently of you, and so long as you call it forth your hand will not open in the right way—like the hand of a child.

Morgan provided a gloss to link the passage back to blind tasting. "If you become the action, and execute the process perfectly, you will become the result," he wrote. "Fear and worry are the heart of failure."

As Morgan saw it, blind tasting well depends first and foremost on sharpening your focus and mental control. You have to keep your mind open to the wine's message at the same time that you silence the doubts that inevitably creep into the edges of your brain to whisper *You always miss Moscato.* "It requires consciousness. It requires attention. It requires saying, 'I'm going to be in tune with my senses, and I'm going to listen to this glass of wine,'" Morgan said.

He prescribed a regimen of yoga, which he said helped him practice turning off parts of his brain and staying present in an action—perfect for blind tasting.

"When I get done with those twenty-five minutes, it doesn't feel like any time has gone by," he said of tasting. "It is the absence of the conscious, yammering mind, right? . . . It's about dissolving into the action. It's about unbecoming yourself and becoming this apparatus that does this. You have to surrender yourself to the wine in order to understand it. Like, I can't force this to be California Chardonnay no matter how hard I fucking try. It's teaching yourself how to listen."

Being attentive to taste—learning how to listen—begins by being open to everything around you, Morgan said. He suggested I practice receiving new experiences anywhere. It could start with something as simple as not wearing headphones on the train. "Pull your own narrative out of your ears," Morgan told me. "You're not stepping on a train being like, 'What's going on today? What's out there in the world?' It's just turning inwards, being self-referential."

Whether it was in downward dog or on the floor of a distributor tasting, there seemed to be few moments in Morgan's life—or his fellow somms'—that were not given over to selling, tasting, reviewing, enjoying, or contemplating wine. "It's one of those fields where whenever you're not studying, you feel super guilty and self-loathing," said one sommelier over coffee. Mia, a female sommelier who had gone to Emerson with Morgan, remarked at one of our morning tastings that she reviewed flash cards on her way to work. A fairly routine activity—except Mia biked to work.

In the restaurant hierarchy, sommeliers were the gentle nerds who carried flash cards and chefs were the sexy bad boys with knives who got the girls. Which, whatever—who cares? The somms didn't have time for that stuff anyway. Twelve- to fourteen-hour shifts were routine, so were six-day workweeks. "Five days is a luxury," Victoria scoffed. On their nights off, generally Monday and Tuesday, they hung out with one another at parties that were mostly excuses to try some special wines. Someone might supply a Methuselah of a twenty-year-old California Cabernet, or a bottle of weed wine, made by tossing marijuana buds into the must. Morgan's friend threw a vino-themed bash—"the *Unfair* Game Party"—where everyone had to bring wines too weird for blind tasting. They traveled around the city in packs, usually arriving at bars long after the civilians had cleared out for the night. "Balance" was only in their vocabulary as it applied to the flavor of a wine.

The extended network of the Court became their de facto family. "They're not driven to go start a family right away, because this is very fulfilling," Master Sommelier Laura Williamson told me. A disproportionate number of the sommeliers I met were dating other sommeliers or, at the most exotic, someone else in the wine world. A girlfriend was not part of the equation for Morgan. Part of the problem, he explained one night, was that he couldn't afford tasting menus for himself and a significant other. And he wasn't about to lose the tasting menus.

CHAPTER THREE

The Showdown

Even as I gained more of a foothold in the wine world, I remained fascinated by the idea of sommelier competitions and was eager to observe one in the flesh. They epitomized what I found endlessly intriguing about the sommeliers, which was the fact that they united extremes of personality—devoutly studious and unrelentingly sybaritic—I'd rarely seen in combination. Given the sheer quantities they drink and the late hours they keep, I had expected them to be extravagant party animals. But instead, they were meticulous, even scholarly, about their hedonistic experiences and their customers', as though Daniel Webster and Keith Richards had spawned a new race (that, like the two of them, was also largely white and male). The somms stressed over the pleasure that was to be had in wine, and dissected every aspect of the experience, from the temperature of a bottle to the placement of a glass. I asked Morgan whether he'd rather spend $300 on a bottle of superb wine or buy three different bottles for $100 each. He grew extremely serious and was quiet for a few moments before answering. "That's a hedonistic calculus of the highest degree for me," he finally said.

Lucky for me, sommelier face-offs are a much more popular activity than I'd ever imagined. There is TexSom, TopSomm, Somm Slam, Somms Under Fire, Best Young Sommelier, Best Sommelier in America, Best Sommelier of the Americas, and World's Best Sommelier, not to mention the long list of blind tasting challenges pegged to specific wine-growing regions. The competitions arrive at a clip of nearly one a month and they devour sommeliers' days off. What is at stake isn't just bragging rights: These are adrenaline-fueled dress rehearsals for the Court of Master Sommeliers' exams, with the bonus perk of offering opportunities to hobnob with power brokers. Winners can also score cash or an all-expenses-paid trip to whatever region happens to be sponsoring the event.

The sommeliers that I knew considered TopSomm the largest, most relevant, and most prestigious of the competitions. Like a sommelier Super Bowl, it puts contestants through multiple elimination rounds to crown the best somm in the country. As far as stateside competitions go, this is Major League tasting—and serving—at its best.

Most weeks, my Saturday blind tasting group would loiter for a while after we'd finished, exchanging restaurant recommendations or trading reviews of the newest book about Barbaresco. On this particular morning, however, everyone hurried through the flights. Now deep into my sixth glass of wine, I was in no condition to tackle a coloring book, let alone a timed test, but the rest of my tasting partners were rushing home to take the TopSomm qualifier. The twenty-minute eighty-question online exam would determine who made it to the first round of the competition.

Since I wanted a front-row seat to whatever Morgan was doing, I asked if I could tag along with him while he did so. Alcohol never seemed to dull Morgan's faculties the way it did mine, or maybe he was just immune by this point. On the L train to Brooklyn, he expounded on the problematic—and prevalent—mentality among American diners of expecting restaurants to humor their every whim, instead of them opening themselves up to the new and unfamiliar.

"You don't go to see fucking *Anna Karenina* and expect her to not die at the end, you fucking dickheads. No, we cannot remove mushrooms from that dish. We cannot make it gluten-free. Because pasta can't be gluten-free, you dongo," he railed. "Should everything be exactly what you want it to be, or should you encounter things that are difficult and challenging and do not live up to your expectations? . . . For me, going to a restaurant is like going to a show. I don't expect to necessarily like it. I expect to see the opinion of the chef and of the wine director and of the service staff."

His monologue continued in this tenor as we walked past a gas station and onto his block. The buildings alternated between shiny, renovated apartments and brick walkups slouching behind chain-link fences. Morgan lived in one of the prewar buildings—more slouching than shiny—with two roommates. Neither of them worked in wine, but they'd evidently given Morgan free rein to decorate.

I bumped into two stacked wine fridges as soon as I walked in. Five large maps of French grape-growing regions, nearly four feet wide each, hung on the walls of the living room. I counted five empty wine bottles on the kitchen counter, an empty liquor bottle on a bookshelf, and on Morgan's desk, an empty bottle of grower Champagne, a trendy, artisanal variation on traditional French sparkling wine that had lately been featured on sommeliers' Instagram accounts. "My aperitif last night," Morgan explained, nodding at the Champagne. Any surface not covered in alcohol was piled with books about alcohol. *1001 Whiskies*, *Jura Wine*, *North American Pinot Noir*, *The Wines of Burgundy*, *Wine Atlas of Germany*, *To Burgundy and Back Again*, *A Short History of Wine*, *Cellarmasters in the Kitchen*, *Reading Between the Vines*, and, the lone exception, *Crime and Punishment.* A wooden crate under one window was jammed with dozens of palm-sized notebooks in which Morgan had scrawled diary entries recording wines and meals. He opened one at random to impressions from a tasting menu he'd eaten alone at Hearth, the sister restaurant to Terroir. *"Hospitality note,"* he'd written, *"You should always have someone at the door to welcome people."*

Morgan puttered around the kitchen brewing coffee and refueling with a bagel, then we sat down at his computer. He had a Post-it note attached to the screen:

Future Morgan, use this time to be productive.

—Past Morgan

The exam was open-book, but you could forget scoring well if you had to spend precious seconds looking up answers. Just in case, Morgan riffled through his crib sheet (116 pages) and flash cards (2,200 of them) to be sure he knew where to find things like the minimum must-weights for Sélection des Grains Nobles wines.

The high scorers on the TopSomm test would be invited to the regional semifinals, which would be held in several cities around the country. From there, the top six sommeliers in each category—TopSomm and TopNewSomm, for entrants under thirty—would fly to California for the finals. Morgan had made it to nationals the past two years in a row, but he'd never taken the top prize. (Past winners aren't allowed to compete.)

"Here goes," Morgan said. He leaned in so his face was only a few inches away from the computer screen.

I caught only snippets of the exam questions. He was answering them faster than I could write them down. "Order the following amari from driest (top) to sweetest (bottom)." "Match the river to the appellation." "Match the country to its approximate current land under vine."

"That is a *terrible* question," Morgan muttered under his breath as he typed and clicked. "Fuck, okay, let's see . . . North to South, Jesus fucking Christ. . . . This is a really hard question because, like, Genshu is undiluted sake. . . . That's a bitch of a question. . . . That's a *whore* of a question. . . ."

He was complaining, but I have to be honest: He looked thrilled.

Morgan qualified for regionals, where he promptly bungled the service section by dropping a silver tray that, to the judges' horror, clattered onto a bare wood floor. He advanced to the finals in spite of this. He'd be shipping out to California for the showdown, which he considered essential for both training and networking. "You just *need* to make it onto that social calendar," he stressed.

I couldn't miss it either. The competition would reflect the real-life scenarios sommeliers face in their jobs, and promised to provide a comprehensive overview of their official duties. More than that, while restaurants sometimes cut corners in the interest of saving time or space, TopSomm holds its competitors to the highest standards of service. The daylong competition would be my chance to witness the Platonic ideal of the sommelier's craft in action. I could also familiarize myself with the standards to which I'd be held when it came time for my own Court exam. As it was, I had only recently discovered that the proper procedure for opening a bottle of sparkling wine is not to jam my thumbs under the cork and take aim at something unbreakable. The cork should be twisted and released into a napkin with a *pffi* sound no louder than—and these are the technical terms I was given—a "nun's fart" or "Queen Elizabeth passing gas."

Though TopSomm's judges typically consist of Master Sommeliers, I was able to convince the competition organizers to include me as a guest judge. I assured them that, in the role of naïve guest, I would bring a unique perspective. I could better judge each competitor's service for its overall . . . feel. Amazingly, it worked.

The competition would include three different events that mirrored the format of the Court's exams. In the theory section, Morgan and the others would be grilled about everything from aging laws to soil types. Blind tasting was self-explanatory. And for service, they'd tend to guests (played by yours truly and the other judges) who would be cheap, chatty, curious, or all three, but definitely annoying.

Where the Court's exams had to stick to some nominal definition of "fair," it seemed that TopSomm just wanted to be equally nightmarish for everyone.

"You just feel for everybody," a past judge warned me. But my instructions were clear: Show no mercy.

Since I try not to make a habit of embarrassing myself in public, I decided it would be wise to do some studying of my own before the competition. It had only been a few months since I'd marched into a wine store demanding a classic bottle of white wine made with Chablis, which is like asking a travel agent to book a one-way ticket to quiche. "Chablis," the clerk said with a smirk, "is a region in France, not a grape." (More specifically, it's a place in Burgundy that makes wine with Chardonnay grapes.)

Such amateur-hour foolishness was behind me. I was going to be a judge. I owed it to the competitors to know my stuff. For starters, I needed to master what grapes were grown where and in what way, along with why, to what effect, and how they were made into wine—for all the winemaking regions in the world. Not only would it help me hold my own at TopSomm, but being a superb blind taster requires a grasp of the facts and forces that can shape the contents of a glass. I had a much better shot at correctly deducing a Riesling from the Mosel if I knew where the Mosel is located (Germany), its climate (cool, continental), its soil (blue and red Devonian slate), what grows there (mainly Riesling, followed by Müller-Thurgau), and how the wines are made (fermented in stainless-steel tanks, rarely touched by oak barrels). Besides, I stood no chance of passing even the first level of the Court's exams without that information—and much more—lodged in my memory.

I created an account with the Guild of Sommeliers, a wine-education organization that runs a website offering study guides and networking for service pros who want to nerd out over yeast species. (The Guild has no formal relation to the Court, despite both groups' shared fondness for the lingo of the ancien régime.) With help from the Guild guides and a stack of wine encyclopedias, I set to work making flash cards on Cram, the study app Morgan referred to as his "good buddy." Priorat's traditional varietals, the soil composition of appellations in Western Australia, mountain ranges in Napa Valley . . . there was no end to the detail. I began to haunt the streets of Manhattan, eyes glazed over, whispering, "Rioja follows the path of the EBRO RIVER through three climatically distinct sub-zones. . . ."

I was still reviewing flash cards on my flight to San Francisco, where I arrived the day before TopSomm began. I'd always thought that the crowds, the neoclassical wineries frosted like birthday cakes, and the precious details ("Zinfandel Lane") could lend California wine country a theme-park vibe. But it was too early in the season for fleets of limos to be ferrying bachelorettes between tasting rooms, and on the afternoon I drove to my hotel in Santa Rosa, a tranquillity had settled over the vineyards. The landscape had a bucolic feel, a reminder that at the end of the day, despite the pretensions often served with each bottle, everything in this business depends on grapes that must be grown, picked, and crushed. Cars shared the road with tractors, rumbling past men in jeans idling at the intersections, hoping to be called for a day's work.

The dress code for that evening's welcome dinner had specified "California casual," but I slipped into heels and a skirt anyway. Since leaving the tech world, where any outfit that needs dry cleaning is guaranteed to be too formal, I'd had to take my wardrobe up a notch. The sommeliers seemed most at home in tailored jackets and black slacks. After a few fashion mishaps, I'd gone digging through my closet for knee-length skirts and suit jackets I'd last worn while interviewing for jobs my senior year of college. Morgan, I learned later, had packed eight pocket squares.

There is something strangely conservative and old-fashioned about sommeliers that can make them—even the women—seem like little old men trapped in twentysomethings' bodies. In addition to dressing like they've raided Jay Gatsby's closet, they spend much of their time thinking about the past, mulling over the traditions of a five-hundred-year-old château, or mooning over a particularly warm spring thirty years ago. The poise they maintain while serving infuses their manner with a formality even off the floor. They are every parent's dream: perfect posture, good eye contact, precisely enunciated full sentences. Morgan was incapable of texting me about "Bandol rosé" or "the Chaîne" without taking the time to insert the proper French accents.

I joined the competitors and the other judges on a luxury tour bus hired to ferry us to a dinner hosted by Rodney Strong, a winery that, if the sommeliers were being honest, they probably wouldn't recommend, not even after it bankrolled the night's festivities. A woman from the winery passed around plastic glasses of Rodney Strong Sauvignon Blanc. For the TopSomm contestants, it was at least their second round of aperitifs. En route from the airport, they'd made their driver stop at a convenience store so they could pick up twelve-packs of Pabst Blue Ribbon and Modelo. Sometimes even the pros want to drink without thinking.

The bus deposited us at an outdoor terrace that looked like a Pinterest mood board come to life. The somms' job came with some definite perks. Musicians, hired for the evening, strummed guitars on a grassy slope. There was a patio overlooking a fire pit and, beyond it, vineyards that vanished into the horizon. Twinkling string lights crisscrossed picnic tables covered with candles and floral linens—and, I noticed warily, no fewer than seven wineglasses per seat.

The conversation during dinner alternated between wines people had drunk in the past, wines they had drunk recently, and wines they hoped to drink in the future. Geoff, one of the Master Sommeliers, polled everyone on what food to pair with his bottle of old Meursault. Oysters, the somms all agreed. Dana, who'd also qualified for the finals, reminisced about the '96 Raveneau Montée de Tonnere he had served at his birthday party a few years ago. He and Morgan recalled with horror the Ruché, a red wine from the Piedmont in Italy, that they'd had to blind taste last year at TopSomm. That reminded Morgan of the white wine he blinded during his

Certified exam a few years ago. He was still scandalized that his fellow test takers had been daft enough to call it Viognier.

"I'm like, 'When have you *ever* had high-acid Viognier *with* residual sugar?' Just call a spade a spade and call it—"

"Acidified Central Coast!" Dana interrupted, cracking up the table with what was evidently a terrific punch line. "Like, 'We just mistakenly dumped a vat of citric acid into our Viognier!' "

"HA! Acidified Central Coast!" guffawed Jackson, a finalist who'd flown in from Seattle. "Does citric acid even come in a bag?"

"Yeah, yes, it does," Dana said.

"For sure," Morgan said.

"I have bags of citric acid at home for making tonic water," said Dana.

"You make your own tonic water?" Jackson asked. "I make my own quinine solution!"

Dana looked unimpressed. "I use cinchona bark instead of quinine," he said with obvious pride.

"Yeah, yeah, I use the bark too," Jackson quickly clarified. "At first I could only find the powder. But then I found a shop that had the actual bark." He tried to compensate for this blunder. "I want to try to make my own vermouth."

I was distracted by a man in a gold-buttoned navy blazer who was parading among the dinner tables, slapping backs and shaking hands. It was Fred Dame, a sixtyish wine distributor and Master Sommelier, who acts as the unofficial mascot for both the Court of Master Sommeliers and Guild of Sommeliers. The visionary who brought the Court from the United Kingdom to the United States, Fred is a connoisseur of exclusive societies for men with money, time, and power. "My wife said, 'No more clubs!' " he roared, in between describing his membership in the Bohemian Club (essentially summer camp for influential men) and the Rancheros Visitadores (essentially cowboy camp for influential men). He taunted the competitors, who were already nervous but trying not to show it.

"How much do you know about Russian wine?" he asked a table of sommeliers. Silence. He squinted at them. "You're all screwed."

He stopped by where Morgan, Dana, and Jackson were sitting and leaned over conspiratorially. "It's a competition, not an exam, so all gamesmanship goes out the window," he reminded them. "The drunker you get your competitor, the worse he'll do."

They seemed to take this advice to heart. After the beers, the wine on the bus, cocktail hour, and the seven glasses of wine at dinner, people were still thirsty. We paused briefly at the hotel to regroup. Someone found an empty martini glass on a coffee table in the lobby. Several somms lined up to smell it.

"I think it's a Grasshopper," one said.

Morgan sniffed and agreed. "It smells like crème de menthe and Galliano."

Morgan led the charge to Russian River, a microbrewery just down the street from our hotel. A chalkboard running the length of the bar listed approximately one thousand beers with baffling names like "Defenestration" and "Damnation." I made the mistake of asking if anyone could recommend something, which was basically like offering myself as chum to a fish tank of half-starved piranhas. Chaos erupted.

I don't know what beer I got in the end. It didn't matter because my glass was immediately whisked out of my hands by one of the sommeliers who wanted to taste it. Everybody traded sips of everything—one more data point in their expanding library of sense memories.

I never finished the beer. By then, it was near midnight, and aside from a girl who had come with her boyfriend, I was the only woman left. The combination of the late hour plus the alcohol plus the gender ratio was moving in a predictable direction. I was learning that while the job does have its perks, for women, who are still in the minority, it can come with less pleasant side effects. Already a judge had volunteered to let me spend the night in his "big" hotel room. (I hadn't asked.) And it was also getting increasingly difficult to ignore one of the sommeliers, who, far from sober, had escalated from awkward attempts at flirting to openly groping me. So I went home. To my regular-sized hotel room.

I arrived at breakfast the next morning just in time to hear two judges trade tasting notes on the tap water.

"Oh, good call on the water," said Jason, a Master Sommelier, gesturing to an Aquafina bottle his fellow Master, Jessica, had brought. "I just had to turn on the tap to realize the $4 were worth it. I was like, 'This water is *corked*.' "

The only competitor who'd dragged himself downstairs was a sommelier in his forties named John. He was getting agitated about where he could find a glass of warm Pinot Grigio at this hour. It was part of his pre-tasting ritual. Like a violinist tuning her instrument, he needed a sip of wine to acclimate his tongue to acid and alcohol. There was no way he could go into his blind tasting without it. "I'm just not sure how I'll get my Pinot Grigio this morning with the Sunday alcohol laws," he fretted. "I bet there isn't a bar in the hotel open."

Jason and Jessica ignored him. They were debating the effect of barometric pressure, altitude, and humidity on people's tasting acuity. A storm rolling in, for instance, could mute the aromas in a wine.

"When I left Hawaii, everything was so much more intense," said Jason.

Jessica nodded. "Everyone should taste in Arizona."

"Do you think they'll have Italian Pinot Grigio?" John asked.

While he went to go worry at the concierge's desk, I left to help the other judges prepare for the first round of blind tastings. TopSomm had commandeered a handful of conference rooms at the Hyatt in Santa Rosa, and we checked that each had a table with six glasses and a few chairs. The competitors would take turns tasting while we sat and scored them. I took a seat across from the flight, and my fellow judge and I welcomed the first contestant.

On the surface, it seemed like the sommeliers all had their own techniques for deciphering the wines. There were sniffers and snorters, guzzlers and sippers, spitters and swallowers, standers and sitters. Some sommeliers spoke into the glass, smelling continuously as they talked. Others needed only a single good sniff or two to evaluate the aromas. Some started with the red wines, others preferred to blind the whites first.

Despite those superficial differences and the fact that this was not an official Court event, their analyses were, without exception, based on the so-called deductive tasting method created by the Court. The Court's "grid," a one-page worksheet, specifies what to examine during the four phases of blind tasting—"sight," "nose," "palate," "conclusion"—and in what order, using which words. The system is intended to make somms "taste with purpose—paying attention to what is tasted," and has shaped the way thousands of sommeliers scrutinize their wines. Other institutions of higher drinking, such as the Wine & Spirit Education Trust, have their own versions of the grid. But big-picture, they're all the same.

Blind tasting is not just a party trick, though I've seen it make for a good one. It's meant to teach sommeliers to recognize quality wines, so they can be savvy about buying bottles and then selling them. When you don't have access to the label, you are forced to focus entirely on what you feel in a wine rather than falling back on what you've been told about it. Eventually, you begin to internalize the flavor signature of grapes, regions, vintages, and quality designations. You get to know which wines are outliers, in both good and bad ways, so you can compensate accordingly. The New Zealand Sauvignon Blanc a distributor offers you might be delicious. But from blind tasting dozens of those wines, you would know that this example tastes more like a Grüner Veltliner from Austria than the zippy bell-pepper lemonade that most people will expect from something with "New Zealand" and "Sauvignon Blanc" on its label. Do you buy it, knowing you'll have to manage guests' expectations and do some explaining? Or do you hold out for something more typical?

Blind tasting also trains sommeliers to snatch up good-value wines that taste more expensive than they actually are. For instance, the wines of Saint-Émilion, an appellation on Bordeaux's right bank, are classified into three grades: Premier Grand Cru Classé A, Premier Grand Cru Classé B, and Grand Cru Classé, in descending order. Provided he splurges now and again, Morgan will ideally have tasted enough of the expensive Premier Grand Cru Classé A and B to know what makes them special. So the day he tries a cheaper Grand Cru Classé that approaches the high-end stuff, he'll think "Bargain!" and snap it up. "Buy low, sell high" applies to restaurants as much as it does to anything else. This is also how Morgan affords his wine-soaked lifestyle: He can buy lots of wine—and lots of great wine—because he has a nose for value.

Morgan, who calls himself an "arbitrage expert," presented me with a situation he would have faced back when he was managing the list for Corkbuzz. Let's say he wanted a Cabernet Sauvignon he could sell for $23 per glass. He'd call all his distributors and ask them to bring him every single Cabernet that cost between $12 and $15 a bottle, wholesale. Then he'd sample each until he found one that tasted like it was worth that $23 a glass. "If none of them do and there's only one of them that tastes like a $20 wine, I'll charge $20 for it," he explained.

Once a bottle hits the restaurant's list, it's the sommelier's job to sell it. Blind tasting comes in handy here too, because it helps somms become fluent in the specialized vocabulary of descriptors—"Grand Marnier," "candied tangerine"—that provide a flavor preview for guests. Sure, it might sound affected to be told a wine has "notes of Earl Grey mingling with cassis" (aka black currant). But it's more informative—and, arguably, more helpful—than "tastes like wine."

It's also critical for somms to learn which wines have similar flavor profiles, even though they were grown on different continents, or made from different grapes. Blind tasting hones this skill so that they can perform the often tricky role of matchmaker on the floor. What if the gentleman at Table 23 wants Tempranillo from Rioja, but there isn't one on the list? The somm can suggest a Sangiovese from Italy that will substitute nicely. Offering up laterals—wines that are alike in style but not in make—ideally keeps diners happy. And knowing wines that are similar in style but not in price keeps restaurants happy.

"So here's an example," Morgan said one afternoon after a tasting. "I've got a four-top and it's Mom and Dad and the kids. Dad is wearing, like, a $50,000 Patek Philippe. She's wearing $75,000 worth of jewelry. They obviously have money. And they're sitting there at this table and the woman says, 'I like Pinot Grigio.' And you know you don't have any Pinot Grigio on your list over $80 a bottle and you're like, 'Fuck, *no.* YOU ARE NOT ALLOWED. DECLINE.'

"So you have to go to Dad and go, 'You know, we only have one bottle of Pinot Grigio on the list.' So you end up selling them a $270 bottle of Grand Cru Chablis because you need to. Because there is no Pinot Grigio that you can sell them that's going to make them happy, or that you want to sell them. Because you will have blocked $220 in revenue for your restaurant, for your floor."

"They haven't looked at their bank statement in ten years!" another sommelier cut in.

"It's figuring out how you get to laterals that will make people happy but cost a lot more money," Morgan concluded. "Because to those people, that amount of money is no money."

When it was Morgan's turn to blind taste, he entered the room and sat down in a leather chair across from the judges. I'd tasted with him enough times to know his routine, which he repeated now. He removed his glasses, as though denying one sense would strengthen the others. Then he shifted the spit cup to his left hand and propped his elbow up on the table.

The clock started as soon as he touched the first glass. He began with the reds, as usual.

"Here we have a clear red wine of moderate-plus concentration with dark ruby at the core and a slightly lighter ruby meniscus, free of gas or sediment," he began, borrowing one of the Court's three approved synonyms for the color "red" ("purple," "ruby," "garnet").

"Clear" suggested the wine might have been fined or filtered, processes that can remove yeast, bacteria, and other particles that can spoil a wine, make it hazy, or, some argue, give it its delicious complexity. "Concentration" referred to the wine's density, or opacity—how easy or hard it is to see through the core of the glass—and "ruby" to its color, both of which could clue Morgan in to grape variety and age. Opacity and hue vary by grape variety. From my tasting-group practice and manic solo studying, I knew, for example, that Syrahs and Zinfandels tend to be purplish and dense, whereas Pinot Noirs are usually a clearer ruby. The wine in Morgan's hand was opaque, and more maroon than eggplant. Syrah, Merlot, Sangiovese, Cabernet Sauvignon, and Tempranillo came to mind. Red wines lose color as they age, while whites (colored "straw," "yellow," "gold," or "amber," in Court parlance) gain color. An orange-toned red wine with a faded, watery meniscus—the edge of the wine where it meets the glass—is likely to be older. Ditto for an amber-colored white. (But—and with wine there's always a "but"—oak aging can also lend some color to white wines.) Morgan's wine was dark ruby at the core, only slightly paler at its rim. It lacked sediment, a by-product of aging that appears around a wine's tenth birthday, when acid, color pigment, and tannin molecules start binding together and settling out of the liquid. Probably under ten years old, I thought.

Morgan lifted the wine to the light.

"It is day bright," he said. The grid allows for "dull," "hazy," "bright," "day bright," or "star bright," with "hazy" sometimes hinting at flaws, and "star bright" often suggesting youth.

He took a sip of the wine and swished it to gauge its texture, rolling the bowl of the glass along the edge of the table, so wine covered its sides. He held the glass up to the light and eyed the liquid as it dripped down. "Our viscosity is moderate-plus." Viscosity: the wine's body, or thickness. The tears of the wine were fat and slow. This suggested higher alcohol—warmer climate.

He was twenty seconds in. Three minutes and forty seconds to go.

Morgan plunged his nose into the glass so that its rim pressed against his cheeks. That first sniff was crucial. If it was intense and unmistakably fruity—plum, fig, cherry, blackberry—that would be a vote for a New World wine, meaning it came from anywhere but Europe. More restrained, savory aromas—dirt, leaves, herbs, even stones—would trigger thoughts of the Old World, aka European wines.

"A moderate intensity of ripe red and black fruits, red and black plum, with a little red and black cassis." I mentally riffled through everything I'd memorized and tasted. That could be New World Cabernet, maybe Merlot? The Court's tasting terminology is so standardized—and the profile of certain varieties so established—that each phrase carries a set of associations that, to the trained ear, hint at possible directions. If you know the language, you can decipher the code. Mentioning rose and lychee is a giveaway that you're heading for Gewürztraminer. Olive, black pepper, and meat mean you're barreling toward Syrah. Plum? Merlot. Cassis? Cabernet.

He rattled off more aromas—rose, fresh-tilled earth, oregano, saddle leather. More Old World than New World, I decided. Consistent with Cabernet or Merlot from France, or Tempranillo, used to make Rioja in Spain.

Sixty seconds down.

"We have a little bit of cinnamon and sort of vanilla, sort of baking spice molasses." Translation: a wine aged in new French oak barrels, which characteristically impart those spicy vanilla caramel tones. This was consistent with Bordeaux, a region in France where winemakers often age Cabernet blends in barrels made with new French oak. Also consistent with Rioja in Spain. Or Napa Valley in California.

"I think there's a little Brett here in this wine, this little sort-of animal character, barnyard, earthiness." That sentence screamed Bordeaux, where Brett (short for Brettanomyces yeast) frequently gives wine the perfume of sweaty Thoroughbreds, which can be as much a flavoring as a flaw.

Two minutes had passed. He was churning through words in a low voice, totally monotone, staring at the glass.

Morgan took a big sip of the wine, slurped, and spit it in a solid stream.

The palate. This includes flavor sensations ("bay leaf," "ashy") and, the ultimate objective evidence, structure (acid, sugar, alcohol, tannin, body). By now Morgan had to have suspicions about what he was drinking, and the structure would help disqualify certain guesses and add weight to others.

"There's a sort of roasted red pepper, roasted tomato that makes me think there's some pyrazine in this wine." That word. Pyrazine. A chemical compound present in green bell peppers, peas, Sauvignon Blanc, and—you guessed it—both Tempranillo and Cabernet Sauvignon grapes.

Three and a half minutes. Thirty seconds to go.

This wine was dry (not sweet). Moderate-plus tannins. It was moderate-plus in acid and moderate-plus in alcohol. Higher acid indicates grapes grown in cooler climates, higher alcohol can mean warmer weather. So it had to be from someplace warm, but not *too* warm. More evidence for Europe over California.

He took another sip. Five seconds left.

I knew, from my own experience, that Morgan had to be racing back over everything he'd said. The vibrancy of the wine's ruby color, plus its sparkle, fruitiness, and highish tannins all suggested a relatively young wine. The tomato, leather, and even the new French oak could be consistent with Spanish Tempranillo. But those layered flavors, with the mixture of plum (hint: Merlot), cassis (hint: Cabernet), and pyrazine (hint: oh *yeah*, Cabernet), pointed to a blend of at least two different kinds of grapes. Winemakers on the left bank of Bordeaux make wine from a blend of Cabernet Sauvignon (mostly) with some Merlot (less) and a few other grapes (even less). Winemakers on the *right* bank of Bordeaux will blend Merlot (mostly) with Cabernet Sauvignon (less) and a few other grapes (even less).

Left bank, I guessed. With that Brett and the oak, it had to be Bordeaux.

Morgan gave his final answer: "This is a Merlot-dominant blend from the right bank of Bordeaux from the village of Saint-Émilion in the 2010 vintage of Grand Cru Classé quality."

One wine down, five to go.

When he finished his flight, Morgan hurried to the lobby to join a gaggle of sommeliers trading notes on what they'd called each wine. They all looked defeated.

"I called it '06 Saint-Émilion," said Mia of wine number four, the one Morgan had tasted first.

"I thought that it had more mid-palate than a Merlot," said Jackson. "I was *totally* on the Saint-Émilion track, then for whatever reason, once it hit the palate I just got, like, the tannins *allllll* up front. It was more mid-palate than front-palate. But otherwise, I was right there with you on Saint-Émilion. All the way."

"How you doing, killer?" said Morgan, inserting himself into their conversation and slapping Jackson on the back.

"Third one I called New Zealand Sauvignon Blanc," said Jackson, ignoring Morgan. He leaned over to tap another guy on the shoulder. "Hey, what'd you call the Sauvignon Blanc?"

"Sancerre," the guy answered.

Jackson paled. "You called *Sancerre*?" He shook his head. "I don't know, man." He reconsidered. Confidence leaked out of him. "It's that weird yeast they use. It makes it have that guava-y . . ." He sighed. "It could totally be Sancerre."

"I called it Sonoma coast," Morgan volunteered. "I was just thinking about the last three Loire vintages. I was like, 'This is really fresh, this is current vintage, and this sort of purity of fruit doesn't make sense for the Loire.' All the thirteens have botrytis on them!"

"Yeah, who the hell decided collectively to make Sauvignon Blanc with botrytis on it?" demanded Jackson, sounding personally wounded by this fact.

I was surprised their guesses were so scattered—France, New Zealand, America. "What was the hardest part of the flight?"

"The hardest part is always yourself," said Jon, the sommelier from my tasting group, who worked at Eleven Madison Park.

"Your brain's in fear mode," Morgan agreed. *"I-want-an-answer-I-want-an-answer-I-want-an-answer."*

"Like on wine number one," said Jon, "I was like, 'Oh, there's a bunch of oak and malo and it's high in alcohol and I don't get much minerality,' so I instinctually called it Cali Chard and moved on. But if my mind was completely open and deductive, I would have been like, 'Well, I'm getting all this sweet citrus and bitterness and banana . . .'" He trailed off. "I became fairly—not frustrated, but . . . scared."

"And that's where it's a mental game," said Morgan. He took a sip from a glass of water that he'd poured earlier from a clear pitcher filled with sliced strawberries and ice water. An expression of surprise passed over Morgan's face, and he cocked his head, trying to process what he'd just held in his mouth. He swallowed and smiled, as if having solved the riddle. "It tastes like strawberry water."

The blind tasting portion of TopSomm gave way to the final two parts of the competition. During theory, my fellow judges behaved. Everyone sat around a table firing questions at the sommeliers from a script prepared in advance by the contest organizers. We pretended to be hapless junior sommeliers struggling to satisfy finicky guests. "My table is trying to decide between young Smaragd Grüner Veltliners from Hirtzberger, Prager, or Veyder-Malberg. Do you know which one is likely to have the most botrytis?" (Answer: the wine made by Hirtzberger.) Or: "One of our customers is interested in vintage Calvados but wants something that's pear driven. What should I suggest?" (Answer: Calvados from Domaine Lemorton in Domfrontais.) And: "One of the customers at the bar is asking questions about our absinthe selection. . . . When did it become legal? What's the typical alcohol range for real absinthe?" (Answer: 2007; 50 to 70 percent.) *Tell her to stop asking so many questions and just enjoy the freaking cocktail* would have been my reply. But the competitors stood erect at the front of the room fielding each question with patience and aplomb.

The judges were most excited about the service section of the competition. There were no rules. It was time for full, unbridled hazing, sommelier-style. The older Master Sommeliers derived a special breed of pleasure from tormenting their juniors.

"Have you taken your man pills?" Fred bellowed when he saw Dana, pounding him on the back. Dana smiled weakly.

He and the other competitors waited outside while the judges and I received our instructions.

"You can be assholes," one of the Master Sommeliers instructed everyone.

"When I lay down and pretend like I'm choking, that's when you know you've really been bad," Fred boomed. "I had one guy once, while he was giving me recommendations I sat there picking my nose.

I go"—he mimed digging into his right nostril—"He was like, '*Aiiiyyaiiiyyaaaiiii.*' "

This was the ultimate fantasy role-play for anyone who's worked in the service industry: It was our turn to act like obnoxious guests. One table was celebrating a birthday and the host, wary of looking cheap in front of his son, would have to intercept the sommelier to explain that he'd be ordering a bottle of Champagne—but *fer chrissakes don't throw me under the bus, keep it under a hundred bucks.* This was Fred's line. A couple at another table would want pairing suggestions, as well as recommendations for which châteaux to visit on their upcoming vacation to France's Loire Valley. They'd try to eat up the sommelier's time (fifteen minutes, total), so it would be nearly impossible for him to rush back to the Champagne table to open and serve the sparkling wine. I was seated with a table of inquisitive history buffs who would order glasses of Madeira, followed by a bottle of red that needed decanting, all with a heaping side of questions.

Morgan came into the room, saw Fred in his section, and immediately swerved away from him to tend to the couple. Jessica, one of the two judges at Morgan's table, asked him about his restaurant's $15 flight of three Loire reds. The menu said each was made with different grape varieties and hailed from different appellations; what were they? Morgan's challenge was to name three specific wines—producer and vintage—that didn't repeat their region or grapes and that his imaginary restaurant could make money selling for $15. Fred crossed his arms and glowered at Morgan from the corner, growing impatient. Jessica also wanted to know what to drink with her chicken. And what pretty castles she should see when she went to the Loire. Oh, and maybe she actually felt like a white—what could Morgan recommend? His voice rose a full octave as he answered her questions and, from the corner of his eye, watched Fred turning red. "So! Superb! Yeah! Superb!" he chirped, desperately trying to extricate himself to get to Fred, who was just then waving down the mock maître d' to complain.

The judges' frowns made it clear where Morgan was messing up. When he poured a taste of Madeira for the Master Sommelier at my table, a splash of wine hit the rim of the glass. The entire table grew silent and not a single person, Morgan included, breathed as we watched the fat, juicy brown droplet roll, as if in slow motion, over the outside rim, along the glass's side, and down the stem to the foot of the glass. It was like a turd smeared on a wedding gown. The Master Sommelier pointedly stopped the drip with his finger just as it was about to bleed onto the tablecloth. "Saved it," he announced, even though it was clear all was lost.

As Morgan finished his turn at service and the next group of competitors cycled in, I sensed that these few minutes of judging had forever spoiled my innocence as a diner. It had ruined the simple, naïve pleasure of eating out by bringing to light the full multitude of sins that sommeliers—and servers—commit at the table. An hour before, I didn't know to be affronted when a sommelier "back-handed" me—pouring the wine so that the back of his hand faced me. But now: *how dare he!* The goal of service isn't just getting the liquid into a glass. Far from it. That's just the grand finale, which has been choreographed with an elaborate set of steps that should build to and enhance the ultimate moment of pleasure: the sip.

The Master Sommeliers walked me through all the "don'ts" of wine service, all of which I'd have to master ahead of my own Certified exam.

Don't lean. Don't slouch. Don't look stiff. Don't cross your arms and don't point. Do not discuss price and do not say your name (what is this, Applebee's?). Don't touch the table, your face, your hair, and never, *ever* touch the guest. Don't forget to polish the glasses. Don't touch anything but their stem. And while you're at it, don't touch the *serviette* to your clothes. Don't let the glasses tinkle. Don't let your hands tremble. Don't even *think* about taking your thumb off the Champagne cork before it's opened. (Don't you want people to live through dinner?)

Do not put an ice bucket on the table. Don't forget to offer the cork. (Didn't you remember two coasters? One for the bottle, one for the cork.)

Don't pour men before women, don't pour hosts before their guests, don't pour more for one person than another. And God help you if you drip. Don't pick up glasses to pour, and don't take more than two pours to fill one glass. Don't empty the bottle the first go-around. Don't ever block the label with your hand. Don't look awkward. Don't fidget. Don't pour from the left. Don't walk clockwise. Don't ever swear. Don't make guests ask you the vintage. Don't be so eager. Don't be so serious—you don't want to be a funeral director, do you? Don't be so shy. Don't say "um." And for the love of God don't look so nervous. This is supposed to be fun.

Once you have them memorized, the mechanical steps of service may sound, if not easy, then at least manageable. But what makes them difficult is that you must do all of these things while making recommendations, running wine up from the cellar, entering orders, acknowledging guests who've just been seated, and offering wine to the woman whose steak just landed, while also making each guest believe you have the luxury to spend all evening satisfying her whims. It must look effortless. "Elegant" came up over and over again. "Graceful." "Really, really soft, really elegant." Posture, the tremor in a voice, pauses in speech, the fluidity bending over a bottle—all of it matters.

"We use the analogy of a swan. We look smooth and calm on top, but we're pedaling frantically underneath," Jon told me during a break. "It has to be perfect."

"What if you have an off night?" I wondered.

"You can't have an off night."

After service was completed, the judges tallied scores while the sommeliers stepped away from the tables to stand with their noses almost touching the walls of the conference room. The ritual was either meant to keep them from seeing the score sheets or haze them, or both. Standing there in their formal attire with their faces pressed against the wallpaper, they looked like naughty CEOs in time out.

Morgan lost points for his drip, but also for being "a little antsy," with an energy that "makes you nervous." Others had their scores docked for missing a wipe, failing to polish their glasses, standing awkwardly, and letting their nerves show. One sommelier made the mistake of being friendly. "He was too familiar," sniffed a judge.

The awards were announced at an Italian restaurant staffed by the mozzarella equivalent of a Master Sommelier. He called himself the Mozz Guy, and he dropped warm balls of curd made of milk sourced from twelve different farms into the outstretched palms of the sommeliers. They stood over him and watched as he massaged the cheese into little tufts of white. He called it "herding the curd." They tried the mozzarella warm, with salt, with olive oil. There was talk of the *terroir* of cheese and the different grasses the cows might have eaten.

Morgan didn't win.

He'd aced the theory questions, as usual. But the droplet of wine during service had killed him, as had his blind tasting. The wine he called a Saint-Émilion, from Bordeaux's right bank, was really a Médoc, from Bordeaux's left bank. He'd missed it by about twenty-four miles, as the crow flies.

CHAPTER FOUR

The Brains

I SHOULD TAKE A STEP BACK AND TELL YOU SOMETHING ABOUT MY physical state at this point. I was drunk most of the time. I was up to three, sometimes four, blind tasting groups a week, which meant I was sober for, on average, a solid six hours a day. When I wasn't tasting, I was smelling—trying to rattle off the scents in my shampoo as I showered—or assembling study guides to wine appellations. But mostly, I was tasting. I had a perpetual headache and I was getting worried about what all this might be doing to my body. "Do you find it's been really hard on your skin?" a friend asked me, her gaze lingering on the puffy areas around my eyes. My dentist gave me a lecture about the dangers of wine's acidity as he poked at my molars. I cringe to think of what appeared in my medical records after a particularly awkward conversation at the doctor's office:

Nurse: Do you currently drink alcohol?

Me: Um, well, I'm training to become a sommelier, so yes I'm currently drinking alcohol. I mean, not *right now* obviously. But I do drink alcohol. But I don't have a problem. But I guess that's what alcoholics say. But I don't think I'm an alcoholic.

Nurse: *(silence)*

In fairness, Matt was getting increasingly concerned about the "Help, I'm hungover" text messages I'd send him at two in the afternoon while he, like most people, was at work and I was stumbling through the subway with red teeth.

Since I probably owed my liver an apology, I at least wanted to know if this training was really helping me live a more flavorful life. I had taken sommeliers at their word when they assured me it was possible to upgrade my senses by following traditional methods passed down through generations of professional drinkers. Then again, this was a group that still believed in the long-since-debunked tongue map, which claims we taste sweet sensations on the tip of our tongues, bitter at the back, and sour and salty on the sides. Was it even possible to hone our senses of taste and smell? Or was I just becoming a good bullshitter? Could science point me toward a better way? My wine-industry mentors had consumed thousands of bottles over many years in a regimen guided more by custom than science. I could never replicate that experience in my limited time horizon. I began to wonder: Could neuroscientists, PhDs, and MDs provide a guide—and maybe even a shortcut—to smarter sensing?

Morgan had promised that what he and his fellow sommeliers did in blind tasting was neither magical nor tied to the luck of the genetic draw. "I am not a wizard," he declared the first time we met. And yet other sommeliers had spoken of a seemingly inborn ability to distinguish nuances in flavors, which made me worry that I might be on a fool's errand. Craig Sindelar, the sommelier who'd worked at Alinea in Chicago, told me about a game he played with his mom growing up: His nose was so sensitive, she'd hide a cookie somewhere in the kitchen, and make him find it by smell alone. When I was the same age, I was eating dog biscuits, which at the time seemed to me like a perfectly reasonable substitute for granola bars.

I wasn't wrong to be worried. Research has found that our genetic makeup does determine our sensitivity to smells and tastes. Some people can only register the stink of, say, blue cheese or malt in extremely high concentrations. For others, low doses are enough to make them wrinkle their noses. That variation has been traced back to our DNA, suggesting each person is born with sensitivity to a unique combination of odors they can and cannot smell well. Someone who is ultrasensitive to Gorgonzola could be nose-blind for violets and just average for the fragrance of rose.

Then there are the "supertasters," who are naturally endowed with princess-and-the-pea palates. About a quarter of the population boasts an exceptionally high concentration of taste receptors on their tongues, which allows them to perceive finer flavor stimuli. These supertasters can discriminate minute changes in flavor and are more sensitive to intense tastes, so cake frosting can be sickeningly sweet or coffee and kale repulsively bitter. They "live in a neon food world compared to the pastel food world," according to University of Florida scientist Linda Bartoshuk, who coined the term "supertaster" in 1991. (Another 25 percent of humans are "nontasters," scientists' callous term for people with normal tongues, and the remaining 50 percent are "tasters," blessed with just a sprinkling of extra receptors.) Studies indicate that supertasters are disproportionately represented among foodies, wine experts, and chefs. My personal experience indicates that supertasters are disproportionately predisposed to lord their status over others. Using a supertaster testing kit I ordered from a company that listed a sketchy apartment over a shoe-repair shop as its return address, I placed a strip of chemically treated paper on my tongue and discovered that I was a "taster." Matt? Smug supertaster. "I'd give you some of my scotch," he offered, swirling it in my face. "But it'd be like taking a blind person to the Louvre."

Even as labs tease out ties between our DNA and our senses, it turns out we are not entirely prisoners to our genes. Thomas Hummel, a professor and physician at Germany's University of Dresden Smell and Taste Clinic, specializes in methods for training the chemical senses of taste and smell (so called because they're stimulated by chemicals that travel through food, liquids, and the air). His lab—"*the* center for smell and taste research in Europe," according to a colleague from Stockholm University—has also become famous, at least in certain circles, for quantifying these seemingly unquantifiable senses and championing them in a discipline that has long dismissed them. He developed the olfactory version of an eye test that's used worldwide to diagnose and measure smell disorders. And more recently, he has led studies probing whether we can improve our sense of smell with practice.

The first time I spoke on the phone with Thomas, he offered to stick a camera up my nose. I liked him immediately. Thomas told me he would be presenting his most recent findings at the annual Clinical Chemosensation Conference he would be hosting at his lab in Dresden. Neuroscientists, physicians, psychologists, flavor chemists, and perfumers from around the world would also be sharing the latest research on taste and smell. He suggested I come. I was already looking for plane tickets.

The 2004 Nobel Prize in Medicine was awarded to two Columbia University biologists who discovered how the olfactory system works. Until their research, wrote the Nobel assembly, smell had remained "the most enigmatic of our senses." And in this case, lack of understanding really was for lack of trying: The Nobel win provided an enormous boost to olfaction, a field that for decades received middling respect, funding, and interest, especially compared to vision, audition, and touch. (Undoubtedly Plato's influence at work.) Among researchers, studying smell (and taste) had long been seen as something you do only "if you have nothing else to do," said Johan Lundström, a neuroscientist at the Monell Chemical Senses Center. "It's like your first girlfriend: 'Oh-*kayyyyy*, but then you have to marry a proper girl.'"

On the flight over to Germany, I perused papers written by the people who'd be presenting at Thomas's conference. I admired the dedication it must have taken to ignore the peer pressure and stick with the chemical senses. But as I dove into their work, I began to think it took a dose of crazy too. Their past research included: how subjects rank the breath of men versus women on a five-day no-oral-hygiene regimen; changes in the pleasantness of human vaginal odors during a woman's menstrual cycle; and the urine odors preferred by "sexually experienced" rats versus rat virgins. In line for croissants the first day of the conference, a cheerful postdoctoral researcher told me that she was currently collecting samples of "aggressive" and "fear" sweat by wiping the armpits of people who had either taken a deliberately impossible test or been made to stand on a building's ledge. She wanted to know why I wasn't getting my PhD, to which I replied that she'd just answered her own question.

We settled into our chairs and Thomas welcomed us. He was a rotund man, solid as a Volkswagen Beetle, with a gargantuan white mustache that would have looked fetching with lederhosen. He made everyone introduce themselves, and I felt as though I'd stumbled into a support group for misfit scientists. "In the real world, there are many people who don't care about the sense of smell. This is what I've experienced a couple of times," Thomas said. Heads nodded in sympathy. He delivered the first lecture, a not-so-thinly-veiled defense of why we should bother with his field.

Even before the lunch break, it became clear that for most of us—the general public outside the chemosensory world—there is a very basic step we can take to improve our senses of taste and smell: Learn which is which.

Flavor, the overall impression we form about food and drink, is made up of tastes, smells, touch sensations, and other stimuli. Yet we have a tendency to attribute any feeling in our mouths as taste. We say something "tastes" good, when really we mean it "flavors." (It would be more accurate to refer to blind tasting as "blind flavoring.") In short, many of us are confused about what taste really feels like, and how to distinguish it from smell. A study conducted at the University of Pennsylvania's Smell and Taste Center by one of the conference attendees found patients who complained about losing their sense of taste were actually three times more likely to be suffering from smell impairment than any taste disorder. Imagine showing up to an ophthalmologist because you're having difficulty reading street signs, only to learn that the problem is hearing-related. It's hard to imagine ever mixing up our other senses in such an elementary way. When I asked one of Thomas's colleagues what the general public misunderstands most about taste and smell, she didn't pause a second before answering: "They don't know what is taste and what is smell."

When he's not using them, Martin Witt keeps his brains in a yellow plastic bucket in the basement of a lecture hall on the University of Dresden campus. I found him and the bucket in a classroom filled with human remains. Skeletons stood guard over a jumble of pelvises and human skulls in Tupperware boxes. Fetuses in formaldehyde peered out from jars on the bookshelves.

It could be the company he keeps, but fiftysomething Martin, an anatomy professor, evokes a skeletal figure himself. Wan complexion, nothing but bones, and skin that stretches tight over his cheeks to reveal a gleaming white grin. He'd brought several specimens, including the brains, with him from his office at the University of Rostock just north of Dresden, and enjoyed recounting his road trips with this unusual cargo. "I remember I vas traveling once between Poland and Chermany vith six fetuses . . ." he said, apropos of nothing, during a cocktail party one evening. He has something less than a surgeon's graceful touch ("Vee dissected that poor guy. It's really difficult, you need a Black and Decker") and an impressively ample repertoire of jokes about dead bodies ("That's a perspective you'll never see in your neighbors—unless you dig somewhere!"). Also, he bears a mysterious grudge against dolphins ("They seem so nice and so social. But really, they're all out for themselves. They have this banker-like mentality").

Martin had been invited to present at the conference, which just so happened to coincide with a visit to Thomas's lab by a class of psychology graduate students. Thomas asked Martin to speak to the budding scientists, and I joined their field trip so I could watch Martin guide them through the human brain—to trace the neurons to the nerves to the brain, and elucidate where one sense ends and the other begins. To properly understand taste and smell, I needed to get back to the most basic, fundamental facts about how these senses work.

Martin reached into his yellow bucket to grab a human head that had been sliced in half by a vertical incision that ran from the crown down through the nose, lips, and chin. "Feel free to touch it," he offered. "If you like you can have it in your hand."

After a brief tour of major anatomical landmarks, he started in on the life of a taste. The bumps on the surface of the tongue each contain clusters of taste buds, around two thousand to ten thousand in total. When wine (or anything else) hits your tongue, saliva dissolves the taste substances into ions and molecules, which enter small pores in the tongue's surface and connect with the gustatory receptor cells at the tip of each taste bud. This triggers a neuron that rushes a signal—Sweet! Salty! Sour!—to the brain.

If you're wondering just how misunderstood our chemical senses have been, consider this: It took almost a century, until about the 1970s, to figure out that the tongue map was bogus, a scientific gaffe arising from a mistranslation of a German student's 1901 PhD dissertation. Contrary to the tongue map's teaching, all areas of the tongue are responsive to each of the five tastes. (Studies suggest the front of the tongue is only ever so slightly more sensitive to sweetness and saltiness, while the soft palate—the roof of your mouth—can pick up more minute levels of bitterness.) Another common misconception is that the tongue is your body's only taste interpreter. In fact, there are taste receptors on your epiglottis, as well as in your throat, stomach, intestines, pancreas, and, if you're a man, your sperm and testes. The idea that humans can perceive only five tastes is also up for debate. Besides sweet, bitter, salty, sour, and umami—that meaty, savory intensity in foods like soy sauce and cooked mushrooms—scientists have argued for expanding the club of basic tastes to include water, calcium, metallic, "soapy," and fat ("oleogustus").

Yet even if "oleogustus" were to take its spot alongside sweet and sour, the range of taste sensations we perceive pales in comparison to our capacity to discern odors. A 2014 paper published in the journal *Science* posited that humans can detect more than 1 trillion odors—many times the number of colors we can see (several million) and tones we hear (nearly 500,000). Other researchers have disputed that 1 trillion figure. But even the more modest estimates, which approximate that humans can distinguish around 10,000 olfactory stimuli, made it clear that to improve my sense of taste (and flavor), what I really needed to do was improve my sense of smell. A German Riesling and a French Chenin Blanc might both taste acidic and a little sweet; it's in the nose where critical differences reveal themselves. I thought of Morgan's stance on Pinot Noir from Burgundy: The pleasure was all in the smell. "I'm going to drink it because that's what you're intended to do with it," he said. "But the aromas to me are 80 percent of the appeal." What we consider "taste" is mostly smell, and it's easy enough to experience it for yourself. Plug your nose and take a sip of coffee. What you're left feeling is taste. Unplug your nose, and the full spectrum of smell and flavor will come rushing back. An espresso *tastes* bitter but *smells* like coffee.

Martin had moved on and was tracing the journey of an aroma on the spongy flesh of his cadaver head. Picture, again, that you're holding a glass of wine. Just above the surface of the liquid are submicroscopically small scented particles that evaporate from the surface of the wine and become airborne. With each sniff, your nostrils suck in those odorant molecules, which travel to the top of your nasal cavity, an air-filled space located just behind your nose and eyes. The odorant molecules, which come in different shapes and weights, hit the olfactory receptor cells that line the tissue in the nasal cavity, and bind to one or more of the receptors. That sends a signal to the olfactory bulb, a crucial relay station that translates "molecule has hit receptor" into a meaningful message in the brain. "Animal character, barnyard, earthiness," it might say if you're Morgan. "Hmmmmm—horse?" it might say if you're me.

Odors, unlike sound waves, are chemically transmitted. Molecules float off the surface of whatever we smell and into our bodies. "Anything you smell, you swallow," is Johan's motto. This is a pleasant thought when it comes to fresh roses or some nice black truffles. It is disturbing when you consider the stink of dog shit. By the time you notice its smell, it's too late: The chemicals wafting off the excrement have already made contact with your nasal cavity, where, Johan assured me, they can enter our bloodstream and continue into the brain. "Which," he unfortunately felt the need to clarify, "means a lot of the shit we smell might end up in the brain."

You continue smelling a wine even after you've lowered the glass from your nose to tip some of the liquid onto your tongue. As you savor that sip, more airborne odorants can travel from your mouth—scientifically speaking, your "oral cavity"—up to your olfactory receptors, a process known as retro-nasal olfaction. Looking at the cadaver, I could clearly see the passageway connecting the very back of the mouth to the nasal cavity. At the moment where a wine would flow past the tongue and down the throat, its aromas could make a sharp turn up, taking the fork in the road back up to the olfactory receptors.

I noticed a strange, pale growth on the underside of the front part of the brain. On the area that sits just behind the eyes, there was something about an inch and a half long, as thin as a rubber band, and with a rounded tip. It looked almost like a smear of bubblegum that had gotten stuck on the bottom of the brain.

"What's that thing sticking out?" I asked Martin.

"Here it is!" he crowed, as if finding an old friend. It was the olfactory bulb.

For something so small, it has created a great deal of trouble. It is the part of the body where smells are born. It is also where our modern olfactory inferiority complex begins.

As early as the fourth century BCE, humans had already given up on smell. This sense is "in our case, not accurate but is worse than with many animals," declared Aristotle in *De Anima*. "For man can smell things only poorly, and he perceives none of the objects of smell unless they are painful or pleasant, because the sense-organ is not accurate." Aristotle, history's first scientist, made the judgment call, and though he couldn't elucidate why we were so terrible at picking up odors, the notion that we possess a poor sense of smell has stuck ever since.

The scientific explanation for the idea that humans are weak smellers finally emerged in the nineteenth century, thanks to the work of a French surgeon, anthropologist, and child prodigy named Paul Broca. Broca, born in 1824 not far from Bordeaux, was seventeen when he entered medical school in Paris, with degrees in literature, math, and physics already under his belt. He would become one of neuroscience's most celebrated figures for discovering the region of the brain responsible for language development, which is still known as "Broca's area."

But the scientists in Dresden see Broca as a troublemaker. He bears the dubious distinction of developing a theory that has dogged their field for nearly two hundred years: He posited—and ostensibly proved—that through evolution, humans had unlearned how to smell.

Smell was not popular among Broca's contemporaries. At the time, researchers viewed olfaction with such condescension that only a "few scattered papers of interest" were published, according to an account of nineteenth-century medical attitudes by historians Anne Harrington and Vernon Rosario. The few scattered papers that did appear mostly confirmed that it was a subject undeserving of more consideration. The loss of smell "barely amounts to a discomfort," asserted a British physician in an 1873 article for *The Lancet*, a medical journal.

Against the backdrop of Darwin's *On the Origin of Species*, olfactory acuity was seen as a relic from our savage ancestors. In a bit of convenient logic, scientists decided that smelling well, a skill they considered lacking among themselves and their enlightened peers, had lost its importance. Thus, they reasoned, it must have disappeared as people became civilized beings. "The habit of living in society and the assurance of finding amongst one's equals the intelligence . . . which has dispensed with the need to have recourse to smell, have left civilized man less sensitive to the impressions that act on that sense, which has therefore lost some of its sensitivity," argued French anatomist Hippolyte Cloquet in an 1821 reference text on olfaction. "Amongst individuals who have not risen in social state, there is a much superior acuity."

Yet it fell to Broca, a big supporter of Darwin, to develop the most convincing proof in support of the hypothesis that modern man "forgot" how to smell. In his lab in Paris, Broca dissected the brains of birds, fish, chimps, rodents, otters, humans, and those bankers of the sea, dolphins, among other animals. He seized on a pattern: As creatures ascend the evolutionary ladder, from sub-mammalian vertebrates to primates to humans, their limbic lobe, an arc-shaped region of the midbrain then believed to control olfaction, "regresses and atrophies." For many years, the limbic lobe was considered the engine for our sense of smell and was thought to include a small, rather unimpressive lump of tissue at the front of the brain—the olfactory bulb. Like his peers, Broca noticed that in higher primates, the olfactory bulb shrank relative to the size of the entire brain. As he noted—and generations of textbooks have repeated since—animals perceived as having superb senses of smell, such as rats and dogs, possess olfactory bulbs that occupy a comparatively huge area of the brain. By contrast, the human olfactory bulb is a puny little thing in relation to our entire mass of gray matter. It's about the same size as the rat's olfactory bulb, while the mass of our full brain is over eight hundred times as large. Broca concluded that these findings illustrated "the diminishment of the importance of olfactory function" to the point that "for the civilized man, the delicacy of his olfactory sense is . . . of no utility in his life."

In a work praising his colleague Broca's contributions, surgeon Samuel Pozzi completed the story line. He articulated the now-prevalent belief that smell became inferior to vision as humans rose off of four limbs and onto two:

> Animals were quadrupeds, a position essentially favorable to the exercise of smell. The primate rose up, man lifted his head forever more away from the earth and directed his sight parallel to the horizon. The hegemony of the visual sense substituted itself for that of olfaction. . . . Is it not curious that the anatomist can legitimately link to this first fact, so apparently simple, the development of the frontal lobe? It is no less curious, from the same point of view, to discover in man's brain the vestiges of that dethroned organ, the limbic lobe. Instead of forming an imposing unit, it is reduced to the state of fragments, barely linked to each other; in other words, a collection of debris.

More simply stated: The olfactory organs are trash. And the better you can smell, the less evolved you must be. That became conventional wisdom, and has been passed along ever since. And according to the experts at the conference, it is wrong.

"I would say that the idea we lost our sense of smell is a myth, period," said Johan Lundström, the neuroscientist. We were chatting in between lectures, and as we nibbled on ham sandwiches, Johan observed that the slices of meat would be much more flavorful if they were a bright color, like neon green. Johan, who specializes in multisensory perception and the chemical senses, splits his time between neuroscience labs at Philadelphia's Monell Center and the Karolinska Institutet in Stockholm, home of the Nobel Committee. (He also once served as Thomas Hummel's research assistant.) Johan spends much of his time watching people's brains while they taste and smell.

Everything he has learned suggests that Broca was wrong—wrong that olfaction died out when we stood up on two legs, wrong that humans are poor smellers, wrong that olfaction is of no use to us whatsoever in our "civilized" existence.

This was working out nicely: I hadn't had to do anything, and I already felt like my sense of smell had improved.

It's true that relative to other animals, humans have a smaller number of functioning olfactory receptor genes. (These encode and produce our smell receptors, which, you'll remember, are what bind with airborne odor molecules to make us aware of aromas.) We have 1,000 of these genes, but only 350 of them are active—significantly fewer than, say, the 1,000 active olfactory receptor genes boasted by rats and mice. Broca and his colleagues might be pleased to know that twenty-first-century scientists have embraced nineteenth-century logic to explain this. They argue that our olfactory receptor genes essentially died off as we developed full color vision.

While our shrunken set of genes and the flimsy size of our olfactory bulb might suggest that we stink at smelling, recent behavioral studies show the opposite. We're much better sniffers than anyone previously thought—probably, notes Johan, because no one bothered to systematically measure our olfactory ability in the first place, including Broca. The explanation for our acuity is still emerging, but one popular theory uses essentially the same evidence observed by Broca to draw the opposite conclusion: Sure, we have only a few hundred olfactory receptor genes and our olfactory bulb is comparatively small. But this equipment is powered by a much larger, more advanced brain, which offsets any loss in size. "Rather than being restricted to a tiny part of the brain, olfactory processing of complex smells, such as those produced by human cuisines, draws on the enlarged processing capacity of the human brain," writes Yale University neurobiologist Gordon Shepherd in a paper for *PLoS Biology*.

Johan directed me to the work of Matthias Laska, a biologist at the Linköping University in Sweden. His research has shown that humans boast a better sense of smell than many of the animals whose noses we've always admired. Rats, for instance, are said to be such olfactory prodigies that they can sniff out land mines and tuberculosis. "We can hardly imagine what such a world is like, our sense of smell is so impoverished," gushes a website for rat fans. Actually, we can imagine it: Laska reviewed all the available data tracking humans' sensitivity to low concentrations of odors, and determined that humans often outperform species long considered to be the über-noses of the animal kingdom: mice, hedgehogs, shrews, pigs, and rabbits, as well as rats, whom we bested on thirty-one of the forty-one odors tested. Humans even trumped dogs on five of the fifteen odors studied.

"If you compare how our sense of smell is doing compared to other animals, we actually beat the crap out of most animals," said Johan.

During one of his lectures, Thomas Hummel presented the findings from a study that pitted undergraduates against well-trained hunting dogs to see if the students could track a scent trail the way man's best friend follows the perfume of pheasants or deer. Dogs, who belong to a supersniffing category of animals that Broca dubbed macrosmats, are celebrated for being able to smell money, bombs, and types of cancer—things we do not necessarily associate with having an odor. Humans, on the other hand, will go a week without removing rotting piles of food from the kitchen trash. The researchers in the tracking study bundled up their subjects to obscure every sense but smell. The students wore long-sleeved jumpsuits, gloves, taped-over goggles, headphones, gray booties, and knee pads, which upped the comfort, but not the dignity, of crawling over the ground on all fours with their noses down and butts in the air. They were released on a grass field through which the researchers had created a scent trail using chocolate essential oil, and tasked with tracking the smell to a designated endpoint. In his lecture, Thomas juxtaposed the paths of a dog in pursuit of a bird and of a student hunting for chocolate: Just like the dog, the person crisscrosses the trail, zigzagging left and right over the chocolate's path until reaching the end. A follow-up to the study found students actually improved with practice. The researchers concluded that "longer-term training would lead to further increases in tracking velocity"—and perhaps a new kind of hunting companion.

We are also capable of smelling warning signals in our environment, just like animals. The sense of smell, our body's alarm system, is constantly on the alert for threats, and subtly nudges our behavior accordingly. The scent of women's tears, for example, has been shown to decrease sexual arousal among men. Johan has found that we can differentiate healthy strangers from sick individuals based solely on their body odors, a cue that may have evolved to help us avoid infection. And of course we can smell some dangers, like smoke or gas, before we see them.

Though we're largely oblivious to it at a conscious level, we exchange social information with each other via smell. Johan's work has determined that humans can distinguish the body odors of twenty-somethings from octogenarians; of friends versus relatives; and of boyfriends versus platonic male friends. Smell can also bring people closer together. One of his studies found that as women fall more in love with their boyfriends, they become worse at identifying the body odors of other men: Romantic love alters women's sense of smell to deflect attention "away from potential new partners," effectively binding them more intensely to their mates. Odors also strengthen the attraction between mothers and their infants, whose natural aroma causes a dopamine surge in the reward areas of the mothers' brains—"almost like they were sniffing some kind of cocaine," said Johan. Pheromones, airborne chemicals we secrete through our bodies, are believed to play a role in bringing couples together in the first place. In the Elizabethan age, long before scientists had developed the pheromone concept, women gave their sweethearts "love apples"—peeled apples the ladies had tucked under their armpits, saturated with their sweat, and then offered to their lovers to inhale. Courtship has come a long way: These days, you can try "smell dating" via a matchmaking service that has strangers sweat into T-shirts, then exchange the BO-soaked clothing with potential mates to sniff.

Even as olfaction guides our behavior like some unseen puppeteer, we consistently underestimate our ability to smell. (One reason may be that the brain is not wired to pay attention to odors, and most smells are processed subconsciously. Olfactory signals, unlike other sensory inputs, bypass the thalamus, a part of the brain that makes us conscious of perceived stimuli.) Not long before we spoke, Johan and his colleagues hosted a party where they did what apparently passes for festive in a neuroscience lab: Johan asked the head of his department to blind smell ten different body odors belonging to each of the man's staff members, then identify which was whose. The department head insisted it wasn't possible. Try, Johan instructed him. With each odor, the man threw up his hands and said he had no clue. And each time, Johan encouraged him to go ahead and guess which person it had come from. Just take a stab at it. Do your best.

In the end, the head of the department correctly identified all but two of the body odors. The pair he mixed up had come from two assistants who had started working with him only a few weeks before.

I was relieved to find that my olfactory skills were better than I'd imagined. Because truth be told, the advice I was getting on how to improve my sense of smell was some strange stuff.

"If you were me and wanted to enhance your senses of taste and smell, what would you do?" I asked Richard Doty, a colleague of Johan's at the Monell Center and one of the world's foremost experts on the chemical senses.

"Cocaine," he said without missing a beat.

Not what I was expecting. He didn't appear to be joking. I told him I didn't quite follow.

He reconsidered. "I think marijuana probably improves them."

I tried to picture myself blind tasting after a few bong rips. "Do you think it would make you taste better?" I wondered. "Or just give you an appetite?"

"Ahhhhh," he said, nodding. "LSD might be better. I've never tested myself on LSD. But it certainly changes vision, so it probably changes taste and smell too. When you manipulate the neurotransmitter systems with drugs, you could probably alter a lot of these things." Something about my expression apparently suggested I'd taken this idea seriously, so he added, "But there aren't good studies on these things."

Perhaps not, though the late neurologist Oliver Sacks did document a case of drug-induced supersmelling. In *The Man Who Mistook His Wife for a Hat*, Sacks tells the story of a twenty-two-year-old medical student who got high as a kite on a cocktail of cocaine, amphetamines, and PCP, a hallucinogen. He dreamed he was a dog and awoke to "a world in which all other sensations, enhanced as they were, paled before smell." "I had never had much of a nose for smells before, but now I distinguished each one instantly—and I found each one unique, evocative, a whole world," the student recounted. He could pick up the identities—and moods—of his friends and patients just by their scent, and tease out the distinct aroma of every street and store in New York. Three weeks later, his senses returned to normal. He called it "a tremendous loss."

Later that afternoon, I added electric shocks to my palate-training to-do list. Olfaction is the most plastic of the senses. Odors can quickly become associated with threatening stimuli, and once the olfactory system is sensitized in this way, it puts the body on high alert for any smells linked to potential dangers. In new research that Johan presented, he had subjects sniff the scent of roses while getting small electric shocks. By the end of the conditioning, the test subjects' sensitivity to the smell of roses had improved.

This, of course, got me thinking. Could I lower my threshold for smelling, say, pyrazines, and never miss a Cabernet Sauvignon, Cabernet Franc, or Sauvignon Blanc again? I consulted Johan on my plan to shock myself while drinking wine. Would it work?

"If you want to be a bit more sensitive to it, yeah," he told me. He suggested an alternative. "One of the best pairings, according to a colleague of mine who's worked with associative learning and conditioning, is to do something while having sex."

As I fell into the flow of the conference's presentations on "Odor Spaces" and "What Is Musk?," I studied the smelling routines of the experts around me. The protocols in the papers that were being presented frequently included helpful tips on minimizing distractions and enhancing sensitivity: no food for an hour before tasting (or smelling); limit sniffs to two to avoid habituation; sniff sitting up, not lying down; and maximize retro-nasal stimulation by gently exhaling over your tongue after swallowing, so aromas are carried from the back of the mouth up into the nasal cavity.

More intriguing and enlightening still were the snatches of time in between the lectures. I saw that, like sommeliers, the researchers at the conference had internalized their own regimens that put taste and smell front and center in their lives. These people had total curiosity and enthusiasm for all things olfactory and gustatory. And that was, without a doubt, the first step to better sensing.

One scientist smelled her children every day. Another was teaching his kids to identify smells. Paul, a fresh-faced postgrad, did a blind taste test of the most expensive and least expensive wines at dinner one night, proclaimed them indistinguishable, then mixed them together into a blend of his own creation. He sipped at it while explaining how he blind taste tests every soda, beer, pudding, and wine he buys to see if the costlier brand name product actually tastes better. "When I'm older, I'm going to fill up nice bottles of wine with cheap wine," he bragged.

Any subject could be tied back to smell or taste in some way. "Strippers make more money when they're ovulating. They don't know if it's that they dance better, or if they release a different smell," I overheard someone say during a cocktail hour. Or: "Flies are lucky because they have taste receptors on their feet." And: "What, exactly, is the purpose of having two nostrils is not exactly clear." Instead of "cheese" when they posed for pictures, the scientists cheered, "The action's in olfaction!"

Every smell, no matter how putrid, had its fanboys. At the tail end of a coffee break on the third afternoon, a dentist specializing in burning-mouth disorder rushed up to me to point out a perfumer she wanted me to meet. "I asked him what smells he's into now and he said urine," she said breathlessly, disappearing before I could ask her to repeat herself because I'd surely misheard.

"So, you're focusing on . . . urine?" I hesitantly asked the man in question, Christian Margot, wary of offending him.

"Oh no," he said, shaking his head, like I was crazy. He stood up a little straighter. "*Stale* urine!" he declared triumphantly.

He developed new flavors and fragrances for Firmenich, which makes everything from the artificial strawberry essence in ice creams to Acqua di Gio perfume. Because Christian examined the psychological effects of chemical stimulants, he liked to call himself a "psychochemist." Emphasis on the psycho. He enjoyed taking the stale urine smell and wafting it in the hall outside his office, so he could watch people's reactions. He giggled over the fact that women, in particular, went nuts. Because I seemed interested, he wanted me to know that he is also working on synthetic indole.

"It's a fecal smell. The smell of feces!" he chirped.

"Why exactly are you doing this?" I asked.

"It is also in muguet and lilies," he said. And then, apparently feeling he had clarified the matter, he excused himself.

It wasn't until the final day of the conference that Thomas's lab presented its most recent findings on olfactory training, which is what I was so keen to understand.

Thomas first started investigating the topic nearly a decade ago in the hope of helping the patients he treated for smell and taste loss. There are estimates that some 6 million Americans—nearly double the population of Los Angeles—suffer from a total loss of smell. The condition, anosmia, is the olfactory equivalent of deafness or blindness. (Ageusia refers to the inability to taste.) But with few known cures for anosmia, doctors have a tendency to shrug when confronted with a problem they can't see, can't necessarily fix, and is not officially designated a disability.

Even Thomas and his chemosensory-minded colleagues will admit that being robbed of smell isn't as debilitating as being deaf or blind. In an informal poll by one of the lecturers, the audience overwhelmingly agreed that if they had to ditch one sense, it would be olfaction. But this is not to say that it doesn't matter. Thomas, who runs a taste and smell clinic in addition to conducting research, says that anosmics endure a more "private" suffering. "They live a more dangerous life. They have more household accidents overall," he told me. "There are many situations where they feel insecure because obviously they know they're missing a signal." He has patients who shower two to three times a day and obsessively reapply deodorant, plagued by paranoia over their own body odors. They fail to detect invisible everyday threats, like spoiled food. Depression and feelings of isolation descend, as social interactions are robbed of their olfactory cues. "I felt untethered from the world," wrote one woman.

Determined to see if his patients could regain what they'd lost, Thomas, in his initial study on the subject, recruited forty people who had lost some or all of their ability to smell. Two-thirds of them followed a training regimen that consisted of smelling four intense odors—rose, eucalyptus, lemon, and cloves—twice a day, for three months. The control group did nothing. At the end of the period, Thomas found the trained patients had "experienced an increase in their olfactory function." Their sensitivity to those odors had improved. This aligned with earlier research, which concluded that repeatedly sniffing an aroma enables individuals to discern it at lower levels.

Thomas tried his training regimen again with patients suffering from Parkinson's disease, which often goes hand in hand with smell loss. Their sense of smell improved. He repeated it again with patients who'd lost the ability to smell because of infection or physical injury, and with children who had a normal sense of smell. Both groups also improved. Thomas determined that adults with a healthy sense of smell who followed the regimen retained their olfactory function (small surprise, since they were normal to begin with). But radical changes had taken place in their olfactory bulbs: They increased significantly in volume. The data were clear—olfactory function, in terms of sensitivity, could be improved through a relatively simple daily exercise.

So Thomas began to refine the training itself. Through a series of studies, he found that inhaling strong-smelling, highly concentrated odors worked better than milder scents. Swapping out the four original odors for four *new* odors after a period of several weeks also enhanced odor discrimination, identification, and sensitivity—telling odors apart, naming the odors, and detecting smaller concentrations of the odors.

Our sense of smell is unique in that it's designed to be flexible and adaptable. The number of visual, auditory, and touch-related receptors in the human body are fixed. But while the *types* of odor receptors we have are also fixed, the receptors themselves regenerate every six to ten weeks as they're exposed to dust and toxins in the air. Every two to four months, our entire stable of olfactory receptor neurons turns over. And in that process, with the right effort, our sense of smell can come back stronger. If an odor becomes more relevant to us, it's possible we may produce more receptors in order to better pick up its scent.

The latest smell training research from Thomas's lab, by his colleague Ilona Croy, has come to another powerful, related conclusion: People can reverse their inability to smell certain odors.

If you've ever sniffed the air, wondering what it was everyone around you claimed to smell, you'll want to know about Ilona's investigation into specific anosmia. The term describes a person's inability to perceive a specific odor, despite otherwise healthy olfactory function. Once considered a rare phenomenon, Ilona concluded from a study of 1,600 subjects that it is likely that every person is hardwired, in their DNA, to be "odor blind" to certain smells. It could be sandalwood for me, the musky sweat smell of pentadecalactone for you, or rotundone for Morgan. But far from a disorder, specific anosmia may be "the rule rather than the exception of olfactory processing," writes Ilona and her coauthors. And it appears to be something we can change.

From the podium in a lecture hall, Ilona recounted how she recruited twenty-five volunteers who had a normal sense of smell and at least one specific anosmia, then had them undergo Thomas's regimen of olfactory training. They received "smell bottles" with dilutions of the odors they were unable to smell, and sniffed them twice a day for ten seconds over the course of two to four months.

Every single person showed "improved perception of the respective odors." Not one of the participants was still odor blind to the smell they'd been unable to distinguish before.

The conclusion is that olfactory training works, even in people with an otherwise healthy sense of smell. We can correct our olfactory blind spots and "see" smells that before wore the olfactory version of an invisibility cloak. Anosmics may be able to bring odors into their world again, while people with a normal sense of smell can enhance their perception. And I might have a chance of growing my acuity to key wine aromas—the pyrazines I was having trouble recognizing, or the scent of vanillin from oak—without undergoing electroshock treatments or licking LSD blotters.

"It's enormous what human noses can do," Thomas said when Ilona had finished her presentation to applause. "That's what I've tried to convey today. When you train, you can get super senses."

My mother phoned me at the Dresden airport just as I was getting ready to board my flight back to New York. My grandmother had died that morning.

She and I had been extremely close. Almost every weekend, I'd ride the train up to her apartment on the way, way Upper West Side of Manhattan to cook with her or tell her about an article I was writing or pry stories out of her about her escape from Slovenia during World War II. We had a special bond. I treasured her.

Back in New York, I pushed my way through customs, anxious to join a small group of relatives that had gathered at my grandmother's apartment. We talked. We cried. Eventually, everyone left, except my mom and me. She closed herself in the guest bedroom to go over the funeral arrangements and find out how much time we'd have before needing to vacate the apartment. There would be the issue of what to do with everything that remained after ninety years of living. Furniture. Tea sets. Clothes.

Clothes. I went to my grandmother's bedroom and slid open the doors to her closet. The past few months, not a day had gone by that I hadn't thought about smell. We would have photographs to remember my grandmother by, even audio recordings of her telling stories that my cousin and I had discreetly made during family meals. But her smell . . .

I was suddenly desperate to hold on to her personal scent, that olfactory fingerprint that belonged to her alone. I stood in front of the pants, skirts, sweaters, and dresses that hung in her closet. I stretched out my arms and gathered as many of them as I could, hugging them against my chest and burying my face in them. I closed my eyes, pressed my nose up against a beige cashmere sweater, and took a deep, long breath. And then another.

The smell felt amazing. I wanted to ingrain it in my mind. I tried to articulate the special mix of aromas in the hope that I could save this part of her, sear it into my brain so I could call it up later, to bring back the sense of being with her in the way only smell can. I inhaled again. It had a softness. I knew it must have traces of her perfume, Eternity, and perhaps the hand cream she used. But I felt like I was guessing. I breathed in that unmistakable Nona smell, at once so moved by the feeling of her presence, and also so frustrated by the knowledge that I was on the verge of losing this aroma—and so much more—forever. Her scent was there. It was disappearing. It would be gone.

I kept returning to this memory later, after the sharp pain of grief had dulled into an ache, and life had nagged me back to my regular routine. I had left Dresden armed with fresh confidence that it actually was possible for me to perceive more and reassured that my senses hadn't been so bad to begin with. But that moment at my grandmother's apartment had revealed a hole in my understanding. Standing at the closet, clinging to her clothes, I could smell perfectly fine. It was just that my brain didn't know what to do with the information. To tune in to the world's sensory signals, I not only had to detect the raw stimulus, but I also needed to transform it into knowledge. So how did the signal become meaningful? What skills did I lack? I plunged into a laundry list of studies—my sole souvenir from Dresden—looking for clues about the nature of olfactory acuity.

Somewhere along the skeptic spectrum between atheists and flat-Earth truthers, there is a sizable contingent of people who believe wine expertise plain just doesn't exist. That sommeliers can't smell or taste any better than the rest of us. That the whole shebang is a sham, so hand over a beer and let's be done with it. Two studies are usually trotted out to prove this point, both of them coauthored by Frédéric Brochet, a former professor at the University of Bordeaux. In one, Brochet's enology students were asked to describe the smell of two wines: a white and a red. Piece of *gâteau*, you're probably thinking. The subjects said the white wine smelled like most white wines—"floral," with hints of "apple, "lychee," and "grapefruit." They characterized the red wine with all the terms commonly reserved for reds, like "cassis," "raspberry," and "prune." Turns out, they'd been sniffing two glasses of the exact same white wine, only one glass had been dyed red. Brochet and his coauthors used these findings to draw a conclusion about language—that we describe wines by likening them to things that are the same color as the wine itself. But the rest of the world concluded that so-called experts can't tell a red from a white. In a second experiment, Brochet made his enology students taste and rate two reds from Bordeaux, one presented to them as a lowly *vin de table*, another bearing the prestigious Grand Cru Classé designation. Of the fifty-seven tasters, forty recommended the Grand Cru as a "good" wine, three hailed it as "excellent," and dozens of students extolled its "balanced," "complex," and "rounded" flavors. When the same group was served the *vin de table*, they choked down what they dismissed as a "feeble," "flat," and "faulty" wine. As you've probably guessed, Brochet had, in fact, poured the "Grand Cru" and the *"vin de table"* from the very same bottle of midrange Bordeaux. Newspapers and blogs declared wine tasting "bullshit" and "junk science." And there's no getting around it: It looks bad for the "experts," who let their senses be swayed.

But before you write them off as frauds, it's important to acknowledge that we know these people *are* different. As I found when I combed through the studies I picked up in Dresden, the answer to what makes a cork dork a cork dork is more complicated than teaching our noses to discriminate ever more minute differences in aroma.

Given that wine pros unleash a torrent of descriptors each time they stick their noses into a glass, you might think that they are far and away more attuned to smells than mere civilians. Not necessarily. There appears to be a cap on the number of discrete odors humans can pick out from a mixture of smells. Even seasoned experts who undergo smell training, like perfumers and sommeliers, can discriminate a maximum of three or four odorants when asked to smell a blend of aromas—the same number as novices. That bouquet of candied ginger, peach, honeysuckle, verbena, and yuzu that your sommelier claims to appreciate in your Chenin Blanc is likely to be the product of industrywide habits—like the Court's deductive tasting method—that condition sommeliers to rattle off terms. Plus, that sort of poetry can help sell bottles.

But there *are* areas where wine experts perform better—much, much better—than regular sniffers. As Thomas and others have shown, training daily with odors, as many experts do, can improve their olfactory sensitivity, so they register subtle smells. Wine pros also excel at odor discrimination: Seasoned experts are more accurate than amateurs when it comes to distinguishing between different smells—say, coriander versus clove—and at picking out nuances between flavors—say, high-alcohol versus low-alcohol liquids. Additionally, their ability to identify those odors and attach names to them improves with practice.

That practice also changes the brains of experts in a dramatic and measurable way. Some of the most convincing scientific evidence that wine and sensory expertise do exist comes from researchers who watched sommeliers' brains while they were tasting wines. In 2005, scientists in Italy published the results of a study they performed in collaboration with neuroscience professor Richard Frackowiak, whose now-famous research proved that as London cabdrivers gain greater and greater fluency navigating the city's streets, their brains undergo structural changes. The scientists recruited seven sommeliers and seven control subjects (amateurs who didn't know much about wine) and had them sip wines from a plastic tube while lying down in an fMRI machine, which measures brain activity by tracking blood flows. The participants tasted several liquids, including red, white, and sweet wines, plus an odorless glucose solution, while following instructions on when to swish and swallow. As they did so, the researchers scanned their heads.

The results were staggering. When the control subjects tasted the wines, their brains showed only a few scattered dots of activity, notably in areas associated with emotional processing. But the brains of experts went wild. They showed more activity, and lit up regions involved in high-level cognitive processing, like memory, planning, and abstract reasoning. In short, there is a distinctive signature of brain activity that sets experts apart from novices. "Our results suggest that the pattern of brain activations is substantially different in experienced sommeliers than controls," wrote the Italian team, which ascribed the difference to sommeliers' "more refined sensitivity" to taste and smell, and their "more analytical" evaluation of the wine. As Alessandro Castriota-Scanderbeg, the study's lead author, observed, "There is clear evidence that the neural connections of the brain change with training and experience." A thought occurred to me: Was my own brain changing?

The French, never ones to let Italians get the final say in matters of wine, conducted a similar study in 2014. A group of neuroscientists from Besançon University Hospital put ten sommeliers and ten amateur wine drinkers into an fMRI. And they found essentially the same results.

So wine expertise is not a sham. (It's worth noting that Brochet, the professor whose studies were touted as proof that wine tasting is "bullshit," did not abandon the world of enology in disgust. Instead, he left academia to make wine at a beautiful château in western France.)

Professional tasters really have taught themselves to experience wine differently from mere amateurs. And the smells in a glass of Cabernet Franc are not, as Broca might have expected, tickling the leftover, primitive side of our gray matter. To the contrary, wine demonstrably activates more advanced, higher-level parts of the brain.

How does that happen? The moral of the story is that smell or taste sensitivity alone is not enough to help people savor more thoughtfully. Sommeliers generally compare their blind tasting practice to exercise, as if stimulating their noses and tongues is akin to weightlifters building muscle as they sweat it out at the bench press. That's not quite accurate. Acquiring wine expertise is more like picking up a new language than it is like pumping iron. We don't master a foreign tongue by improving our hearing so that we can make out extremely subtle noises. We learn by expanding our conceptual knowledge. Before I started studying Chinese, it was just sounds—*nihaowodemingzijiaobaobian*. I didn't need to get my ears checked in order to make sense of that. I had to connect meaning with sounds ("*wo*" means I). I had to encounter those sounds over and over again (*wo, wo, wo*). And I had to develop a larger framework in which to orient the significance of those sounds (I is *wo*, you is *ni*). With time, that acoustic mess separated into: *Nihao, wode mingzi jiao bao bian,* or "Hi, my name is Bianca."

Similarly, wine expertise comes by paying attention, sensing clearly, and then imposing meaning onto those physical sensations. Language, for instance, is thought to play a key role in boosting odor discrimination. The pros improve their olfactory skills as they learn to assign names and meanings to smells (that sour, red fruit aroma is cranberry), as they encounter those smells over and over (*cranberry, cranberry, cranberry*), and as they develop a framework in which to orient the significance of those smells (*cranberry* often appears in Sangiovese from Tuscany). "A large part of the wine taster's skill comes from being able to develop some sort of classification system, and then to associate words/categories with smells," said Tim Jacob, a smell specialist and professor emeritus at the University of Cardiff. By learning those labels and schemes, as reported in a paper published in *Frontiers in Psychology*, an individual can acquire "perceptual abilities reports incredibly superior to that of an untrained person."

In other words, Matt could take his supertaster status and shove it. It's not that we have to be supertasters (or supersmellers) to appreciate all the subtleties of wine. It's more important to be superthinkers. (Though even then, you can still take pleasure in wine just by being super relaxed, super in need of a glass of Pinot, or super anything.) What I needed was to have a conceptual structure in place so that I could classify and comprehend the aromas I smelled.

Armed with this new knowledge, I decided to accelerate my training by working at it from both angles, body and brain. I switched up my daily routine to incorporate the olfactory training regimen developed by Thomas and his team in Dresden. I invested in Le Nez du Vin, a kit with fifty-four aromatic essences that commonly occur in wine, from musk to melon. (One of the World's Best Sommelier winners deemed it a "precious companion.") Adapting Thomas and Ilona's methodology slightly, I picked five new vials from Le Nez du Vin each week to smell for thirty seconds each, twice a day, while trying to imprint their names and associations on my memory. *Saffron,* I would recite, holding the thimble-sized glass under each nostril. *Saffron, saffron, saffron.* As perfumers had coached me, I tried to associate it with images—an orange star—and describe its smell—soapy, metallic undertone, paprika-ish. I attempted, unsuccessfully, to get Morgan on the olfactory training bandwagon, assuring him he might be able to cure his rotundone anosmia. He preferred to do things the old-fashioned way.

I also redoubled my efforts at studying wine theory. Correctly identifying the scent of vanilla, dill, and coconut wasn't enough. Expertise meant having the framework to ascribe meaning to those smells: knowing that vanilla, dill, and coconut suggest a wine aged in barrels made with American oak, a trademark of Spanish and Argentinean winemakers, particularly those in Rioja and Mendoza, who make wine with Tempranillo and Malbec grapes, respectively.

But even as I undertook this more scientific approach to improving my blind tasting, I knew it wouldn't teach me anything about how to cater to other peoples' noses and tongues. After all, cork dorks cultivate their senses not only for their own pleasure but to curate flavor experiences for their guests. In order to learn more about how to help others taste, I needed access to civilians. I needed a restaurant.

CHAPTER FIVE

The Magic Kingdom

LOOKING OVER THE COURT OF MASTER SOMMELIERS' SERVICE GUIDE, I found worrisome hints that the sommelier's job bears more than a little in common with a hostage negotiator. The Court's instructions made it sound like somms grapple with unstable strangers who are one wrong glance away from doing something drastic. "Pay close attention to guest response, speaking manner, and body language," instructs the official guidelines on the "Demeanor of the Professional Sommelier." "Maintain eye contact with guests as appropriate." "SMILE." *No sudden movements*, I wanted to add.

This was a wake-up call. While my tasting skills, buttressed by science, were progressing nicely, my service abilities were nonexistent. Here, Martin Witt and his buckets of brains could be of no help. One evening at home, I practiced decanting wine over a candle and successfully singed part of a kitchen cabinet. At this rate I'd never pass the Court's Certified Sommelier Exam and I'd never have a shot at working the floor.

To master service, there is no substitute for restaurant experience. Most sommeliers, in the course of their careers, will do "trails," where they shadow colleagues at other restaurants, just to be sure they can nimbly handle diverse wine lists or more formal styles of service. In the weeks before a Court exam, someone who somms at a happy-hour-special type of place might seek a refresher in upper-crust dining, and spend a few nights pairing forty-year-old Brunellos with tasting menus. Someone else might call in a favor so she can somm for an evening under the watchful gaze of a Master Sommelier, who can critique her at the end of the shift. This is referred to by its French name as a *stage*, pronounced *staahge*. Less a prerequisite to becoming a sommelier, it is more often a way of fine-tuning existing skills.

I wanted—and desperately needed—to do a *stage*, though in my case, I wouldn't be honing skills so much as trying to get them in the first place. It was crucial for my exam that I become fluent in the formalities of serving wine, and I also wanted to witness top-tier cork dorks on the floor to understand how real-life formal service compares to the Court's textbook version. Of course, there was also a chance that in the course of trailing with a restaurant's team—sommeliers' version of networking—I might also hit it off with people who could eventually help me get a job on the floor.

Just as I was getting ready to leave my cellar-rat post after four months of heavy lifting at L'Apicio, I'd persuaded Joe to let me trail Lara during service so I could get a feel for life in the line of fire. At the last minute, however, Joe had changed his mind. Fortunately, I wasn't too crushed by his decision because I'd already set my sights on something higher.

At the same Wine Bar War festival where I'd met Morgan, I'd gotten to know a wine wunderkind, Victoria James, who was everything I aspired to be. At twenty-four, she had to be the city's youngest sommelier, and she was already working at Marea, one of New York's high temples of haute cuisine. It was a place I dreamed of going for a *stage*. After a few weeks of badgering and an overly generous description of my former responsibilities at L'Apicio, I persuaded Victoria to convince her bosses to let me shadow her.

Marea is the kind of place that comes to mind when people call Manhattan a "playground for the rich." Chef Michael White's gastronomic landmark serves Ossetra caviar ($385 per ounce) and

Pacific langoustine crudo near a stretch of Central Park known as billionaire's row. The area boasts what has to be the world's highest concentration of Michelin stars. Within a block of Marea (two stars) are Jean-Georges (three stars), Per Se (three stars), and Masa (three stars). Servers call this level of fine dining "high-stakes." Guests know the best, expect the best, and at the prices they're paying, will settle for nothing less. Three sommeliers stalk the floor at Marea each night, selling a combined $20,000 to $35,000 of wine. "We never go below fifteen," said Victoria. "Except when Hurricane Sandy hit." Marea's reservationists are required to Google every one of its guests, though George, the smooth-talking maître d', already knows every socialite in the city and has a gift for strategically arranging feuding celebrities around the dining room so they never lay eyes on one another. Marea's attention to the finer points of hospitality, which has been recognized with a James Beard Award for service, was one reason I was so keen to embed with Victoria. The other was that while Masa feeds around thirty-five people each night, Marea serves well over three hundred. It's white-glove quality at Chipotle volumes, which made me think it would be a particularly fitting place to see how the Platonic ideals of service fare in real-world conditions. As a bonus, I'd get to try some outrageously fancy wines. It seems counterintuitive that the world's best restaurants would be the ones where sommeliers help themselves to your wine even before you, the guest, get to taste it. But at places of Marea's caliber, the protocol requires somms to taste each bottle before they serve it, just to be sure there's nothing wrong with it. They'd argue a little sip is merely proper service, since it guarantees no guest is served a faulty wine. But none of them would deny getting a thrill from dipping into the fine bottles they summon from the cellar. I was certainly looking forward to it.

I was also curious to get the perspective of a female sommelier. Women have only recently invaded the boys' club that has long ruled the restaurant wine scene. America's first upscale restaurants imported not only Europe's pomp and circumstance around wine but also the tradition of an all-male staff. New York City's earliest known reference to sommeliers appeared in 1852, in a classified ad directing somms-for-hire to an address that, appropriately, was only a few blocks from Wall Street. It wasn't until 1943, nearly a full century later, that the *New York Times* profiled the city's first and then only female wine steward. She "has learned the knack—the envy of many a wife—of being respectful yet not obsequious; of getting her way without offending male vanity," wrote the *Times*, which reported that the woman got along well with men because she "sticks to things she knows something about." "I never try to advise a man on hard liquors," the "*sommelière*" is quoted as saying. "New Yorkers don't need any help in that department. They usually know exactly what they want. Sometimes too well." By 1970, a full 92 percent of food servers were female, but women in the cellar were still rare. "When I started out, there were almost no other women," said Madeline Triffon, who became the first female Master Sommelier in 1987. Even now, 86 percent of Masters are men.

If there was anyone who could shake up the patriarchy, it was Victoria. She reminded me of a femme fatale out of an old noir film: a classic beauty with round eyes and ivory skin, and a won't-take-shit-from-nobody attitude. She grew up on the Upper West Side of Manhattan with four siblings. Money was tight, so when she turned thirteen, she got a job waitressing from four p.m. to two a.m. in the smoking section of a Greek diner willing to look the other way on child labor laws. Victoria enrolled at Fordham University to study psychology, but missed the manic energy of restaurants. So, three years before she could legally drink, she bartended at a little Italian place near Times Square and took wine courses on the sly. She soon started working as a cellar rat, then dropped out of college. As soon as she turned twenty-one, she talked her way into a sommelier job at Aureole, pre-dating Morgan by just a few years. She'd moved up the ranks faster than anyone I'd met, and considered wine her career, hobby, calling, passion, and everything in between. She grew Pinot

Noir on her fire escape and spent her free time foraging for wild herbs, which she made into homemade amaro, aged in a barrel in her kitchen. "Wine is freedom," Victoria had told me. "It gives you freedom to meet people you wouldn't otherwise meet, go places you wouldn't go, and try things you otherwise wouldn't get to try."

I was about to get access to a world that few people ever got to see, and even fewer got to work in. So her observation was certainly true for me.

I arrived at Marea at three p.m. on a Thursday in an outfit that Victoria had vetted in advance. That might seem excessive—how do you go wrong with a black blazer and black skirt? But restaurants at Marea's level fastidiously monitor the appearance of their front-of-the-house staff—including the somms, servers, runners, bussers, and so forth—so I couldn't be too careful. (The back of the house belongs to the chef, sous-chefs, line cooks, dishwashers, and other kitchen crew.) Even getting to choose my outfit was lax by the standards at Eleven Madison Park, where sommeliers are dressed in matching Victorinox suits. Per Se is known for bringing in ballet dancers to teach its staff to move with grace. And Jean-Georges provides guidelines on both walking *and* attire, handing out instruction manuals that cover the nitty-gritty of lipstick hue, jewelry style, nail color, and nail length, while also dosing out advice on good posture. Earlier that week, Victoria had chopped her long brown hair into a chin-length bob because her boss suggested this hairstyle would be "more appropriate." When I met her, she had on her own black blazer, paired with black ballet flats and a no-nonsense dress. Neither of us wore jewelry—we couldn't risk upstaging a guest—or any kind of fragrance. I'd heard of a female somm who'd been reprimanded for using a shampoo that smelled too strong.

Victoria walked me through Marea's house rules. Restaurants often massage the steps of service to save time, money, or space, and certain conventions contradicted the Court's code of conduct. Don't open the wine tableside—so "bistro," Victoria instructed. That should happen out of sight, by the sommeliers' station—ahem, *credenza*—at the rear of the dining room. Don't bring the cork unless asked. "It's like presenting garbage to the table." Always taste the wine before serving it, just to be sure there's nothing wrong with it. Always pour women, then men. "Oh, clergy!" Victoria corrected herself. "God's first." The details of good service might change from restaurant to restaurant. But as the Master Sommeliers at TopSomm drilled into me, every action should strive for elegance. Our ultimate goal was to disappear. "If the customer's having a good experience, they shouldn't remember anyone's faces that served them," Victoria said. "Things are magically supposed to fall in front of you."

She steered me past the maître d's podium, through the dining room, and, in the back near the kitchen, to the sommeliers' station. We faced a wall of shelves shimmering with glasses of various heights and girths. Victoria pointed to a bulbous model that looked like a transparent grapefruit plopped on a pedestal. That was for red Burgundy and other "aromatic" wines. "Because if you have more surface area, there's more your nose is exposed to," she explained. Riesling and dessert wines were to be served in the shorter, narrower glasses over there. The tall ones almost double their height, so comically big and unwieldy they resembled goldfish bowls stuck on glass stems, were meant for Cabernet Sauvignon, Syrah, and Nebbiolo.

To the connoisseur, the pairing of wine and glass demands as much care as the pairing of wine and food. At Alinea, the sommeliers audition three glasses for each wine until they find one that brings out the quality they hope to highlight. Glassmakers claim the shape of a glass's bowl accentuates certain flavors and textures in the wine—sometimes, ostensibly, by controlling where the wine hits the tongue, or how much air hits the surface of the wine. Riedel, an industry leader, goes so far as to sell glasses customized to more than a dozen grapes and regions, including one glass for "Bordeaux Grand Cru"

($125 each) and a different one for "Mature Bordeaux" ($99 apiece). Pity the rube who desecrates a Chablis by pouring it into Riedel's "Alsace" glass. They come with pseudoscientific explanations that should set off anyone's bullshit-o-meter—use Riedel's pear-shaped glass to enhance pear aromas!—and yet devotees swear a carefully engineered curve can transform the drinking experience.

Let me pause momentarily to say that like so much with wine, this is partially, but not *entirely*, bullshit. I'd always wondered whether people were justified in fussing over rim diameter and bowl angle, so I went digging through the surprisingly ample library of scientific research that exists on this topic. The short answer: Yes, they are justified (and no, Solo cups aren't a substitute). Five different studies have shown glass shape can, in subtle but noticeable ways, mute or enhance wine aromatics, though not necessarily in the specific manner Riedel, Zalto, and other glassmakers claim. In general, glasses that are wider around the middle and narrower at the top increase the aromatic intensity of the wine more than other models. In one study, these even enhanced the fruitiness of the wine. Japanese researchers used an adorably named "sniffer-camera" to show why this may be. They observed that the curve of a wineglass concentrates the ethanol vapors against the sides, creating a clear area at the center where drinkers can sniff their wine without the aroma-killing interference of evaporating alcohol. In martini glasses and highballs, the ethanol vapors are all over the place.

I followed Victoria to the first of Marea's three "cellars." It was actually a tall fridge sandwiched between two pairs of heavy swinging doors that, when in motion, left something smaller than a me-sized space between them. One pair led into the kitchen, where a trio of men was steaming individual wineglasses to glimmering fingerprintless perfection. The second set of doors was covered in glossy dark wood and swung into the dining room. Someone flew past with a tray of dirty plates and I threw myself onto Victoria to try to avoid being crushed by the swaying gates of death. "They're like vertical guillotines," Victoria warned me, only a little too late.

She explained how Marea's cellars had about 1,400 different types of wines spread over 10,000 bottles that were collectively worth more than $800,000. Most wines on the list were marked up around three times: More expensive wines had a slimmer markup, while the cheaper bottles might have more padding. Victoria was introducing me to the wine runner, whose job was fetching bottles from the basement during service, when the heavy wooden door to my right slammed into my shoulder, hard. I tried to act like I didn't think it was dislocated. "Be careful, yeah?" said the wine runner, looking concerned. Victoria eyed me suspiciously, as though just realizing I might be more trouble than I was worth. She turned and pushed her way into the kitchen.

"You're going to die," she called over her shoulder.

Restaurants like Marea are Disneylands for moguls. From the matching ties worn by the servers to the cloth napkins in the bathrooms, no errant detail is permitted to spoil the fantasy of an enchanted kingdom where ordering the risotto with a $150 serving of shaved white truffle is not only good but right. Like all well-designed theme parks, the surroundings are meticulously calibrated to bring the dream to life. Polished Indonesian rosewood the color of chocolate frames the restaurant's banquettes. Behind the bar, there is a wall running the full length of the restaurant that glows gold with backlit honey onyx, its long stripes reminiscent of tiger fur. It makes you want to touch something, preferably something expensive and rare. Gilded conch shells are placed on the windowsills in a nod to Marea's maritime menu. The whole dining room could pass for the interior of an oligarch's yacht, so it must look familiar to many of Marea's guests. All of this has a Cinderella feel, as though diners become Masters of the Universe—if they weren't already—just by settling into one of the leather bucket seats. The courteous and deferential staff, the sparkle of the glasses—all of it imparts the sense that even if life outside the dining room is chaos, for two hours at Marea, all is right with the world. And you deserve it. All of it. Including the Ossetra caviar.

The perfectly staged fiction of tasteful order and equal-opportunity elitism came crashing down even before the dinner service started. This was merely a veneer, under which lay a chaotic world of shouting, blisters, and greased-palm dealings.

At five p.m., half an hour before the first reservation, I gathered with the rest of the staff for lineup, the daily pre-service meeting. Michael, the assistant general manager, eyed Victoria's black flats as we sat down. "There's a lot of foot exposure with those shoes," he remarked, raising an eyebrow. I took a seat next to Victoria and the two other sommeliers who were on duty that evening. There was Liz, a woman in her thirties with big hair and a tight smile, and Marea's beverage director Francesco, a delicate, petite man, Italian by way of New Jersey.

The chef introduced a six-inch half pipe of bone marrow that was new to the menu. A pastry chef recited the petits fours she'd be serving that evening. Michael pleaded with the staff to be more careful with the olive oil cruets. The maître d', George, however, was the main event.

"We have Octavia Sansone, wine PX, at six fifteen," he bellowed. "Adesh Patel, a regular guest here. Mr. Bennett Davis, wine PX. Miss Georgina Wilde, two people at six thirty—another wine PX. Alex Wang, another wine PX."

PX, Victoria explained, is short for *personne extraordinaire*, restaurant code for "spends dough." It's appended to reservations made by big spenders, owners' friends, high-rolling regulars, and special guests, like Chef Daniel Humm of Eleven Madison Park, who'd be coming in tonight at eight. They are to be coddled, spoiled, humored, and upsold at all costs. Marea keeps files on its guests—their pet peeves, personal quirks, dining histories, and importance to the restaurant—and communicates the information to the staff via *soignés*, paper tickets that print as soon as a table is seated, so everyone on duty knows how to treat the group.

Some restaurants will get no more detailed than "VIP," "PX," or "BLR" (short for "baller"). But the most ambitious dining institutions scrutinize their guests almost as much as the food they send out to the tables. The more someone can—or does—spend on their meal, the more they're investigated, and they can be flagged as opportunities long before they sit down. A *soigné* marked "ATG" means "according to Google," as in "ATG investment banking analyst at Barclays Capital." Marea sorts its clientele into niches that include "occasional wine PX," "wine PX has-been," and "PPX" (*personne particulièrement extraordinaire*). There is also "F/O" for "friend of"—"F/O Francesco," "F/O George," "F/O Owner." You could be a "regular," "blogger," "press," "previous complaint." A temper tantrum will get you labeled "HWC" ("handle with care"), which is what other restaurants call "SOE" ("sense of entitlement") and the servers call "This motherfucker was *crazy* last time." Be very, *very* bad and you'll be "86 DO NOT ACCEPT." Be very, *very* good—and very profligate—and you just might be crowned "NEVER REFUSE."

George rattled off several more names, building to the "big wine PX on Table Eight"—a corner booth that's one of the two most coveted tables in the dining room. "Señor Peralta from Brazil," he elaborated. "Wealthy Brazilian."

I followed the sommeliers back to the credenza and asked what it took to become a wine PX.

Liz looked at me like I was mentally deficient. "They . . . spend . . . money," she said extremely slowly.

I reached for what seemed like an outrageous sum for a bottle of wine. "So spending, what, $300?"

One of the servers, a balding man named George, blinked at me. He exchanged glances with Liz. "Per . . . person?"

Per bottle, I clarified.

He laughed out loud. "That's *average*."

"So, like, if someone spends five hundred plus"—per bottle—"we're going to be like, 'This person drops *real* money,'" Liz explained.

"I'm probably going to write down the bottle that they had because then the next time that person calls for a reservation, and we see this, even if we didn't have that seven o'clock party for two, we're probably going to try to give them a table because they've previously come in and spent money. . . . The wine team has annual and monthly sales goals. Then the other reason is just that it will ultimately affect sales for the night, and we work on a tip pool, so a higher check means a higher tip. Which means more money for everyone."

That seemed to get her excited and she scanned the dining room. "I'm going to take a loop around," she said, sashaying off.

Unlike in other restaurants, Liz, Victoria, and Francesco weren't assigned to specific sections. Marea so valued PXs and personal relationships, it offered its sommeliers total flexibility to flutter around the dining room, pampering regulars they knew well, regardless of where they were seated. These wine PXs earned privileges beyond the personal touch or hard-to-get reservation. One PX, a regular and a regular drunk, had, on previous occasions, thrown up in the dining room, stuffed a whole fish down his shirt, and entertained himself by whispering obscene come-ons to the female staff. He wasn't banned—just banned from having female servers.

"He spends *so* much money," one of them told me. "They *can't* ban him."

The dining room was still relatively empty. Then again, this was "amateur hour," when, as it was explained to me, the inexperienced diners came out to eat. "Who goes out to dinner at five p.m.?" Victoria wondered. She scanned the tables to see who had their wine lists open, and who'd already consulted and closed them.

She took a spin past two women at the bar. One was a regular who enjoyed white Burgundy from Chablis and Meursault. She wasn't ready to order. Victoria spotted an elderly couple seated on the banquette, under a window overlooking Central Park.

"Hi, how are you tonight?" Victoria asked.

The wife, who held the wine list and appeared to be in her seventies, looked Victoria up and down. Then she peered around the dining room as if expecting someone else to appear. "Are you the wine—the wine lady? Person?"

Victoria said she was. The woman asked her to recommend something cold and crisp, like a Chablis or Sancerre. These are both citrusy, savory wines that have the flavor equivalent of sharp corners thanks to their high acid. Victoria asked a few questions, then went to the cellar to fetch a bottle that, Victoria said, was the Italian version of a fat, buttery Chardonnay. This made no sense: It was like someone asking which salad to order, then settling on birthday cake.

"Sometimes what people say they want is not what they really want," Victoria whispered on her pass back to the table with the open bottle. She poured the guest a taste.

"Oh!" exclaimed the elderly woman after taking a sip. She smiled at Victoria. "I love it."

I didn't hear anything else because just then Victoria's boss, Francesco, jerked me backward, away from the table and toward the wall.

"Would you mind just hanging back a little bit? Just because to be totally honest with you, the guests can be very particular and inquisitive, and they can be set off by really ludicrous things," he said. I thought back to the Court's guidelines. *Pay close attention to guest response, speaking manner, and body language.* Do not approach the cage. "If you won't mind just being a few steps away, or just casually moving around—pretending not to be observing . . ."

I hurried to catch up with Victoria as soon as she left the table. She had mastered the art of moving extremely quickly while looking like she was walking at a normal pace, and I was scrambling to keep up with her. I asked what I'd missed of her conversation with the older couple.

"They just wanted to talk about their travels. Their fancy stuff," Victoria said as we clattered back downstairs to the basement cellar.

It was divided into two refrigerated units, one for expensive wine and one for extremely expensive wine. A gold engraved sign that hung on the door read NO SPITTING. "When you think about it, you're like the servant. Wine is just the vehicle through which you serve these people. So you have to flatter and make them feel at home and comfortable and recognized, and validate their feelings." In this case, Victoria was required to smile and nod while the couple recounted their recent trip to Piedmont.

Victoria conferred with the host at an eight-top of Japanese businessmen, fetched their two magnums of 1997 Renaissance Cabernet, deposited a cork at Table 25, swung by the kitchen for a shot of espresso, and refilled a table's wineglasses because the server, whose responsibility it is to do so, apparently forgot. I made a note of this: full glasses = proper service. Plus, continuous refills hurry a table through one bottle and on to their second. And if they're not on bottle two by the time the entrées arrive, you're past the point of no return, Victoria warned.

While we waited for a group of men in ties to take a spin through the list, Victoria decoded how to make sense of guests' sometimes irrational statements about their taste in wines. Every night, someone professes a preference for dry red wines, even though virtually every red wine is dry. "You can't correct it, but you look at the psychology behind it," Victoria said. "When they say that, they want a wine that dries out their mouth. Tannin is what they're talking about." So maybe a Brunello di Montalcino or Chianti Classico from Italy. People also ask for wines because they sound like what they're supposed to want to order. They crave something that tastes like Cabernet, but they want to call it "Pinot." They claim to despise all Chardonnay, then demand Chablis, which is almost exclusively made with—you guessed it—Chardonnay. Guests reject wines for reasons that have nothing to do with taste. Pinot Grigio was tacky, but Sauvignon Blanc was trendy. Cabernet was too old-fashioned. A woman near the bar told Victoria she loved whites from Burgundy but hated wines that were fresh, green, or mineral—qualities often associated with whites from Burgundy. Victoria tried to narrow it by asking the woman who her favorite producers were. Since the guest couldn't name one, "then she probably drinks—not necessarily shitty, but *generic* international styles of white Burgundy. So this"—Victoria wiggled the bottle in her hand—"should be perfect."

If you've ever ordered wine at a restaurant, you know how excruciating the experience can be. First, there's the uncomfortable conversation about what everyone is in the mood for, with no one eager to venture an opinion for fear of picking wines other people don't like, or sounding like the kind of ignorant philistine who orders—ugh—Pinot Grigio. Then there's price. Again, only inarticulate murmurings—no one wants to stake a claim. Since you're holding the list, it's up to you. Great. When you finally pick a number, you either feel like a cheapskate or a large-livin' Texas oil baron, and either way you feel like your choice has spoiled the mood. To make it worse, you've got the sommelier hovering over you the whole time, watching, waiting, breathing, despite the fact that you have no idea what to say to her. Name your favorite Burgundy producers? You're still struggling to pick a color.

What's hard on you is doubly challenging for the sommelier. At least you know, deep down, what you want to spend and what you like. You'll recognize the answer when you see it. Victoria is on the hook to narrow a thousand options into two or three suggestions that fit your palate and wallet, even though you're probably not going to be able to articulate either. She'll get to ask about three questions, max. With that information, she'll have to home in on a region and style, then point out three bottles, at wildly different price ranges—$85, $225, and $495—to see where you flinch. And meanwhile, she has to intuit what you want emotionally out of this experience, so she can play to that in how she pitches the wine.

Given how much she has to glean in so little time, I asked Victoria if she ever stereotyped her guests.

"Definitely," she said. The minute she lays eyes on a table, she begins sizing them up. Table 46, with the Japanese men: Asian guests usually start a meal with hot water and lemon, so the wine she'll recommend will need to have at least as much acid, or it'll taste flat. Table 27 was all men in suits, which hinted at a business dinner. That either meant a $200 cap per bottle or "the market's doing well, so they want to spend thousands of dollars." The young couple on the banquette and the couple at the center table were on dates. They'd go for something boring, out of fear of picking the wrong thing. Old money—Table 22, in turtlenecks—would want the classics. Table 9 would want to show off. They were "new money," Victoria said, and would order "to impress me."

As corkscrews flew in and out of bottles back at the sommeliers' station, I mentioned a somm at Le Bernardin (three stars) who'd memorized men's luxury watches so he could pick out a Jaeger-LeCoultre, then recommend big bottles to match it. His colleague studied rings, jewelry, bags, and shoes to calculate how astronomic she could get with her wine suggestions.

Rookie move, Liz and Victoria agreed. Carats were deceiving.

"We get all these nouveau-riche people here, so there'll be, like, a family in sweatpants and they're going to order a $3,000 wine," said Liz. "So I don't think you should necessarily approach people with stereotypes. Because then there's people like the girl at the bar. She's in Chanel and has giant rocks on her hands and she's like—"

George, the server, stuck his hip out and put on a nasal falsetto: "DO YOO HAV PINEAPPLE JOOOOOCE?"

"Yeah! She's like, 'Where's the Prosecco?' And you want to be like, '*C'mon.* You can buy something nicer than that.'"

Victoria was also conscious of ways that tables were stereotyping her. With the older guests, she'd be extra demure and courteous. "The second they see me, they're going to think, 'Who is this young girl? Why the hell is she trying to sell us wine? To rip us off? She has no idea what she's doing,' " she said. "The first thing you want to do is show them respect. Always." She wouldn't offer to "help" the older guests with the list. She'd ask if she could "bring" something for them. "You never want to make it look like you're trying to teach them something. These people are, like, seventy. They don't need a new lesson."

Wives were land mines for a young, attractive *sommelière* like Victoria. Her manager had warned her to watch out for them when she first started. Sure enough, they'd been a problem. When she worked at Morini, Marea's sister restaurant on the Upper East Side, a woman eviscerated Victoria in an online review because she suspected Victoria of hitting on her husband. Now, Victoria always makes a point to smile at the wife. To pointedly inquire what *she* likes to drink. To ask her if she would like to taste the wine. "To pull up my shirt so it's not too low."

Liz wholly agreed. "Especially if it's a couple, you always want to go up and smile at the wife—'Hi, how are you, how are you doing?'—so she's not like, 'Who's this bitch who's trying to get my husband to spend lots of money?' "

Men were extremely receptive to Victoria. She milked it for all it was worth. "You go up to men and, you know, let's already get past that they're going to sexualize you," she said. "If you go up to a table of young guys, they're all ears. You can tell them anything you want. They're interested in what you have to say. Maybe because they want to sleep with you, or maybe just because they're more on your level."

Ultimately, the most important thing was to seize on what the guest wanted from the interaction, and deliver that along with the wine. The elderly couple sought an audience to admire their jet-setting lifestyle. Men often craved simple adoration.

"Like, it sounds terrible, but men want to be acknowledged," she said. "Stroke their ego a little bit. Great choice. You have a great palate. Congratulations, you have a very big penis. It's a great bottle of wine."

I started paying more attention to Victoria's word choices after that, though it was difficult to hear over the din while also maintaining a safe distance from her tables. It was past seven p.m. and we were well into the second seating. The dining room was full, but the hit—the busiest part of the night—was still coming. The prices of the bottles we grabbed from the cellar were going up: 2012 Miani Ribolla Gialla ($250), 2004 Dauvissat Premier Cru Chablis ($275), 2011 D'Angerville Premier Cru Volnay ($400), 2011 Quilceda Creek Cabernet Sauvignon ($525). Victoria and I tasted every wine we opened, and we reveled in the cross section of classics we were drinking. "Instead of waiting on wealthy people, you're waiting on billionaires, which is nice because they'll order anything," she said with a grin. Francesco snuck me a splash of his table's Bordeaux—2004 Château Léoville Las Cases ($495)—while griping that the people who'd ordered it didn't want it decanted, but should have, since it needed to open up. (Not everyone agrees decanting can help with that: Émile Peynaud protested that doing so could harm wines' delicate aromas, while food science obsessive Nathan Myhrvold, author of *Modernist Cuisine*, advises "hyperdecanting" old Bordeaux by whipping it to a froth in a blender.) As the night went on, the incoming guests were, for lack of a better word, softer. Everything they wore seemed to be made of cashmere and silk and the skin of baby animals. Rhinestones glittered off one woman's cape.

I watched Victoria pour a $300 bottle down the drain. It was corked—a bit of the chemical trichloroanisole had contaminated the bottle's cork, lending the wine a wet-cardboard stench. Someone else spent $190 on two glasses of Château d'Yquem, a sweet wine from Bordeaux. The private dinner downstairs ordered a round of Pappy Van Winkle whiskey, at the cost of approximately a semester's college tuition. I thought about the bathroom in Morgan's apartment. There was mildew crawling down the walls and the handle had broken off his toilet, so I had to reach into the tank to flush. Victoria lived on the Upper, Upper, *Upper* West Side, a part of Manhattan that most of Marea's clientele would probably only glimpse while being chauffeured to Westchester County Airport, a hub for private jets.

"Is it weird being around all these people who drop a month's rent in a few hours?" I wondered aloud after a hike back up from the cellar.

Liz rolled her eyes. "This is *New York*."

The truth was, she and the other servers could get annoyed when people didn't spend, and took pleasure when they did. Each time the sommeliers reconvened at the credenza to open bottles, they discussed who'd ordered an "exciting wine"—"an expensive wine," Liz translated. For Victoria, "exciting" wasn't necessarily pricey. It could be something unusual she didn't get to taste very often.

"Guess what: Table Fourteen isn't drinking. She's pregnant," Victoria informed Liz. They exchanged a long look.

Still, it wasn't a wholly mercenary endeavor. The sommeliers were salespeople, not predators. They wanted to do their jobs and bring in money for the restaurant. That was how Marea stayed in business and met payroll. There's a limit on what restaurants can charge for a plate of pasta. Wine, like a progressive tax rate, is the industry's way of price discriminating among its customers. At the same time, Victoria and the other somms also wanted to delight their guests and earn their trust, which was ultimately more profitable in the long run. Ask for a bottle in the $200 range, and Victoria would steer you to a wine comfortably under that, just to show she wasn't trying to take you for all you were worth. Hopefully, she'd gain your confidence so she could recommend a second bottle later that evening, or later that year. And yes, they were buttering up the wine PXs. But then what regular doesn't expect some reward, some extra effort, after thousands of dollars and years of loyal patronage?

This was the sommeliers' career, and they had bigger concerns than one evening's tip pool. Some sommeliers, albeit not at Marea, are paid a salary, so the price of the wines they sell is divorced from their personal bottom line. But even when it isn't, wine is almost always more sacred than money. Sommeliers want their clients to drink well, first and foremost. Because wine is meant to be savored. It should spark epiphanies and be shared. Even at Marea, there was more than one way to be a wine PX, and open, obvious curiosity was a good place to start.

As the night went on, I began to lose all sense of time. Intervals were now measured in bottles opened, not minutes passed. I was getting wrapped into the swirl, the spectacle, the adrenaline rush of the dining room. There were bottles to be summoned, corks to be recovered, sediment to be filtered out. I dropped coasters on tables and fetched wines from the cellars. Our small corner, at the back of the dining room, pulsed with manic energy. We had to be calm and collected, smile and fawn. We have all the time in the world for you, sir. When really, we were two indecisive tables away from the whole illusion crashing down in a flame of irate PXs.

More and more people were waiting by the front door. The maître d' was saying yes to everyone. The staff had a glint in their eyes. I couldn't tell if it was the shine of scared animals being chased or the gleam of hunters on the prowl. I felt a contact high. It was electric. There were four tables that suddenly wanted to order wine, Table 57 was running low, 25 couldn't decide what to get, the wine for 31 was down in the basement, and the bottle for 12 was oxidized and there wasn't another. I tried to keep up with Victoria, who was gliding from the Japanese businessmen to the table of women with facelifts to the four-top of Spaniards and back again, all with practiced ease. I was constantly underfoot. The "hit" had hit. I was caught in the dance around me, getting pressed into walls, ducking through seats, dodging glasses stacked on trays. As soon as I paused in place—"Behind you," someone snapped. I put myself somewhere else, then felt someone reaching toward my thighs to nudge me over.

I'd blocked the silverware. A server elbowed me aside as she reached for bottles of water. Trays of food rushed at me. "Behind!" Bottles going to a table, plates coming from it. I stepped back to avoid a tray of six Burgundy glasses, but before I put my foot down I was rocking forward again to avoid the fusilli coming from the kitchen. And always the threat of those swinging doors. I retreated to the credenza, where people were grabbing glasses from shelves and putting new ones back. I'd never been so conscious of my body's size. There wasn't room for any of us. Michael glimpsed a big woman sidling up to the bar with a puffy jacket, a large purse, and two enormous shopping bags. "Uh-oh, that's a problem," he said, striding toward her. "She's got to go." Michael tried to steer her toward a low-traffic corner of the room while whisking her bags to the coat check.

I found a place to park my body by wedging myself into a ten-inch crevice in between the bottom of a silver railing and the edge of the credenza. The servers and sommeliers flowed in and out of the station to fire entrées (place orders) and drop glasses (set glassware). I took refuge next to the railing and listened as the staff discussed their tables:

> "These are for Forty-Six, but it's red and so they wanted it decanted now."
>
> "Two Bordeauxs and a coaster on Fifty-Eight, please."
>
> "Can I have the wine on Fifty-Seven?"
>
> "Fire the pastas."
>
> "I'm not going back to Table Five ever again. She's just so crazy."
>
> "Bordeauxs on Thirty. Three's a heavy smoker."

"Tequila PX. I asked if I could bring her the lime juice on the side and her response was, 'Do I look like a bartender? I will do nothing. You will do it for me.' Sweet."

"I've got the Cloudy Bay. Seat one or two?"

"Wow. Thank you for your *terrible* fucking tip."

"That guy there just reeks of sex."

"If I flip out it's because *they're* flipping out."

"She left the tag on her jacket. Look there. Look!"

"New. Money."

"She just fucking lost her shit. She was like, 'You had one job.' I can't—they're never going to change, you know?"

"Aww, that's so sweet—kitchen tour for that kid on Twenty-Eight's seventeenth birthday. Let some of those line cooks slap some sense into him."

George, the maître d', shook hands with a F/O his and glided toward my hideout. He stopped and directed my attention to an attractive young couple sitting at the bar, whom he wanted me to appreciate. She wore a leather jacket and a model's pout, he a white shirt and a tan. They didn't have a reservation, but George wanted to put them at one of the best tables anyway—2 or 8, the corner tables overlooking the dining room.

"You want people to look around and say, 'Oh my God! There is a couple sitting in the corner that is *soooo* gorgeous,'" he murmured to me. "You have to dress the room."

Victoria beat Liz to Chef Humm's table. More than actors or politicians, to Marea's staff, Chef Humm was a celebrity sighting. There had been some excited whispers when George escorted him to his table, and Liz had just assumed that Francesco, as senior-most somm, would do the honors tending to the star of the night. But Francesco was busy with a regular, and Victoria swooped in. Chef Humm order-fired a red wine, pointing at it on the wine list without so much as a word of discussion.

Victoria was also first to get to the wealthy Brazilian—the big wine PX at Table 8. Victoria smiled at his date, then at him. The woman pulled out a cell phone, so Victoria sidled up to the man to discuss Barolos. I wondered if she was relieved by the date's disinterest. I'd been told that women were notorious "cork blocks" who always talked their husbands down from exciting wine. ("You don't want the wine list to get passed to a woman," a sommelier informed me. "You want the guy to lay his fucking timber on the table.") Not knowing Victoria had already been, Liz dropped by Table 8, expecting her wealthy Brazilian to pick out his usual PPX bottle. Instead, he ordered only a single glass—*a single glass!*—of white Burgundy. And not even Grand Cru stuff, but measly Village level, if you can imagine that. Liz was close to hyperventilating when Victoria and I reappeared with his wine. Victoria displayed his order: a 1997 Bruno Giacosa Barolo, $745. An exciting bottle. All was right with the world. He would start with a glass of white, then move up from there.

Victoria's background in psychology seemed to be coming in handy. Surprisingly little of her time was spent taking care of the wine—opening it, decanting it, and chilling it. Mostly, she was reading people. She had to decipher when guests were no longer describing the wine they wanted but the person they hoped to be—powerful, manly, strong—and advise accordingly.

Victoria went to help a table of four guys in button-down shirts and loafers. Probably bankers, she guessed.

"I want something full, rich—the biggest wine you can give me," one of the guys instructed. She suggested three different wines. They settled on an Amarone, an Italian red that's the closest a red fine wine can get to cough syrup. It's the thing you want with wild boar and steak, not Marea's dover sole and sea urchin, but they ordered it. After Victoria served them the bottle, the men kept her at their table longer than was necessary. Were they hitting on her? "I can't tell," she said. "I mean, they have on wedding rings, but let's be honest—that never stops anyone."

It struck me that Victoria was saddled with an extra burden when she helped men on the floor each evening. Morgan just had to command authority. Victoria had to command authority *and* seduce. Not that she wanted to date the bankers. But she had to flatter them by giving the impression that she wasn't closed to the possibility and humor their advances, at least until the check arrived. As another sommelier more crassly put it, "I want those guys to feel like they can pick me up. But to pick me up, they're going to have to spend some fucking cake."

The four-top in button-downs polished off the bottle of Amarone and Victoria returned. Their party had grown to six. One of the men asked Victoria what she would drink with their meal. Not the Amarone, she admitted. She showed him an entirely different wine—the 2011 Domaine Jamet, a leaner Syrah, but still big and plenty rich, she promised. It was her favorite on the list. She'd won them over with the first bottle, so they agreed to try the Syrah. At $295, it was $100 cheaper than what they'd ordered before.

Her candor surprised me given that what people so often crave from sommeliers—and what sommeliers provide—is reassurance. Every sommelier I'd met had a go-to empty endorsement. It was the line they pulled out to flatter, without sincerely praising, a guest's truly awful choice in wine. Victoria resorted to reciting the facts:

The Amarone comes from the Veneto, it's a blend of Corvina, Corvinone, and Rondinella grapes. Andrea at Jean-Georges fell back on, "It achieves what it's trying to do." Jane, a sommelier at Del Frisco's, would murmur, "This is very, very classic." Morgan's thinly veiled reply was, "It's very pleasant," or "It's highly drinkable," or "It's a lovely picnic wine."

From my perch backstage, where I could see Victoria and the others shed their polite façades as they moved from the guests' tables to the credenza, the studied courtesy could appear manipulative, even conniving. "I call sommeliers 'some liars,'" Michael cracked when Liz, Francesco, and Victoria were out of earshot.

Only, they weren't lying, exactly. They were lying in the same way an actor feigns emotion while reciting Shakespeare, or a ballerina pretends her feet aren't killing her when she runs tiptoe for *Swan Lake*'s punishing *pas de bourrées*. The sommeliers were using pleasantries and feigned smiles to keep their diners in an alternate reality where everything is elegant, polished, and uplifting. Where you, the guest, are always right. And clever and classy and erudite and distinguished. Victoria and the others were briefly helping to make up for bad marriages and demeaning bosses. They were an escape from the ordinary and unspectacular. They were, with a reassuring nod or smile, helping to ease the sting of delinquent children or failed deals. People had come to Marea only in part for the food and the wine. An egg sandwich at Morgan's favorite diner would have satisfied their hunger just as well as the butter-poached Nova Scotia lobster. But it wouldn't have satiated the spirit—or the ego—in quite the same way.

"You want it to be like a magical experience," Victoria said, once she'd caught her breath. She saw it as her duty to create pleasure. In one way, this was an unnecessary luxury. In another way, it was the best favor a stranger could perform for another person. And when she failed, Victoria was crushed. "I got into hospitality because I want to make people happy. I like being a host, and I can make people happy with wine and food. It's what I do best. The hardest part is not being able to do that sometimes—when a table doesn't like you or they don't want to be helped or you're just not good with them," she told me. "It's like being in a relationship and you love them and you want to be with them forever, but they just don't feel the same way about you. That sucks. And to get your heart broken, like, all the time—that's the worst part."

Marea's guests were reluctant to leave. The six finance guys ordered another bottle of the Syrah that Victoria had recommended. And then another. Midnight rolled around. Other guests had trickled out, but Chef Humm and the bankers remained.

The three servers who were left took bets on who was winning, meaning losing, because they would have the last table to leave. While they watched the final few guests linger, they regaled me with horror stories from the floor. Katy got punched in the face while trying to keep a man from taking a picture of Ryan Seacrest. There was that time a woman came in reeking of piss, so George, the maître d', covertly spritzed the area around her table with his bottle of Chanel cologne. Another night, an octogenarian was taking too long to eat, and since George needed to turn the table, he started spoon-feeding the old man to hurry him along. Darnelle, a slender black woman working in a sea of mostly white, mostly older diners, got it bad. There was the table that told her to calm the hell down because *her* president was in office; the one that told her she looked like that actress who won an Oscar for playing a slave; the one that said it was "unfortunate" she'd grown up in Haiti.

The bankers got up to leave and Darnelle went to retrieve the wine they hadn't finished, along with their signed check. The women all cracked up when they saw it. Someone had scrawled "call me" on the receipt. He'd been too drunk to leave a number.

They'd also left about a third of the bottle of the Domaine Jamet.

On other nights, in other restaurants, the leftovers might have been saved to resell as a by-the-glass special, or repurposed to pour for someone who'd ordered wine pairings with their tasting menu. Not a dollar would go to waste. But this was too good to save.

"Oh my *God*. You guys *have* to taste that," Victoria said, grabbing a few glasses and pouring a splash from the bottle for each of the servers. "It's like the best bottle ever. It's my favorite red wine in the entire world. Hands down. You have to taste it."

Darnelle was a budding wine lover, and while the other servers sipped, she took her time getting to the glass. Being around so much great wine and food hadn't jaded her to its appeal. If anything, it increased it. This was the way it went: Despite seeing the machinations behind the scenes, the servers and sommeliers who sustained the mirage of elegance and magic craved that experience on their nights out. The show was so convincing and delightful that even its actors looked forward to being in the audience. They spent their evenings off in leather bucket seats, in the same position as the people they served. They drank the oak-aged Kool-Aid. Morgan sipped it solo over his tasting menus.

"Before I started working in the restaurant business, I thought Olive Garden was the *shit*. That's where I'd go on Sunday with the family," said Darnelle, swirling the Syrah in her glass. "And now I'm like, 'Hey, why don't we go to Ai Fiori?' "—Michael White's other Michelin-starred restaurant. "It just makes me happy, you know? You go somewhere, and you sit at the bar, and you eat good food, and you drink, and then you're like, 'Hey, I'm lucky to be alive and to be me.'

"The minute you say the word 'sommelier,' people get intimidated. When I go to a restaurant, as broke as I am, I want to see the somm. I'm like, 'Hey, I can only afford $80. Yeah. That's a nice bottle, you know? Okay, give me the nicest red you have for $80 and we're good,' " she said. "If people are embarrassed to be coming to a restaurant like this when they don't have a lot of money, it's like, no, not all of us are rich. Go ahead, don't be embarrassed to say 'That's what I can afford.' "

She finally brought the wine to her nose and inhaled. She thought about it, and then, at last, raised it to her lips. "My first sip here I'm like, 'Ooohmmm.'" Her voice dropped an octave. She gave a throaty purr. "That's *sooooo* good."

Darnelle closed her eyes and she took another sip. She swayed her hips side to side. "My second sip, I just want to da-*ance*!" She sashayed to the rhythm of a silent music, and rolled her shoulders to its beat. She kept her eyes closed and smelled the wine again. "I swear," she whispered. "Once you start getting that little taste, that little taste bud starts growing. You just can't go back."

CHAPTER SIX

The Orgy

I WASN'T A WINE PX, BUT I WAS STARTING TO DRINK LIKE ONE. I WAS trying more wines than ever, and trying better wines too. In addition to my tasting groups, Morgan and Victoria were passing along invitations to all sorts of events: distributor tastings, wine seminars, parties, lunches. I was shocked by how much great wine I could drink for free, or close to it. And, whenever possible, I was blind tasting it all.

As the months went on, I was improving. When it was my turn to blind taste, I no longer behaved as though I'd recently suffered a stroke—chirping out half-formed words and panicking over why I couldn't smell anything in the glass. I was figuring out how to discern the wine's message. Peach yogurt said "Zinfandel"; notes of caramel, butterscotch, and baking spices hinted at a wine aged in new French oak barrels. There were moments I barely recognized my own brain. I'd come across a Chardonnay with a yogurty, popcorn-butter flavor and think, *Ahh—malolactic fermentation.* There was a time I wouldn't have been able to spell that, much less tell you it was a winemaking technique that converts fermented grapes' malic acid (also found in apples) into lactic acid (present in milk) and diacetyl (used in artificial butter flavoring). Thanks to my twice-daily routine of sniffing and naming essential oils, scents like raspberry or tobacco would reveal themselves in a glass like familiar faces glimpsed at a party. I still had bad blind tasting days when I thought there was something medically wrong with me. But on the good days, which were becoming more frequent, I would nail one or two of the six wines dead-on—vintage, grape, region. I'd get around four glasses directionally correct—usually right grape, wrong region—and completely flub only a couple. I'd recently rejoined a tasting group I hadn't seen in a few months, and the sommeliers were stunned. "Who have you been tasting with?" one of them asked. "Because whoever it is, we want their number."

A glass of wine was no longer just good or bad, empty or full. It was high-acid or low-acid; possibly Pinot Noir or maybe Cabernet Franc; typical or an intriguing outlier. Each bottle was a chance to reexamine patterns I'd learned about what to expect from regions or grapes. I drank not because I was thirsty but because I was, for the first time in my life, genuinely curious about the bottles I encountered. Did this one live up to Morgan's hype? Was this producer as delicious as I'd been told? It was a puzzle. I'd scan the shelves for winemakers I'd heard sommeliers discuss, keen to experience this thing that was as much a cultural touchstone in my adopted circle as Beyoncé's new single was to the wider world. I felt I was going beyond knowing *what* I liked to grasp *why* I liked it.

I finally had the words and knowledge to ask for the flavors I craved, and I could seek out specific experiences with the bottles I chose. Certain wines could change my mood or mental state, and not only because of the alcohol. One dreary, wet Manhattan morning, I stuck my nose into a glass of white, and in a flash, I was back to a mid-July car ride with Matt, where we'd driven to the beach with the windows down and Stevie Wonder cranked up, past green pastures full of yellow wildflowers fluttering in a warm wind. Smell, curator and keeper of memory, allowed me to be a time traveler, and more than ever before I had control over my destination: I could pick a scent or a wine, then whisk myself to a time, feeling, or place. (Andy Warhol, I learned, would often do the same. "If I've been wearing one perfume for three months," the artist wrote, "I force myself to give it up, even if I still feel like wearing it . . . so whenever I smell it again it will always remind me of those three months.") Aromas bypassed my conscious brain, and their hit was instantaneous. Rosemary sent me back to walks with my grandmother when I was little, Viogniers were the scent of middle-school beach holidays. Hedonism was not a thing that had to exist at a distance from everyday life—something to be cherished at a four-star restaurant, or hunted down after a long red-eye to a town on the Amalfi coast. Smell and flavor delivered momentary escapes into pleasure for the sake of pleasure and these escapes showed up anywhere I was open to them.

My relationship with food was evolving too. Cooking, once a chore, was now an experiment. I ditched recipes and threw together ingredients guided by the logic of wine pairings: Opposites attract. Sweet wines play nicely with spicy foods; high-acid wines with high-fat foods; bitter, tannic wines with salt. A chicken's honey-plum sauce got chilies; creamy soups got lemon zest; and my friend's iced coffee took a packet of salt. (I was hoping to mute its bitter taste. I failed.) I confess: I'd also become more high maintenance. I sent back wines at restaurants if they weren't adequately chilled, and refused glasses that smelled of anything except air. "You look like an asshole swirling your wine like that," my friend Chris informed me over dinner one evening.

Still, I was a long way from Morgan and true cork dork territory. Seeing all the money changing hands on "exciting" bottles at Marea, I'd left my trail with Victoria more curious than ever to explore what serious wine lovers derive from wine. Is the best thing about a bottle how it tickles their senses? Flatters their egos? Gets them hammered?

I couldn't speak for the civilians, but I saw that for Morgan and the other somms, a great wine went beyond physical pleasure to move them at a level both intellectual and spiritual.

I got a taste of this one night just before a party hosted by the Guild of Sommeliers, when Morgan invited me over to Dana's apartment to pregame. Now, I know I'm stereotyping here, but when two bachelors throw a "pregame," my expectations for what we'll eat are low. Like, stale chips and old salsa low. So low that when Morgan asked me to bring cheese, I instinctively bought about $45 worth of crackers and dairy, figuring that would have to suffice as dinner.

Cut to a three-course meal prepared entirely by Dana and his sous-vide machine in a kitchen the size of an airplane bathroom. Even before we got to the sea bass with hedgehog and black trumpet mushrooms in a sunchoke and ancho chili broth; and the individual portions of sliced tuna belly on a bed of watercress, spring garlic, potato, dashi, and grated Meyer lemon; and our perfectly spiced pork chop with a gastrique made of hand-pressed apple juice, rum, German Riesling, cider, honey, star anise, cloves, peppercorns, and vinegar—even before all that, my cheese was immediately upstaged by Dana's homemade duck prosciutto, cured and dried to perfection in his wine fridge. I'd only narrowly missed the chance to try his cured pork jowls and his pickles—fermented with lactobacilli bacteria, not pickled with vinegar, *obviously*. "I totally, one hundred percent believe in pickles being fermented," said Dana with the conviction you'd usually hear in relation to banning concealed-weapons permits. Dana treated us to some of his homemade tonic water, and he and Morgan took it upon themselves to blind taste my cheeses. They correctly deduced a French Brillat-Savarin and Piedmontese sheep's milk cheese. I'd spent about half an hour stressing over what to buy—*you* try picking food for people who argue over whether the leg of Mangalitsa they shared should be classified as *prosciutto* or *jamón*—and I glowed with pride when Morgan complimented me on letting the cheeses come to room temperature. "That was a classy thing to do!" he said. "Just figuring out how to live your life!"

If that was the cheese, you can imagine the scrutiny they devoted to the wine. We'd already drank and discussed three bottles when Dana brought out the Fine de Bourgogne, a brandy, and a forty-year-old German Eiswein, an ice wine made with grapes left to freeze on the vine, so the cold concentrates their sugar. Dana had been saving the Eiswein for a special occasion and wanted to bring it to the Guild party. Being an only child, I asked why he wouldn't wait to open the bottle when there might be fewer people to share it with, so he could drink more of it himself.

"Because these are people who understand it and appreciate it," said Dana, of the Guild guests.

"Because they're people who are primed to receive such a wine," Morgan echoed. "At least five to twelve people who taste that wine today will be like, 'Holy shit, I have been recontextualized. My place in this universe and the person that I am and the way that I relate to the product I sell on a day-to-day basis has been recontextualized.'"

This was the pinnacle of what wine could do for its drinker. Philosophers like Kant and Burke argued that taste and smell, which are incapable of creating any "grand sensation," cannot produce aesthetic experiences on par with sonatas or still lifes. To Morgan, that was insane. Good wine was transformational. It changed how he related to the world around him and how he saw life.

"I've had experiences with wine in which I've felt small in a way that happens when you see Modigliani's *Reclining Nude.* When I see that painting, I'm like, 'There is something that is outside of myself and bigger than me,'" Morgan explained. "Wine for me is just a touch point to a wider world view: That I am not important. That I am a sack of water and organs that's going to be here on Earth for eighty years if I'm lucky. And so I should figure out some way to make that count."

A sip of wine didn't rouse some wild animal chained up inside of Morgan. Give him a glass of Condrieu, and he could decode, through its flavor, the blood, sweat, tears, and hopes that the pickers, farmers, and vintners had poured into that wine. He was sensitive to the human contributions and natural metamorphoses represented by the craftsmanship of that bottle, along with the moral and historical dimensions of each. "I'm understanding what people are like when I taste their wine," he said.

As Dana and Morgan saw it, not everyone was ready to receive the epiphany that certain fermented grapes had to offer. And being able to afford these wines was not the same as deserving them.

The evening was my first glimpse at how these sommeliers considered themselves custodians of the rare wines that could generate such revelations. Morgan, Dana, and others felt protective of these bottles. They believed they should be saved for those who were prepared to grasp all the layers of the wine's magnificence. Giving the bottles to people who weren't ready, or wouldn't appreciate them, was no better than pouring them down the drain. It was sacrilege. But in the right mouths, they could do glorious things. For this reason, somms will sometimes, for the right customer, reduce the markup on expensive wines. They'd rather be paid less for the wine and ensure it's drunk by someone who'll cherish it.

Morgan admitted that for special wines that Aureole had in extremely limited quantities, he picked which guests got to have them, not the other way around.

"I would just like to make sure the wine's in good hands, right?" he said. "There's almost more responsibility because it could be a transformative experience. You could serve that bottle to someone and they would really fucking love that wine and it'll totally fucking blow their mind."

This got Morgan and Dana reminiscing about past bottles that had totally fucking blown their minds. The '69 Chateau Musar Blanc, '90 Noël Verset Cornas, '98 Jean-Louis Chave Hermitage Blanc—"revelatory," "more cerebral than rawly hedonistic." They got worked up about tasting experiences they'd had, and Dana grabbed his laptop so he could pull up wine lists from the last five birthday parties he'd thrown himself. He read each list out loud from beginning to end. He and Morgan agreed it was tragic these wines had been drunk by people who couldn't fully appreciate what the bottles had to say. For Morgan, it was "heartbreaking."

I was curious to know how they judged if someone had been

moved—really, truly *moved*—by a bottle, while trying to remember how I'd acted when I tasted the wines they'd opened that evening. How could they tell that someone had not really appreciated a wine?

"Because," Morgan said, all hopped up on Chablis, "it doesn't look like they've been *harpooned* in the fucking *chest* when they fucking *drank* the fucking thing."

As a sommelier, Morgan's job is not to recontextualize his own place in the world. It's to find wines that do that for his customers. But was that what they wanted? Did wine-crazy civilians crave certain bottles because they loved feeling like sacks of water and organs? I wondered how this world looked from the wine PX's point of view and what was the joy they took in wine.

Most of what I knew about this elite stratum of drinkers had come secondhand via sommeliers. I could tell they were grateful for these high rollers, whose expensive tastes and large bank accounts offered opportunities to try wines the somms would otherwise only read about in books. Almost all of them worked in places where—like at Marea—they taste-tested each bottle they served. And like Victoria sharing her favorite Syrah with the servers, they looked for chances to spread the love, knowing that sips of the really good stuff were hard to come by. After a blind tasting at EMP one Tuesday, Jon surprised us with a bottle of late-harvest 1989 Trimbach Clos Ste. Hune Hors Choix, a $1,765 Riesling from Alsace that a two-top the night before hadn't finished. "One of the canonical all-time bottlings," Morgan said, licking his lips. "They only made two vintages: '59 and '89. I've never even seen a bottle in person." Aside from covert trips to the bathroom to snort lines of cocaine, the two men who'd bought the wine had been ideal guests. They dropped four grand on food and $14,000 on wine, and didn't talk price once. "Rich people are awesome," said Jon, beaming as he poured us each a splash. The sommeliers, who often came from middle-class backgrounds, didn't resent the big spenders' extravagance. They might poke fun at them, like the batty socialite who brought her wine sloshing in a Ziploc bag to Jean-Georges, thinking no cork meant no corkage fee. And yet they ultimately had affection for their PX patrons, and during the hours they spent caring for them each night, even developed a certain rapport, like Pharaoh's cupbearer-confidants of bygone days. ("Robert De Niro money isn't *real* money," I overheard a sommelier scoff, sounding very much the wealth-weary investment banker gossiping at his country club.) At best, rich civilians shared the somms' obsession with great wine. At worst, they bankrolled the staff. The only group that earned somms' full contempt were the cheapskates who whined about the price of $21 salads, and didn't get it through their thick skulls that the price took into account not just leaves of lettuce but the cost of the restaurant's rent, insurance, utilities, staff pay, linen service, toilet paper in the bathroom, and so on.

The truth of the matter is that as much as sommeliers drink—and even they deem themselves "functioning alcoholics"—they are not the ones who keep the fine-wine industry in business. That falls to the people they serve. There are collectors who amass tens of thousands of bottles in their personal cellars, more than they can drink in a lifetime. The most expensive bottle of wine in history was sold in 2010 for $304,375. You could have bought a house, two full college tuitions, or five Porsche SUVs with what was spent on that 1947 Château Cheval Blanc, which, despite being called "pure perfection," will eventually be destroyed and converted into extremely expensive urine. ("That's why it's so beautiful and temporary!" Morgan once insisted. "Because you're going to pee it out in four hours!") The flavor of those wines can reduce titans to tears. I watched an ABC News interview in which billionaire Bill Koch gets choked up thinking about his cellar—this from the unsentimental oil magnate who waged a brutal twenty-year legal battle against his own brothers. "Can any wine be worth $25,000 or $100,000 a bottle?" a reporter asks Koch. "A normal person says, 'Hell no, it isn't,'" Koch replies. "But for me, the art"—here Koch clears his throat—"craftsmanship"—his voice cracks on the final syllable and he blinks a few times to stop the tears that have started to come. He attempts a thin smile. "Excuse me." He clears his throat once more, coughs, then throws up his hands as if to say *I can't believe this is happening to me.* The reporter looks embarrassed for Koch and tries to help him out. "You care about this," he offers. Koch lifts himself up and rearranges himself in his chair: *"Oh yeah."*

I didn't fully understand why oenophiles splurged on wines and stalked labels, but I hoped to. To do that, I needed to drink with these big-bottle hunters and get into their heads. But talking to large numbers of such people is not, strictly speaking, easy. You do not merely go to Marea or Eleven Madison Park, ask the sommelier to point out the wine PXs, and begin peppering them with questions about their wine habit, unless you have a burning desire to be banned from such restaurants.

Over Dana's duck prosciutto, Dana and Morgan had mentioned an upcoming event called La Paulée de New York, a celebration of the wines of Burgundy inspired by a century-old French tradition of the same name. Most of the somms, distributors, journalists, and importers in the city were also buzzing about it. Being an aficionado of Burgundy, hailed as one of the world's best wine regions, requires an investment of cash and time that only the most die-hard—and wealthy—wine fanatics can dedicate, and La Paulée was said to be the most extravagant gathering of collectors anywhere on the planet. The weeklong festival included a dozen dinners and tastings, culminating with the grand finale: a $1,500 BYOB gala dinner to which attendees are instructed to bring "treasures from their cellar." (Yes, you read that right—your ticket buys you no alcohol except a "free" glass of Champagne.) More than a million dollars' worth of wine shows up for the final dinner, I was told. The dump buckets alone would contain some $200,000 worth of tossed Pinot and Chardonnay. "La Paulée is the kind of thing that starts revolutions in countries," said a collector who'd attended in years past.

Demand is so high, you can't pay your way in to La Paulée. You have to know someone who knows someone. Merely getting to pour there is a privilege, and sommeliers milk every connection they can to work the floor, for free, during La Paulée. They know the gig offers tastes of wines that are worth a week's salary. Dana told Morgan and me he'd been angling to get an "in" by double-dating with La Paulée's chief sommelier, the guy who picks which somms will pour. "You dirty slut," said Morgan admiringly.

Hoping to avoid playing politics, I went straight to the top. I called Daniel Johnnes, the creator of La Paulée de New York, who also imports Burgundy and serves as wine director for Chef Daniel Boulud's restaurant group.

"This is sold out, that's sold out—that's been sold out for *months*," he said, ticking through the Domaine Michel Lafarge Rare Wine Dinner ($1,500 per person), lunch with winemakers Jean-Marc Roulot and Christophe Roumier ($1,200), and the Legends Dinner at Boulud's Daniel featuring bottles from Domaine Leflaive and Domaine de la Romanée-Conti ($7,250). There was the possibility of getting me into the "off-grid" tasting on Tuesday—at $95, the equivalent of a free gift bag. But no one went for "off-grid" at La Paulée. You were there for the treasures. After a few more rounds of negotiations, in which I bartered an article for a luxury travel magazine, as well as my pride, Daniel added my name to the list for two different tastings and—with some additional pleading—the gala dinner.

Burgundy has a reputation as the most overwhelmingly complex wine region on the planet, which is exactly what its devotees love about it. You don't just decide to be a Burgundy fan. You have to earn it. "Keep in mind that understanding this region is a lifelong pursuit," warns the Guild of Sommeliers in its guide to what it deems an "impossible to master" corner of France. Sommeliers have a grudging respect for civilians who make Burgundy their mission, and it's by definition more mission than interest. "The people who do Bordeaux are businessmen," said a sommelier in my Tuesday tasting group. "The people who do Burgundy are passionate."

Just the names of the wines are intimidating. If you were to sidle up to Marea's bar and scan the wine list for a glass of Burgundy, here is the brainteaser you'd encounter by way of an option:

CHASSAGNE-MONTRACHET 1ER CRU, *LES CHAMPS GAINS*
F. & L. PILLOT (BURGUNDY, FR.) 2013 34

Let's unpack that. First the easy stuff: This wine is from Burgundy, an area in east-central France slightly larger in size than the state of Massachusetts. The 34 refers to the price per glass, 2013 to the wine's vintage. Good? Good. Other regions might not get more specific than that, but this is Burgundy. Chassagne-Montrachet is the name of the village where the wine was made; it takes its name from the town Chassagne and the Grand Cru vineyard within it, Montrachet. Premier (1er) Cru is the quality designation, the second highest of four recognized by Burgundian wine designations. Les Champs Gains is the specific vineyard, twenty-six acres in size, where the grapes were grown. And F. & L. Pillot is shorthand for the producer, Domaine Fernand & Laurent Pillot. So, pop quiz: is the wine red or white? And what grape is it made with? If you're a Burgundy nut, you'll know that Chassagne-Montrachet is legendary for its whites, and that to be labeled Premier Cru, the bottle would have to have been made with Chardonnay. If you don't know that, well, you might have given up and gone with a gin and tonic.

To be fair, in certain respects Burgundy is a much simpler region than others. With a few exceptions, Burgundy's white wines are made from Chardonnay and its reds from Gamay or Pinot Noir, a fussy weakling of a grape that's far more delicate and disease-prone than its happy-go-lucky cousin Cabernet Sauvignon.

But that is where Burgundy's simplicity ends. Whereas Bordeaux helpfully ranks its top sixty-one producers into a hierarchy of "First

Growths" (best of the best) through "Fifth Growths" (worst of the best), Burgundy holds itself to no such logic. It can be thought of as having four quality designations (Grand Cru, Premier Cru, Village, and Bourgogne, in descending order); five distinct wine-growing areas (Yonne, Côte d'Or, Côte Chalonnaise, the Mâconnais, and Beaujolais); and approximately one hundred different appellations. (You can look them up.) But knowing the reputation of each appellation will help you only so much, because what also matters is the vineyard site *within* that appellation. (There are around six hundred Premier Cru vineyards alone, so don't bother trying to memorize them.) And within that vineyard, quality can swing from marvelous to meh, depending on which part of the vineyard you're in and who's making wine from those vines. (Multiple winemakers will share a single vineyard.) You can't just rely on a producer's reputation either. A single Burgundian winemaker, and there are thousands of them, might produce as many as twenty different types of wines, each drawn from different vineyards, appellations, and quality designations. Oh, and good luck getting the scoop from them, because they don't much care for discussing their wines with outsiders.

Some of the most expensive wines in the world are from Burgundy. Also, many of the most unreliable wines in the world are from Burgundy. "Pinot from Burgundy is such a whore," Morgan lamented. "It's like the boyfriend who generally treats you like shit but shows up at the right time with flowers and chocolates. Of four bottles, two of them will be like, 'Wow, that was really good, but I definitely paid for that.' One will be like, 'Fuck, this is so depressing, I spent all this money and this wine *sucks*.' And the fourth bottle will be like, 'WHY DO I EVER DRINK ANYTHING ELSE?'" I've never watched someone open what was supposed to be an outstanding bottle of Burgundy without a look of mild terror on her face. The wines oxidize, they get reductive, they are fickle in mediocre vintages, and they go through awkward phases in their youth. The people who adore these wines tend to have a masochistic streak, and when you meet a Burgundy fanatic, it's hard not to puzzle over what trauma—*were they hugged enough as kids?*—might have compelled them to attempt to master this region.

Because nothing prepares you for a long, drunken night of drinking amazing Burgundy like a long, drunken morning of drinking amazing Burgundy, La Paulée's Grand Tasting was held the morning of the Gala Dinner. Each producer was assigned his own tablecloth-covered table, in front of which wriggled a tangle of arms, as Pauléers thrust their glasses at the somms and jostled for tastes. An older man with cheeks the color of rosé scored a pour and lifted his glass for a toast. *"À tout les jeunes filles!"* he crowed, bouncing his glass off his buddy's. *"À les jolies jeunes filles!"* the guy, equally pink, hollered back. Most people were "well fed"—Morgan's euphemism for well-off civilians—and being under thirty, with breasts and a full head of hair, put me in the minority. I stalked the floor, pressing the people around me to share what had kindled their obsession with wine.

I met a man who'd brought his own wineglasses with him from Los Angeles because he felt La Paulée's stemware didn't do justice to Burgundy's subtle aromas. To him, tasting wines from producers he knew well was like checking in on friends. He had an emotional connection with the wines. "When I see bottles, it's like a group of people."

For others, wine was their way of bonding with actual people. A couple in their late twenties—him, finance; her, interior design—got married in Burgundy. Funny I should ask about their wine hobby—the husband had been bidding on bottles at an auction just that morning. They held each other with the hands they weren't using to swirl their glasses. Why wine? "It's something we share," said the wife. "And a colleague of mine is a big collector," said the husband.

There were acquisitive types, like a round German restaurateur who answered my questions while picking lint off my sweater. He'd come to taste the 2012 vintage because he was accumulating sixty thousand bottles for a wine bar he would soon open in Berlin. What pleasure did he take in wine? "What's the pleasure about having sex, you know?" he said. "For me, wine is part of my life. And I can't live without." So why wine and not, say, fast cars? "Yeah, well, okay, to be honest, fast cars is another passion of mine. But if I would have to decide to either give up my wine cellar or my car collection, I'd give up my car collection."

Some collected experiences. A woman from Israel who bought a pass to La Paulée's nine fanciest events ($14,500) had flown into New York at the beginning of the month for La Festa del Barolo, another wine festival. Rather than going home, she'd decided to hang out in the city for three weeks. She couldn't risk missing La Paulée. "It's an art," she said of the wines. "It's truly an art. The aficionado who comes to taste tastes the art of the winemaking." She'd tried most of the hundred or so bottles on offer at the Grand Tasting, but she refused to spit. "Spitting burns my palate. And in any case, only swallowing gives me the true experience. So anyway, I have a very big problem with alcohol consumption."

I squeezed through tables, bottles, and blazers on the lookout for an old La Paulée hand who could teach me the ropes. I stopped next to a tall, bald man in a houndstooth sports coat. I was drawn to him by his spitting. It was gorgeous: He could shoot a neat stream of Pinot into a bucket three feet below his mouth and a foot to his right, without leaning over. Assuming such elegant expectoration could only have come from years of practice, I introduced myself. His name was Richard and he'd attended La Paulée religiously since it started, in 2000. In fact, he and his wife, Isabella—he waved over a woman with waist-length black hair—were hosting this year's guest of honor, winemaker Michel Lafarge. Richard tottered off to find Michel and drink some more. I stayed behind with Isabella, who was considerably younger than Richard but not eyebrow-raisingly so. She wore a Barbour jacket, jeans, a ring the size of a shih tzu, and a bored expression. She'd already made a pass through the tables and said her palate was fried—abso-*lute*-ly fried!

"I can't do this every day," she said with a sigh, as if it might have been an option. "We follow the whole circuit. We go to Burgundy once a year. Then we'll go for special events. So we went to a 450th anniversary last year and it was off the charts. . . . The 450th anniversary of—something. I don't know. I walked off the plane and I was like"—she waved a hand in front of her face to suggest *totally blotto*. "It was a seven-hour lunch-dinner. We were *all* there. All of the growers in Burgundy. It was off the *freaking* charts. A lot of growers came from *Ee-tah-lee*"—she pronounced the country with a French accent. "We *lit*-uh-rally walked off the plane into this once-in-a-lifetime de-*bah*-cle! The ladies, they couldn't find their husbands! But the next morning they found three of them sleeping in a field at the château! Com-*plete*-ly hammered!" She giggled at the memory. Richard came by with a sip of a Clos de la Roche Grand Cru. Isabella swallowed it and made a face. "Oh, look!" she brightened. "My God, that looks like a château that we were in last year! It probably is! I have no idea what it is. I just know we landed and it's outside of Burgundy. It's phe-*no*-menal." She offered a cheek to two friends, who leaned in for an air kiss. One was a Rockefeller. The other's name I'd seen plastered over major construction sites. "We have many wine societies," Isabella continued. "So we have wine-geek societies, clubs. We have wine dinners in clubs. All of our clubs in the city. And a lot of people like Brian"—she wiggled her fingers in greeting at someone across the room—"and other people, we follow the whole dinner thing together. Côtes du Rhône, Bordeaux, and Burgundy. The Commanderie de Bordeaux. Next weekend we have another dinner at another club of ours in Tuxedo Park," as in upstate New York. Someone called Michael gave Isabella a hug. "Oh, it *is* exhausting! I just went to *Pair-ree* for ten days. Just to sleep. Just. To. *Sleep*." She marveled at her husband's stamina the night before. "They were out last night until three a.m. Everyone had a huge dinner at

Dan-*yelle*"—the Legends Dinner, I figured—"and then an after-party until three in the morning. There's only so much you can put in your veins! If I was out until three a.m. at that dinner I would not have made it here today. I definitely would not have made it to SoulCycle. Because I've done it and overdone it and continue to do it and sometimes overdo it, so I know when it's time to say, okay, you're done. And I'm totally done. And I'm very happy. I'm very satiated. At least until tonight."

I had to excuse myself. The Grand Tasting was winding down, the Gala Dinner would be starting in a few hours, and I still didn't have anything approaching a treasure to bring. I'd been putting off buying a wine as long as possible, especially after Morgan suggested it would be appropriate if I spent at least $500 on a bottle, if not double that. I thought he'd been exaggerating, but the Israeli woman had me worried. "You can wear anything you want," she'd told me. "But what to bring, *that's* an issue."

I went to the Burgundy Wine Company, a shop conveniently only a few blocks away from the tasting, and told the manager that I needed a bottle for La Paulée. I gave him my price range. He squinted at me. "What's your *absolute* cap?" The wine I brought was essentially my pickup line, he explained. People got up from their assigned seats during dinner to walk around and pour tastes for one another. If I wanted to get in with the wine PXs, I better have something good to share. "You need to make a show of strength," he advised. The golden rule of La Paulée was bring the best you can bring. Whether you're a hedge fund CEO or an unemployed journalist, it should hurt just a little.

I spent ninety minutes in the wine shop sweating profusely, alternately consulting the manager, texting Morgan, and looking up online reviews for every bottle he had in my budget. With some prodding from Morgan, I settled on the 1990 Louis Latour Corton-Charlemagne, a white wine nearly as old as I am. It had a not insignificant chance of being off, Morgan warned. It cost me $275. It was, from my perspective, a treasure.

A few hours later, I arrived at the Gala Dinner clutching my bottle to my chest like the precious cargo it was. I weaved past black SUVs double-parked by the curb, and up the scuffed steps of the Metropolitan Pavilion, a charmless space more typically rented out for sample sales and bridal shows. There had been minimal effort to gussy it up. Floor-to-ceiling photographs of Burgundian vineyards covered the white walls. The wines, not the décor, were clearly meant to be the highlight.

A man in a suit offered to help me check my wine, and I reluctantly handed over the bottle.

"From eleven to now, I spent all afternoon at galleries," said a man in line behind me at the coat check.

"I need wine to go to galleries," his friend answered.

"See, if I do that," the first man replied, "I go in and I just say, 'Oh, I'll take all of it.' "

The Gala Dinner's four hundred attendees were dispersed among tables named after vineyards. The Grand Cru humans—big names or big collectors or big winemakers—were placed at the Grand Cru tables. I looked for my place card in between names like Jay McInerney and Neil deGrasse Tyson, both of whom were assigned to the Romanée-Conti table.

I took my seat and introduced myself to the woman to my right, Suzanne, a blonde in her forties who was there with her husband for their sixth La Paulée. On my left was Laurent, the French winemaker who'd been assigned to our table. He was a La Paulée virgin, like me.

The lights dimmed and Daniel Johnnes bounded onstage to introduce the sommeliers who'd be serving us. When he got to the names of Rajat Parr, Patrick Cappiello, and Larry Stone—three of the industry's celebrity somms—people around me audibly gasped.

"Ohhhhhh maaannnnnn," Suzanne said, grinning at her husband.

Daniel handed off the microphone to a giddy winemaker, who proposed a toast to "resounding intoxication." "That ees all I wish on you tonight!" he cheered, raising his glass. We all cheered back. It was at this point that I realized we were in a room with no windows. This suddenly seemed like good planning. "At eleven, all hell breaks loose," Suzanne whispered knowingly.

It was eight p.m. and already it was chaos. Sommeliers were making the rounds with bottles of wine the size of sturdy toddlers. A troupe of rotund Frenchmen with white mustaches, matching page-boy hats, and big glasses of red wine had replaced Daniel onstage. They were belting out "Ban Bourguignon," Burgundy's version of a drinking song, which also involves doing a dance that's basically a lazier hokey pokey. Raise your right hand in the air and twist; raise your left hand in the air and twist; repeat, pausing only to lift the glass in your right hand to your lips.

No one was really there for the food. I glanced at the menu anyway. Six famous chefs, six courses, starting with tête de cochon (pig's head) and ending with a golden egg (your guess is as good as mine). Laurent tapped me on the arm, and I turned around just as he handed me a bread plate. My memory of the evening is hazy, but I'm pretty sure I gasped. The plate was stacked high with freshly shaved black truffles on a bed of more black truffles. I must have looked confused, because Laurent jerked his head toward the end of our table. A barrel-chested Frenchman, built like a truffle himself, sat gripping a black truffle the size of a baseball in one pudgy fist and in the other a silver slicer he'd brought from home. He had a round, red face and a meaty arm slung across an enormous sack of truffles, like a fungus Santa Claus.

The six wineglasses arranged in front of me filled up quickly as the somm army began their rounds. The first wine I tried, according to my notes, was the 1988 Joseph Drouhin Clos des Mouches Premier Cru. Medium-plus acidity, with notes of red raspberry and damp dirt.

That's about all I can tell you about the wines that I drank. Savor? I barely had a chance to swallow. At first, I tried to take notes on each wine. Then I attempted to, at the very least, write down their names. That devolved into numbers—2008, 1993, 1962. And then I just tried to jot a check mark for every wine. I lost count around twenty-six. Suzanne couldn't get through her story about attending Chef Ferran Adrià's private dinner at Eleven Madison Park without being interrupted twice by offers for more wine. The man next to Suzanne couldn't get through *his* story about the cellar at his vacation home in the Bahamas without being interrupted by offers for more wine. The bottles came at us faster than we could handle, and we kept running out of glasses. Sip, dump, sip, dump, sip, dump—I would taste a wine for the first time just as I went to dump it, so I could make room for whatever the sommelier held in her hand. I tasted my favorite wine of the night and I had no idea what it was.

"Do you think wine can ever be better than sex?" I heard the hedge-fund manager next to Laurent ask his date.

"Vega Sicilia," she answered, without missing a beat. "It's a joy to the world."

No one was spitting, so neither was I. I was starting to feel very warm. The singers raised their volume and stamped their feet. "*La la la la lalalalalère*," they chanted. Laurent dropped his notebook of tasting notes and didn't bother picking it up.

"It's a feeding frenzy!" cried an auctioneer behind us, lifting his glass for a toast. "People get caught up, it's like blood in the water and *naahgnaahgnaahgnaahgnaaahhhhhhh*"—he gnashed his teeth in the air—"We are destroying a ton of wine. It's so wonderful! And it's so sad!"

More wine!

"It's like an orgy!" the hedge-fund manager shouted back. "You can't fall in love with the person you're with!"

White wine, red wine, wine orange from age. I said yes to everything. We all did. More. More! *Lalalalalalère!*

My face was hot and the dancers seemed blurrier than before. The dance was silly. How jolly! Laurent and I practiced our lazy hokey pokey. The sommelier for our table brought me my bottle, finally, cradling it carefully. Would I like to pour it, or should he? *Take it!* someone screamed, I think Suzanne. I poured, we toasted, we drank. It felt like melted butter and silk lingerie. Suzanne's eyes rolled back in pleasure. I walked around with my bottle and glass outstretched in front of me, like a beacon. Women in shiny clothes and men with shiny hair and sommeliers with shiny glasses. I locked eyes with a white-haired man, a distributor with a fluffy mustache who I think was nicknamed "The Walrus." It was too *lalalalala*-loud to hear. He kissed my hand and poured me some Champagne. "French Alka-Seltzer! Champagne is the ultimate palate cleanser!" A tan guy from Connecticut was begging sommeliers for selfies. "Jane! Jane! Get a picture with Wasserman!" the hedge-fund manager yelled, pointing at the importer Paul Wasserman. The singers bellowed. The men bellowed. The wine went into glasses. The wine went into us. The Walrus and I put our right hands in the air and twisted, our left hands in the air and twisted, and our right hands to our mouths and drank.

I did not hear tasting notes about the bottles, just unsolicited observations about me. "Jesus Christ, the difference between your fake and real smile is unbelievable. Fake is not so good," announced a man named Lenny. Someone else: "I like the way your hair falls in your eyes." A man I'd never met was introducing me to people as his "future ex-wife." "I need her for eleven minutes, ten of which are cuddling," he roared to a group of men I'd never met. Three different men asked me if there was anyone waiting for me at home. Was I married? For how long? Not even a year? My answers seemed more an invitation than a deterrent. Wine and sex have always gone together, I tried to remind myself. Ancient tradition. The Romans and their sommelier-lovers. I'd read that Dionysus, the god of wine, did double duty as the god of "the wild, weird and exotic; god of the ecstatic, sexual and fertile; god of mystery, madness and the irrational; god of passion, comedy and tragedy; god of bloody raw feasts and secret initiation rites. . . ."

Yes, it was, in its own way, an orgy. A bachanna-*lalalalala*. It was sick. It was indulgent. It was messy—"like two thousand pounds of foie gras just shoveled in your face," one of the sommeliers, a friend of Morgan's, yelled into my ear. We were greedy. We wanted to consume it all. We weren't hungry, but we had a voracious appetite. It was overkill and we were overserved.

But there was an openness too. People were receptive to raw experience in a way I'd almost never seen in a city like New York, where everyone usually shrugs off excitement with a "been there, done that" attitude. People wanted to be titillated. They wanted to titillate. Laurent and I decided my Latour paired perfectly with the shaved black truffles, and we stumbled around the room making people try our pairing creation. *"Tiens, goute ça et ça,"* said Laurent, placing a truffle on the tongue of someone called Pierre while I poured the Latour into Pierre's glass. *"La densité, la profoundeur . . ."* All of us in this windowless room chugging to the tune of the "Ban Bourguignon" had come together over a shared fascination with the physical. Joe Campanale found me and pushed me toward some special wine; my sommelier friend from EMP rushed over with a 1959 I *had* to try. Everyone was doing something to someone else's body; everyone wanted to stimulate someone else into feeling pleasure. A man in a suit fed another man cheese. "Buttery," the eater moaned. "Delicious." Strangers approached strangers with things to put into their mouths. "Can you have an orgasm standing up?" a man asked me, pouring wine into my glass. Lenny lined up three wines from three different years. "I'm going to do weird things to you," he said. Isabella handed me her glass. "Just smell it." "Oh my God, Jane. That's so decadent," said the hedge-fund manager to his date. "Fuck. *Me*," she said, taking the wine he offered. "Fuck *me*, this is crazy."

I found an unattended bottle of Domaine de la Romanée-Conti La Tâche, a legendary and supposedly heavenly wine. I tried to pour myself a glass. Empty. I imagined how delicious it might have been. I turned my back on my bottle and it was gone. People grabbed plates of the gold-leafed dessert from seats that weren't theirs. People grabbed dates that weren't theirs. The *lalalalère* got replaced by big hits by the Rolling Stones. The chefs sprinted out of the kitchen for a victory lap. Chef Daniel Humm, Chef Michel Troisgros, Chef Dominique Ansel. People in suits climbed onto their chairs, fists pumping. We all waved napkins in the air. The guys waved their ties. "Not only are these the best chefs in the world *BUT THEY'RE CRAYZEEEEEEEEE*!" whooped Chef Daniel Boulud before the other chefs threw him over their shoulders. He was crowd surfing. Then Daniel Johnnes was crowd surfing. Someone waving a napkin did a belly-flop onto his tablemates. "New York, New York" came on. *Come to the after-party*, my future ex-husband yelled to me. Sinatra was going at it. We were all going at it. Arms on shoulders, ties in air, yelling out the words, all wanting to wake up in the city that never sleeps,

And find I'm A-number-one, top of the list,
King of the hiiiillllll, Ayyyyyeeeee numberrrrr ooooooonnnnnnnnne . . .

After my hangover wore off, I was left trying to make sense of what I'd seen. In one way—in a big way—it had been an appalling display of excess. I'd gone to La Paulée thinking I'd find a group of connoisseurs who relished the sensory experience of wine. Instead, we dumped bottles that in other scenarios would have been the best things we drank all year. We barely paused to savor them before tendering our glasses for more.

Despite the waste and the gluttony, however, I realized that, in a strange way, I *had* found the sensory connoisseurs I'd anticipated. It was just that I needed to expand my definition of flavor and savoring.

The Paulée-goers did relish these wines, though not necessarily with their noses and tongues. La Paulée was, in its own way, a laboratory that proved flavor does not come only from our nostrils and mouth, as we often assume. We savor with our minds.

Price is the most powerful spice of all, and with our $1,500 tickets in hand, we entered that dining room primed to receive these wines and love them. What I'd experienced anecdotally at La Paulée has been proven scientifically. Researchers at Stanford University and CalTech put test subjects in an fMRI machine and had them taste five bottles of Cabernet Sauvignon priced from $5 to $90 each. The tasters predictably panned the cheap $5 and $10 wines, while applauding the pricier $35, $45, and $90 bottles, which made their brains' pleasure centers go nuts with glee. But there was a twist: The bottle that cost $5 had been served a second time, disguised as a $45 wine, and the $10 wine had actually been poured from the $90 bottle. The supermarket swill was deplorable when it cost $5, and divine when accompanied by a $45 price tag.

The scientists concluded that our brains derive satisfaction not solely from what we experience—those aromatic molecules tickling our noses and tongues. Rather, we're delighted by what we *expect* we'll perceive. In other words, all that careful attention to flavors, aging, and vintages could, for some tasters, be overshadowed just by saying a $50 Chardonnay is really a two-buck chuck. Knowing my Latour cost $275 might have enhanced its flavor as much as the oak barrels it was aged in.

From its exclusivity to its prices, La Paulée was perfectly engineered to raise our expectations. The feeling of entering the Gala Dinner—a rarefied environment reserved for the wine elite—paired with the promise of "treasures" from the best cellars in the city meant that even before the somms poured a single glass, we were prepared to think each wine would be delicious, regardless of whether it was flawed or fake. In fact, La Paulée is the former stomping grounds of Rudy Kurniawan, a convicted wine forger who, perhaps understanding the psychological element of wine appreciation, poured liberally from his cellar at Gala Dinners, and may have passed off phonies in the sanctum sanctorum of Burgundy connoisseurship. "It was a spectacularly beautiful wine, and I still have no idea if it was authentic," admitted a wine expert who'd guzzled one of Kurniawan's treasures. "It didn't really matter, to be honest."

Besides the dollar signs, the flavor of the wines that night could also have been influenced by the stature of the sommeliers, the color of the tablecloths, even the sound track for the evening. Though we think of our senses as separate and distinct, we are by nature multisensory beings and the senses act upon one another in powerful ways. Charles Spence, an experimental psychologist at Oxford University, has shown in numerous studies how colors affect tastes, sounds affect smells, and sights affect the touch sensations we register. Flavor is not only determined by what we taste and smell, but also by what we see, hear, and feel. He argues there are so many overlaps between our senses that it "appears likely that crossmodal correspondences exist between *all* possible pairings of sensory modalities." His research indicates that the very same glass of Rioja smells fruitier when sipped in a red-hued room with legato music piped in, but takes on a "fresher" character under green lights and a staccato sound track. Pairing a piece of toffee with "sweet" music—a track with high-pitched piano notes—makes the candy taste sweeter, while it becomes more bitter when eaten in the presence of "bitter" rhythms—a low-pitched piece featuring bass and trombone. MIT research scientist Coco Krumme found that a bottle of wine could be made to taste either jammier or earthier depending on whether drinkers wrote their tasting notes on purple-tinged notecards with pictures of fruit (jammier) or green-hued index cards with drawings of leaves (earthier).

With so many forces influencing what we perceive, evaluating wine objectively may be impossible. And so what? say some experts. Objectivity is not something we should necessarily aspire to, argues

Columbia University neuroscientist Daniel Salzman, a wine obsessive and past La Paulée attendee. "We'd probably enjoy the wine a lot less," he told me. "Knowing what wine you are drinking is part of the enjoyment of the wine."

Part of me still believed in striving for a more objective drinking experience. Our tendency to minimize and even disregard our senses of taste and smell leaves us open to letting context pervert our perception, and I wanted to know all of the ways I was outsourcing my experience of flavor to my more dominant faculties, like vision. At the very least, I was interested in understanding the influence of loud noise (dulls tastes) or the color green (evokes acidity) so I could control for their effects in those moments when I did aspire to purer, more critical sensing. I learned, for example, to be wary of the shape of foods after reading about a scandal that rocked the chocolate world. In the UK, lovers of Cadbury's Dairy Milk bars drew up a petition to protest an act of "cultural vandalism": The company had tweaked the candy's recipe, making it taste "sweeter," "sickly," "artificial," and "slightly nuttier," the chocoholics ranted. In reality, only the candy's silhouette had changed. The rectangular, straight-edged Dairy Milk bar, with its grid of chocolate squares, had been rounded off to form a single line of smooth, oval pieces. That transformed the flavor, since we "associate sweetness with roundness and angularity with bitterness," Spence explained. His research, and others', shows a drink smells fruitier if it's dyed red than if it's clear, and that wine tastes sweeter and fruitier if sipped under red lights, so I also filed away color as something to be conscious of when blind tasting. And context shapes everything. Scientists created a mixture of isovaleric and butyric acid, which reek of dirty feet and puke, respectively, then gave it to subjects to sniff. When people were told they were inhaling the perfume of Parmesan cheese, they gave the scent high ratings, on par with something delightful, like fresh cucumber. When they smelled the mixture again and were informed it was the scent of vomit, they were repulsed and docked its score by more than half.

But I also conceded that Daniel had a point. Since we know flavor is muddled by expectations and context, perhaps we could make peace with that fact and embrace all those inputs—label cost, color, music—as part of the flavor experience. There are countless articles suggesting sommeliers are frauds because they fall for fake bottles, or wax poetic about some Grand Cru right up until the moment it turns out to be a lousy *vin de table*. Instead, maybe the point should be: So what? The pleasure people get from those bottles, regardless of what causes it, is real. I've felt it. The people at La Paulée felt it. The Stanford scientists saw it: The price tags generated real, measurable happiness in their subjects' brains.

Sommeliers and wine distributors talk about a kind of "honeymoon effect" with wine. Say you taste a wine on your honeymoon in the south of France, then order that same phenomenal bottle again later. It will disappoint. Without fail. No wine is ever as delicious as it was when you tried it at the winery while some suave winemaker walked you through his family's two-hundred-year-old cellar and offered cheese made from his own goats. Whether it's La Paulée's illuminati image or the European countryside, all those things and more are part of the flavor, even if they're not contained in the bottle. And just as flavor is not constrained by the contents of a bottle, neither is the pleasure that the big-bottle hunters take in wine. What some Paulée-goers relished about their Burgundy extravaganza had little to do with the Pinot Noir on offer. They could have been drinking Barolo or martinis for all they cared. They appreciated the wine because it was their conduit into a lifestyle that made them feel special.

What Morgan knew intuitively was right: We love our bottles best when we are primed to receive them. And maybe the subjective experience isn't something to fear or belittle. We don't "blind read" books. When we delve into Hemingway, we don't remove all the context—the author's name, the year and circumstances in which it was written—and analyze it in a literary vacuum. Knowing about

Hemingway's life and the time period in which he wrote enhances our ability to appreciate the story. And that's considered a good thing. So why not with wine? Knowing that a bottle comes from an eight-hundred-year-old estate, costs as much as a car, and was beloved by Louis XV's mistress helps us gauge if the wine lives up to its reputation and fulfills its ambitions, as with any creation. If we can embrace the experience on the full terms on which it is presented, we might enjoy it more.

I soon had a chance to put this logic to the test. A mutual friend had introduced me to a wine collector—a PPX-, NEVER REFUSE–level collector—whom I will call Pierre after his favorite French winemaker. The financial markets were very good to Pierre. Pierre was very good to himself. And recently, Pierre had been very good to me.

He appointed himself my palate patron, and over one long weekend in Bordeaux, I joined Pierre for a series of formal dinners hosted in wineries' private rooms, which sagged with the weight of their silk brocade curtains. We were served by French maids, in French-maid uniforms, and propped up in overstuffed chairs so large my toes barely touched the floor. I knew the literature on priming and perception well enough to be skeptical of any pleasure I might take in the iconic bottles Pierre planned to serve. Expectations drastically alter sensory experience—yeah, yeah, I got it. Thanks to my flash cards, I also knew enough to appreciate that the wines Pierre was pouring were very big deals. If you'll indulge my name dropping: 1893 Château Montrose, one of Bordeaux's Second Growth estates; 1967 and 1974 Château Cheval Blanc, one of just four famed Saint-Émilion producers to be awarded the top rank of Premier Grand Cru Classé A; and three vintages—1989, 1942, and 1921—of Château d'Yquem. All of those wines left me feeling, to Morgan's point, like I'd been "harpooned in the fucking chest." But in the course of studying the wine canon, Château d'Yquem in particular had acquired an almost mythic status in my mind. Made in the Sauternes region of Bordeaux, this sweet wine—which goes by the nickname "nectar of the gods"—

is held to such high standards that, in crummy vintages, the winemaker scraps a year's worth of work and releases no wine at all. (Ironically, the secret to making this "nectar" is perfectly rotten grapes: It relies on Sauvignon Blanc and Sémillon berries that have been attacked by *Botrytis cinerea*, a necrotrophic fungus that dehydrates the fruit, shrivels the grapes, and concentrates their sugar.) The most expensive white wine ever sold was a bottle of Château d'Yquem. The second most expensive? Ditto. Thomas Jefferson was a fan, and ordered extra Yquem to share with George Washington.

I had all these facts in mind when I tasted the Yquem. I could lie and say I was indifferent to the bottles, or that they were overrated. And my life would be simpler if that had been the case—I wouldn't have been left aching for the ghost of flavors I'll never have again.

The truth is that the wine was incredible. Each sip took me by surprise. The younger wines smelled of orange, grapefruit, caramel, saffron, and vanilla; the older ones had developed a nuttiness and that rich, savory flavor that comes from age. But such a literal description fails to capture their full effect. As Château d'Yquem's consulting winemaker, Denis Dubourdieu, ranted when I spoke to him, "My grandfather would never have described a wine by comparing his dear bottles to little fruits that you could find for three francs at the market. He would have found that extremely trivial! Vulgar!" The Château d'Yquem tasted like the sun. It tasted like an experience that would never repeat itself, one I had better enjoy, surrender myself to, and be alert to. It compelled me to be present with the glass, so much so that tiny details about the night are still etched in my mind. I can feel the coarse weave of the tan linen tablecloth on my fingers, and hear my tablemate's cracks about botrytis—"A magic mushroom!" Where the taste of Yquem and the idea of its taste begin and end is impossible to say. In the moment, that question paled in comparison to the intense pleasure of the flavor and the compulsion I felt to absorb it.

But the encounter raised another question: If we can't really tell the difference between wines, or if we're so easily affected by extrinsic factors, then what *is* the difference? Why couldn't I have come to La Paulée with a $27 bottle of whatever I found at the corner store?

As I was going back over my notes from the day of the Grand Tasting, I found a comment I'd forgotten, or possibly blocked out. It was something the manager at the Burgundy Wine Company had told me as I was paying. It was the last thing I wanted to hear after spending almost $300 on a bottle of wine.

"Of course," he'd said, "the dirty secret of this business is that a $1,000 bottle of wine is maybe two percent better than the $50 bottle of wine. And sometimes, even, it isn't."

CHAPTER SEVEN

The Quality Control

Lei Mikawa runs one of the only wine operations in Napa that doesn't want you to come visit. Honestly, you can't even really find it. Or at least I was hopelessly turned around.

I'd come to California wine country and wound up lost on Route 218 because I'd gotten lost in a figurative sense. Since my pillage of Yquem and other once-in-a-lifetime bottles, I'd struggled to answer what had initially appeared like a relatively simple question: What is "good" wine? In my blind tasting groups, I was learning to distinguish classic Chenin Blancs from classic Pinot Gris. These were differences in type, not in quality, and I wasn't sure what ruler to use in measuring whether they were any good. Given all the bickering that somms did over bottles, I'd also gleaned that identifying a wine is much less contentious than determining how good it is.

For the better part of half an hour, I'd been making U-turns on gravel roads in a hapless search for Lei's research lab. That's where Lei, a sensory scientist, analyzes what regular humans—not critics or sommeliers—enjoy about wine. She works as the sensory insights manager for Treasury Wine Estates, one of the world's largest wine companies, which produces more than seventy labels that pump out more than 30 million cases of wine each year, ranging from the swanky Syrah your uncle might serve at Thanksgiving dinner to the plastic mini-bottles of Pinot Grigio you knock back on airplanes. I was more interested in the latter. And I was a long way from the treasures of La Paulée.

"Bad" is how most oenophiles would refer to Treasury's budget wines. Treasury calls them "commercial"—bottles sold for $10 or less—or "masstige"—a portmanteau of "mass" and "prestige," referring to wines under $20 each. This is the grape juice that ends up in most Americans' stomachs. In 2015, the world's wine auctions sold a combined $346 million worth of fine wine, like Château d'Yquem, to PXs like Pierre. That same year, Americans spent almost $2 billion on five "bad" wines alone: Barefoot, Sutter Home, Woodbridge, Franzia, and Yellow Tail—smash hits from Treasury's biggest competitors. The average price Americans paid for a bottle hit a record high in 2015, when it reached a grand total of $9.73.

The labels "commercial" and "masstige" refer broadly to price categories. A $15.99 bottle of Verdelho from the Barberani family's biodynamic, no-machines-ever vineyard in Umbria could technically be "masstige." But the term is more often used by conglomerates who produce a very particular type of commercial and masstige wine: not only cheap but engineered to taste the same year after year, developed to have mass appeal, and churned out in Walmart volumes. These mass-market wines are what you see over and over again in every liquor store you visit, or on the laminated menus in chain restaurants. They usually have critters on the label, or puns that get chuckles around the office water cooler ("Marilyn Merlot," "Seven Deadly Zins"). And they drive oenophiles crazy. Wines like Yellow Tail have all the delicacy of "raspberry motor oil," railed biodynamic winemaker and cellar celebrity Randall Grahm in one of his newsletters. To the elite, these are overmanipulated, nurture-trumps-nature, factory-made Frankenwines. They are dismissed as the wine version of a soft drink. Which, I was to learn, is more or less the idea.

Rather than take someone else's word for it, I wanted to develop my own metric to gauge what made these wines worse—if indeed they were. Knowing, by a wine's flavor, not only what it is, but whether it is good, great, or bad—and articulating why—seemed fundamental to having a discerning palate. Any reasonable person who eats out should want to comprehend why she'd spend $150 on a wine when $15 buys her the same quantity of fermented grape juice, as well as how to judge what she's drinking. And any decent sommelier should be capable of explaining that to her.

But the somms I knew had been little to no help whatsoever in articulating how they recognize quality. A great wine, they said, is "like a splash of cold water on the face," or "moments when you're standing at the top of the mountain." It has "more intensity," "more expressiveness," "more *wineness* to the wine."

Even Morgan, usually patient with my prying, had grown agitated when I brought up the quality question at a distributor tasting. A sip from a $1,200 bottle of Rousseau Clos de Bèze, a Grand Cru from Burgundy, had stunned him into uncharacteristic silence. I asked what distinguished it from a bottle a twentieth the price that we'd tasted earlier. "Why can't the answer be there isn't a fucking answer?" Morgan erupted. "Like, God, America, SHUT *UP.* I don't need to provide the answer to this question, because why don't we have some goddamn mystery left in the world? . . . It's in your heart. It's spiritual. It has nothing to do with quantification. And to me, at least, in a world where everything is quantified and everything is measured, thank God there's still something on this planet that belongs completely to the process and the mysterious and the aesthetic."

I assumed that instructing inquisitive guests to *shut up because we need some goddamn mystery left in the world* probably wouldn't fly in most restaurants. Nor did it satisfy me. And so I went hunting for answers.

One of the oldest ways of judging a bottle is to consider how, where, and when it was made. The ancient Egyptians tracked vintages—1272 BCE was reportedly "*nfr-nfr,*" very good—and the ancient Romans, who knew which vines thrived in certain soils and climates, paid close attention to a wine's origins. They used the method by which it was made as a proxy for how it would taste. We still do the same. My Guild study guides assert that the best Chablis vineyards sit on Kimmeridgian marl—a limestone-clay hybrid sprinkled with fossilized oyster shells. Morgan memorizes vintage charts so he knows which year Germany's vines got scorched (2003) or drenched (2014), since both conditions should affect the flavor. And producers around the world rely on quality designations, like Italy's "DOCG" imprimatur, to indicate that they've made their wines while observing rules meant to yield better bottles—culling their vines to concentrate flavor in the remaining grapes, for example, or aging wines that are too harsh in their youth. In Spain, wines bearing the Gran Reserva label will be left in wooden casks for a year (or more) longer than wines with the Crianza designation, a process that should soften tannins and add more complex flavors. Almost every region has its own quality hierarchy. In France, AOC (Appellation d'Origine Contrôlée) trumps simple Vin de France. In Germany, Qualitätswein beats Deutscher Wein. Both somms and drinkers are guided by these terms, which are meant to designate a wine's quality and style.

This sounds so easy, right? Basically, we can rely on the wine's label to tell us whether it's excellent, fine, or just so-so. Simple. Case closed. What's all the fuss about?

Not so fast. Unfortunately, it's not that straightforward. Despite its longevity, this classification system is often unreliable. The titles on labels are supposed to correspond with quality, but in practice, not every Grand Cru necessarily beats a Premier Cru, or even a Village wine. (One producer's Village wine can be several times as valuable as another's Grand Cru.) Some of Italy's best modern winemakers threw out the rulebook to create prized wines like Sassicaia, a blend of French grapes that, for years, was officially classified as a lowly *vino da tavola*, a table wine. Bordeaux fans use the nickname "Super

Seconds" to describe outstanding Second Growth wines that are every bit the equals of the ostensibly superior First Growths. And besides, instead of measuring quality by what went on in the vineyard, shouldn't we gauge the wine's success by what happens in the glass—how it tastes, smells, and makes us feel?

So classifications couldn't be trusted entirely. Next, I considered price. Concrete, quantifiable price. A $60 bottle of wine tastes much better than a $6 bottle, and way worse than a $600 bottle—right? Why else would we splurge?

I posed this question to wine economist Karl Storchmann, an NYU professor who runs the *Journal of Wine Economics* and, an oenophile himself, blind tastes weekly with friends. He agreed with my simplistic logic: Price does correspond with quality—but only up to a point. There's a price threshold at which a wine is likely to have been manufactured; another, higher one at which it's probably been handcrafted; and yet a third, even higher price point beyond which it becomes a status symbol. Fine wines may taste better—and set you back more—because they've been made with higher-quality inputs that are expensive and bump up the price. A single barrel fashioned from premium French oak can run $1,000. An acre in Napa Valley—where grapes are pampered with just the right amount of sun and rain—sells for around $300,000, many times the cost of land in boxed-wine country, like the scorching hot Central Valley. Cellaring a wine for years, so it can age and mature, also adds up. All those outlays are passed along to the drinker.

Karl estimates that quality steadily creeps up with price until around $50 or $60 per bottle. After that, brand, reputation, and scarcity start to nudge up a bottle's cost, such that for "a wine that costs $50 and a wine that costs $150, the physical traits of the wines are probably the same," said Karl. Burgundy's Domaine de la Romanée-Conti averages just 8,000 cases of wine a year, whereas Treasury's Beringer Vineyards pumps out around 3.5 million cases annually. The laws of supply and demand allow the Domaine to sell 750 milliliters of fermented grapes for prices normally reserved for down payments on homes. When the price of a wine hits the triple digits and beyond, it might say more about the bottle's value as an investment or heirloom, and less about its deliciousness as a beverage. "Anything that costs $500, it's not about wine. You're not buying wine. That's a collectible," said Orley Ashenfelter, a Princeton University econometrics professor who collaborates with Karl on the *Journal of Wine Economics*. Putting aside speculation or sentimental value, when it comes to flavor, "there's no justification for a $500 bottle of wine. I guarantee you I can get you one that will cost only $100 and you won't be able to tell it apart," he said. "The world is full of people buying bullshit."

Their argument, backed by the sober weight of the dismal science, was persuasive. But the emperor-has-no-clothes take also felt reductive. I had met lots of people who had staked their careers and lives—and fortunes—on the idea that there is a difference. And I'd seen that price could guide our perception of quality, more than purely reflecting it.

Which led me to science. This, I thought, could be the bullshit antidote. Maybe there was something unique, at a chemical level, about top-tier wines?

Enologix, a Sonoma-based wine consultant, argues there is. Using proprietary "quality recognition software," Enologix claims it can analyze the chemical makeup of a wine to predict its taste and quality, as measured by the scores it will receive from influential outlets like *Wine Spectator* or Robert Parker's *Wine Advocate*. Enologix has built a brisk business telling winemakers how to harvest and age their wines so they'll hit target ratios for the hundred or so compounds that Enologix has identified as critical for a high score. The chemicals they measure range from the typical—alcohol, sugar, acidity—to the more exotic—terpenes, anthocyanins, polyphenols.

But there's a "but" here too: Many winemakers protest that Enologix's "quality index" is fine-tuned to yield a specific style of heavy, fruity wine that only certain drinkers like. In other words, Enologix's formula might only produce the "best" wines for a particular palate. On top of that, experts' ratings can't necessarily be trusted as a measure of quality, if you consider quality to mean "people like to drink it." Tragon, a market research firm that specializes in helping companies craft hit wines, concluded that the relationship between wines that critics rate highly and wines that consumers enjoy is . . . zero. Point scores "are NOT reflective of *any* demographic or preference groups' liking," Tragon wrote in a report.

And finally, a study published in 2015 by the University of California, Davis—the "Harvard of enology"—suggests the relationship between wine quality and wine chemistry is not clear-cut. Scientists tested the chemical makeup of twenty-seven bottles of California Cabernet Sauvignon that, among other attributes, varied by price (from $9.99 to $70) and score (from 82 to 98 points, out of 100). They observed some trends: For example, bottles with concentrations of the elements europium, barium, and gallium were more likely to get higher scores from reviewers. But on the whole, the researchers failed to find any chemical components that could positively predict a wine's quality. With perhaps as many as one thousand different compounds in each wine, it might not help much even if they did. It's unlikely that we love a certain bottle because there's a touch of gallium, just as it's doubtful that we appreciate van Gogh's *Starry Night* simply because it happens to have a dab of cobalt blue. And good luck getting anything but blank stares if you ask a sommelier for a bottle that has a hint of barium with undertones of europium. Even if the study did decode the chemistry of quality, it might not be too useful at the dinner table.

Let's not forget that science has also determined that each of us perceives flavor differently. In light of that, could it be that the definition of "good" wine is entirely subjective?

That's probably the first answer you'd get from a sommelier if you asked. The relativists argue that the benchmark for quality varies from person to person, or even within the same person over time. I knew this to be at least partially true because my own tastes had changed so drastically. Since my palate training began, I'd ditched the liquefied-Cool-Whip-in-a-bottle white wine I used to love—a $14.99 Chardonnay from California—and I'd upgraded to the painfully hip Vin Jaune from the Jura, in France. This is a style of wine that, at its best, tastes like seawater mixed with rancid Martinelli's cider. (It's delicious, really. Don't knock it till you've tried it.)

There is, however, a subtle but important distinction between a wine that's good to *me* and a wine that's good—full stop. While everyone can (and should) decide their favorites for themselves, experts do attempt to grade quality according to certain objective standards. By those criteria, a wine can be great even if the drinker doesn't like it. "'Good' exists independently of one's personal preference," writes *Wine Spectator* critic Matt Kramer. Jamie Goode, author of *The Science of Wine*, concurs, asserting that wine quality "is something 'outside ourselves.' In wine appreciation, we are effectively tapping into an aesthetic system or culture that is outside our own biological preferences."

This sounds promising. So perhaps this "aesthetic system" is the answer. Though most critics each have their own take on that "system," there are three key attributes that pros consistently consider when rating a wine: its balance, complexity, and finish. An unbalanced wine will have flavors that stick out in awkward and unpleasant ways—maybe the alcohol burns too much after you swallow, or the acid overwhelms the fruit—while a balanced wine brings its disparate parts into harmony. Complexity is the capacity for a wine to keep delighting, with layers and depth and variety. The finish describes the length of time the wine's flavor lingers in your mouth after you've spit or swallowed. A mediocre wine finishes quickly, a good one sticks around. This checklist is supposed to help drinkers judge the inherent, objective "goodness" of a wine, which is reflected in the point scores it receives. A critic's rating is meant to indicate whether a bottle is superb or mediocre, irrespective of how much the reviewer liked it personally. A 92/100 is the grade for the wine, not how much pleasure the judge took in it.

But if these traits really do provide an objective ruler for quality, then why do judges disagree so much with one another—and even with themselves—over which wines are good? If quality was inherent and this "aesthetic system" could recognize it, then you'd expect the same wines to get the same scores (or very close to the same scores). At the bare minimum, they should get the same scores from the same critics.

That's not always what happens in the real world. A study published in the *Journal of Wine Economics* tracked the reliability of wine judges at a major California wine competition over three years. At every contest, around seventy judges would each taste thirty glasses of wine, some of which had been poured in triplicate from the same bottle, and then award the wines gold, silver, bronze, or no medal. The results were, at best, an embarrassment: Only 10 percent of the judges were consistent in their scores. Most of them gave the same bottle entirely contradictory ratings each time they tasted it. One judge awarded a wine 90 points (silver) the first time he tried it, then gave it 80 points (no medal) when he tasted it a few minutes later, and finally decided it deserved a nearly perfect score of 96 (gold) when he drank it for a third time. The study's author concluded that the bottles' medals were essentially handed out at random. "It is reasonable to predict that any wine earning *any* medal could in another competition earn *any other* medal, or none at all," he wrote.

This instills little confidence in the "aesthetic system" that's supposed to provide a dependable definition of "good." Especially because the study only backs up what others have observed. A report, published by *The Grapevine*, a California newsletter, tracked four thousand wines entered across a dozen competitions and found more than one thousand of them had won gold medals in certain competitions while failing to place entirely in others. Author and physicist Leonard

Mlodinow recounted in the *Wall Street Journal* how a vintner entered the same wine, under three different labels, to a single competition. Two of those bottles were dismissed entirely (one deemed "undrinkable") and the third, identical wine won a double gold medal.

The study on California wine competitions did find that there was one situation where the judges were extremely consistent: rating wines they did not like. Quality is elusive. But bad wine can't hide.

These definitions of quality swirled in my head on the drive from San Francisco to St. Helena, where Lei runs her lab. Since "good" wine resisted a coherent description, I'd decided to pay a visit to the epicenter of "bad" wine—more accurately "mass-market" wine—to see if I could better define quality in its absence.

The highway was lined with tasting rooms housed in Queen Anne mansions sitting in gardens as meticulously groomed as sheared poodles. Most of the wineries I passed worried about their *Wine Spectator* scores, or how they'd fare at competitions like those the *Journal of Wine Economics* had eviscerated. But for mass-market bottlings, producers like Treasury are usually more concerned with winning "share of stomach" than scoring points: The goal is wooing drinkers away from Bud Light and vodka sodas. During Lei's tenure, Treasury had gone after beer-loving bros with Sledgehammer, a fist-pumping line of red wines that brag they're "literally a hammer blow to your taste buds!" (Its motto, which appears on its website next to a bottle of Zinfandel exploding from a ball of flames, was written to be grunted: "Meat. Wine. Good.") Treasury has likewise tried to attract the Skinnygirl Margarita demographic with Be., a label that uses *Cosmo*-style quizzes to pair ladies with its Pink Moscato (called "Be. Flirty") or Riesling ("Be. Radiant"), depending on whether they prefer sky-high stilettos or polka-dotted ballet flats, respectively. A press release toasts Be. as Treasury's first line of wines "designed to appeal to the increasingly influential wine demographic of Millennial women." Consider that for a second: a wine not "made" but "designed." Elsewhere, someone referred to Be.-style wines as "developed," and it occurred to me that this was the first time since leaving the tech world that I'd heard "develop" used as a synonym for "create."

I finally found Lei's lab off a side street bordered by ranch houses, in a mustard-yellow office building tucked behind a row of low concrete warehouses. NO TASTING OR TOURS, warned a sign at the entrance, not that there was anything remotely enticing about the complex of parking lots.

Lei was in her early thirties and had rejected the wine-country uniform of jeans and a Carhartt jacket for a black dress with black stockings and black suede boots. She led me up carpeted steps to the lab, a sparse, bright room where an assistant was mixing canned mushrooms, black pepper, and cranberries into glasses of red wine lined up on Formica counters. One side of the room had a narrow row of brightly lit white booths, each one just barely wide enough to fit a chair, a person, and a tiny built-in counter. Lei brought her test subjects here to taste wines, and the sterile booths were designed to eliminate potential sensory distractions, like stray odors, or bright colors. A chain of paper letters pinned near the door spelled out PARTY TIME.

Before joining Treasury in 2010, Lei spent five years at Jack in the Box, the fast-food company, testing trans-fat-free cooking oils in a hunt for the tastiest way to fry up everything from French fries to chicken nuggets. Working on wine was "almost the same thing" as developing fast food, she said. I was surprised to hear this. Critics sneer that so-called designed wines, like Sledgehammer, are no better than the sodas at drive-thrus. Gulpable, but cloying. Consistent, but boring. Industrially manufactured. Was Lei's work really turning wine into a kind of alcoholic Coca-Cola, like they claimed? "It looks like it's coming to that." She shrugged. "One of the wines that was super popular a few years ago was Moscato. It almost tasted just like a soft drink."

Treasury's sensory research lab, the first of its kind at a winery when it opened in 1989, was founded in part on the principle that wine is more like snack foods or soda than it might seem. No company would ever launch a new flavor of potato chips or energy drinks without market research, sensory evaluation, and consumer testing. They need data, numbers, and analysis. Why should wine be any different? The sensory research lab that Lei inherited was created under the oversight of Beringer Vineyards, an iconic California property pre-dating Prohibition that was then owned by Nestlé. (Treasury has owned Beringer since 2011.) Nestlé had ample experience developing supermarket staples like Lean Cuisine, Häagen-Dazs, and Coffee-mate, so when Beringer's team had the idea to put its wines through sensory analysis to understand what drinkers actually enjoy in a red or white, the powers that be agreed it made perfect sense.

But wine had never really worked that way. Wineries traditionally rely on a small team of experts, led by a winemaker, to create a wine that satisfies their vision of "goodness." The bottles that recontextualize Morgan's place in the universe are almost always made in this fashion, crafted by oeno-*artistes* following their gut instinct for quality. To consult the drinkers would be like Monet running focus groups to decide the colors for his next canvas.

In a break from the tried-and-true process, Beringer—and now Treasury Wine Estates—embraced winemaking by committee. They experimented with having the tastes of amateurs, not only professionals, guide the profiles of their commercial and masstige bottles, an approach that can also be used—and has been—by the winemakers who make Beringer's fine wines. (It's just one more tool to make them a success.) The sensory analysis marked a radical new philosophy: Instead of bringing wine as it is to people, the producers began bringing people as they are to wine. That approach spread to other giants, such as E.&J. Gallo (of André, Carlo Rossi, and Barefoot fame) and Constellation Brands (owner of Woodbridge, Robert

Mondavi, and Ravenswood, among other labels). Both currently run their own sensory research divisions. Tragon offers similar services to wineries that can't afford in-house labs.

Lei had invited me to watch the first step in developing a wine that, in industry terms, was "created from the consumer backwards." Shortly after I arrived, a group of volunteers—all Treasury staff—settled into a conference room to drink and describe the fourteen wines that made up Lei's latest study. Though Lei wouldn't identify the bottles, they were likely a mix of existing Treasury products, new prototypes, and hit wines made by Treasury's competitors, whose profiles Lei and her colleagues might want to copy. In the session I visited, she asked the volunteers to discuss what words they'd use to describe each of the wines. She needed to be sure everyone had the same definition of "fruity" or "earthy," and offered up the glasses of mushrooms and cranberries I'd seen earlier, just in case anyone needed to remind themselves of a scent. Lei's "sensory measuring devices," aka the drinkers, didn't have to be wine connoisseurs, just relatively sensitive to differences in what they eat, which can't be taken for granted. According to Tragon, roughly 30 percent of any population "cannot discriminate differences at better than chance among products they regularly consume."

In a few days, the employees would head into the tasting booths to evaluate the character of each wine. Next, more than one hundred amateur drinkers (not the Treasury staff) would rate how much they liked each of the fourteen samples. By comparing these two data sets—the sensory profile of the wines, and which ones consumers enjoy most—Lei would understand what her target buyers crave. Maybe they want purplish wines with blackberry aromas and low acidity. Or maybe the new trend would be for wines in a pinker shade of red that are unoaked, low in alcohol, and have a hint of sweetness. Whatever it was, Treasury's winemakers could fine-tune their formula to please drinkers' palates. They might adjust their blends, aging process, yeast strains, harvest time, plantings, rootstock, or oak usage, among other tweaks. "If we see that Wine A scores much higher than Wine B, and if Wine A had a significantly higher sugar level, then we know that we just need to add a little bit more sugar to it," Lei explained. Tasters tend to perceive opaque, dark-hued wines as more delicious than pale, translucent wines, like Pinot Noir, so Treasury might decide to bump up the color of its wine. Amateur wine buyers have been known to teach experts a thing or two about up-and-coming wine trends. During the '90s, boom years for big, buttery Chardonnays, one of Tragon's tasting panels rejected the oaky styles that were then en vogue. The drinkers preferred a $4, unoaked bottle to everything else they tried. But when the researchers told their client to consider designing a line of unoaked whites, the winery that commissioned the study kicked them out. "They said, 'You're crazy. Get out of my office,'" recalled Rebecca Bleibaum, Tragon's "Chief Sensory Officer." These days, it's the leaner, unoaked Chardonnays that are all the rage.

I sipped the wines that Lei put out for her panel to try. I could see how they would evoke something from a 7-Eleven. They reminded me of blueberry smoothies with a shot of vodka and Hershey's syrup stirred in. But I was trying to keep an open mind. *Price is a spice*, I reminded myself, *don't be such a snob.* Truth be told, I didn't want to finish them. There was nothing new that revealed itself after the second sip. The wines were rich, syrupy, and heavy.

In this sense, they aligned nicely with the tastes of commercial and masstige buyers, who tend to prefer sweet and fruity wines that are low in astringency, bitterness, and complexity. That also made these bottles pretty much the antithesis of what the wine cognoscenti would consider "good." I thought back to a blind tasting session in which a sommelier from Jean-Georges had recounted the horror of attending a wedding where Beringer wines had been served. "My friend and I kind of dared each other to try the Chardonnay. And we were like 'Eeeeeeewwwwww!'" she complained, to sympathetic nods. "I drank a lot of scotch and soda that night." Lei's wines were about as similar to Morgan's earthy $1,200 Rousseau as a Snickers is to roasted quail.

Though Morgan might refuse to swallow any of Lei's samples, making bottles "from the consumer backwards" has transformed the pleasure that people take in wine. In 2007, it was the rare Sledgehammer-type bottle that could meet the minimum score that Tragon considers necessary for a product to be viable in the marketplace. Drinkers choked down these wines, assigning them the same low ratings as spinach and frozen peas. Bearable, but not at all pleasant. Now, as mass-market wines have gotten better at satisfying drinkers' tastes, panelists routinely award these bottles the same high scores as upper-end ice creams, like Häagen-Dazs. "You're getting wines to get up into that sort of indulgent 'love it' category," said Rebecca. "On a blind basis, consumers *love* them." Acidic, mouth-puckering Bordeaux can be an acquired taste. Yellow Tail or Sledgehammer, with their intense fruity notes and sweet aftertaste, are a more natural fit for drinkers who, like many of us, stick to a diet of sugary Pumpkin Spice lattes and Vitamin Waters. People like Lei and Rebecca have a motto: "Marketing will get you to buy a wine once. Sensory will get you to buy it twice." (John Thorngate, the director of Constellation's sensory department, cautioned that logic doesn't apply at the luxury level. Those drinkers are totally irrational: "People who drink Screaming Eagle"—yours for the low, low price of $1,000—"who *don't* like it will keep drinking it because it makes them feel good.")

This was not yielding the tidy answer to the quality question that I had hoped for. Counterintuitively, then, "bad" wine was really wine that tasted *good*, at least to large numbers of wine drinkers.

Producers like Treasury have embraced a definition of quality that is far simpler than Robert Parker's or the Court of Master Sommeliers': A wine is good if lots of people like it intuitively, without having to know anything about balance or finish. These "bad" bottles are engineered for maximum pleasure, so they can be enjoyed without a user's manual and appeal to drinkers' natural inclinations. And what was so bad about that? Parallel trends exist in music, fashion, movies, and art, where the lowbrow and highbrow manage to coexist. You wouldn't want to hear Felix Mendelssohn at a rave, but same goes for walking down the aisle to Miley Cyrus's "Wrecking Ball."

While in California, I took a detour to meet Tim Hanni, a former Beringer employee and one of the first two Americans to become a Master of Wine, a superlative distinction awarded by the Institute of Masters of Wine. Despite the fancy title, Tim has been nicknamed the "wine antisnob" for lobbying his peers to rethink the rules of wine appreciation. More specifically: He wants them to ditch the current playbook entirely. He pooh-poohs the laws of food and wine pairing, has given gold medals to wines most connoisseurs wouldn't touch ("Chocolate Cherry Truffle," anyone?), and considers teaching drinkers to appreciate Grand Crus over Sledgehammer a misguided and condescending approach. At a Starbucks not far from Lei's lab, Tim argued that oenophiles' definition of "good" wine has nothing to do with its flavor or how it was made. Rather, he says, it has its basis in peer pressure and a herd mentality. Hoping for acceptance among the wine "in" crowd, wannabe snobs mimic the tastes of the snobs, and those preferences trickle down from there. If you don't know much about wine, you might assume you're a tabula rasa and bias-free. Now think of the word "Bordeaux." If something, anything, came to mind—maybe you immediately associated it with castles, or rich people, or tradition—it's because somewhere along the way, some article, or offhand comment by a friend, has colored what you consider good taste.

To take pleasure in critically acclaimed bottles, "you really have to give up your natural likings and inclinations and adopt the collective delusions about what wine is," said Tim. And this is from someone who, before coming to terms with his alcoholism, tasted more than his fair share of the classics. Tim contends that we each have unique sensitivities to flavors that should steer us toward the wines we like. Wine lovers are expected to rave over tannic, bitter Barolos, even though as children we instinctively covet sweet things and scrunch our faces at bitter flavors, an evolutionary defense against ingesting toxic foods. If you learn to love Barolo, "your palate's not 'maturing,' it's actually becoming unnatural," Tim said. "You dispose of your natural taste for sweetness and whatever, and even learn to make faces. And not only about the wine, but about the people because it's part of the criticism. You learn what you're supposed to like, and you also learn what you're *not* supposed to like, and *who* you're not supposed to like by association of what you're not supposed to like. You learn to criticize not only the fucking wine, but the fucking people who like that wine."

Tim's argument is not a new one. It recalls a theory proposed by French sociologist Pierre Bourdieu in his 1984 book, *Distinction: A Social Critique of the Judgement of Taste*. Bourdieu contends that we learn to appreciate things—golf, skinny arms, the opera, Champagne—because of the social and cultural capital we derive from embracing certain pursuits and rejecting others. As Bourdieu sees it, no taste is pure. As we interact with our social circle, we absorb cues about the things we should—and shouldn't—celebrate in order to gain acceptance from our peers. In the end, we admire whatever will make us admirable. "Taste classifies, and it classifies the classifier," writes Bourdieu. Lusting after Domaine de la Romanée-Conti appears more arbitrary—and even a little sinister—through this lens. A "good" wine is whatever a certain stratum of society christens a "good" wine, for reasons that might have little to do with the contents of the bottle. And we use peoples' judgment in wines to, in turn, judge them. This puts a new, unflattering spin on the sommelier's job: By guiding their guests to quality wines, somms essentially help the upper classes to differentiate themselves from the hoi polloi through this rather arbitrary notion of "good."

Tim was giving voice to a nagging misgiving that had been part of what fascinated me about wine in the first place. I didn't believe in any mass conspiracy to dictate the world's tastes. But it seemed possible that even the experts were guilty of appreciating wines not because those bottles were good but because they'd learned to *say* those bottles were good. What they picked as their favorites reflected their identity. I found it telling that while other people post selfies to Instagram, sommeliers share snapshots of bottles they've drunk. Those labels said something about who they were as people, and many ended their shifts by uploading "#bestbottleofthenight" photos, to show off what they'd tried. Morgan admitted feeling frustrated by the pressure to conform to the tastes of the moment. He griped about somms attacking people who didn't get on board with the idea that some trendy new Champagne maker was the best thing to happen to sparkling wine since the invention of the cork. "They get all Jesuitical about it," he complained. "There's this whole issue where if people spend $350 for a bottle of wine, they don't want to admit they don't like it."

Perhaps "bad" wine wasn't really *so* bad. At the very least, it offered an inviting welcome for people who might otherwise never have picked up a glass. "A lot of people start out with a sweet wine and then they'll eventually leave and they'll actually go to the luxury level and become a wine collector or a wine consumer or a wine snob," said Lei. She saw her bottles as training wheels for future oenophiles. The drinkers who love their Sledgehammer now might be only a few bottles away from becoming snobs who dismiss those same wines as trash.

Before leaving Lei's lab, I'd spotted a small plastic package on a shelf in her office. It contained wooden chips that appeared to be a kind of seasoning for wine. BUTTERSCOTCH & CHOCOLATE STAVE SAMPLES, the label read.

Given everything I'd learned, it seemed tricky to deem these mass-market wines "bad" based purely on their taste. But was there something problematic about the way they were made—or rather, designed?

Each year, 14,000 winemakers and grape growers descend on the Sacramento convention center for the Unified Wine & Grape Symposium, a trade show where producers go to buy their bungs, barrels, bottles, corks, capsules, centrifuges, concentrates, color stabilizers, crush pads, flavoring agents, enzymes, electrodialysis machines, infusion tubes, tanks, presses, and pumps. The only winery staple not on offer: romance.

Lei and Tim were both going. And so was I. "If you're not at that show, then you're not in business," a Tragon staffer informed me.

When Lei told me all the ways that Treasury could tweak its wines to suit consumers' tastes, she'd described a degree of control over the winemaking process that didn't seem possible. Color, bitterness, tannin, even aromas of blackberry, cherry, and plum—each could be cranked up or down according to drinkers' desires. It sounded as though the winemakers had a dial on each individual attribute of the wine.

Because they do. I hadn't fully grasped how this could be accomplished with such precision until I joined herds of men in fleece vests and work boots on the trade-show floor. The products I passed had futuristic-sounding names that suggested sci-fi feats of flavor manipulation: Accuvin, UberVine, Dynamos, Nutristart, Turbicel, Zyme-O-Clear, the Thor. They were a far cry from the homey labels like "Barefoot" and "Naked Grape" you might peruse at your neighborhood wine shop.

Zyme-O-Clear and the Thor don't usually feature in the story of how wine gets made. The big-picture, tradition-heavy, utterly stereotypical, and non-nuanced account of where fine wine comes from, as recited in stores and on vineyard tours, will go something like this: First, the winemaker plants his vines on a certain plot of land with the ideal terroir for whatever variety he wants to grow. Then, as fruit begins to form, because he is a farmer and healthy crops rely on good weather, he curses the sun/clouds/rain/sky because it's too hot/cold/rainy/dry and the grapes are too sweet/sour/mildewed/desiccated for the ideal wine. Eventually he harvests the grapes, sorts them, crushes them, and pours the mixture into some sort of container, like a stainless-steel tank. Yeast, either naturally occurring on the skins of the grapes themselves or added separately, kicks off fermentation. The fungi consume the sugar in the fruit, then release it as (among other things) alcohol, carbon dioxide, and the aromatic compounds that contribute to a wine's perfume. Once the juice has fermented, the winemaker might choose to put the wine into barrels, so that small doses of oxygen seep in through the porous surface of the wood, or the oak flavors the wine. He might also leave the wine in its stainless-steel tank to preserve freshness and fruit flavors, or maybe move it to an egg-shaped concrete tank for something in between the effects of oak and stainless steel. Finally, he bottles his juice, then ships it off.

Drinkers tend to picture all wine, no matter its price or origin, as the product of this traditional, agrarian process. It's hard to blame them, since wine producers often play up the artisanal angle, even when it doesn't quite apply. The labels on bottles from Sutter Home feature a bucolic scene of grapevines nestled next to a Victorian house, with FAMILY VINEYARDS SINCE 1890 and FAMILY OWNED IN THE NAPA VALLEY emblazoned beneath. It suggests a personal mom-and-pop operation. From our family to yours. Never you mind that the winery churns out an industrial-sized 120 million bottles each year, enough to give a few bottles to every family in the fifty states.

The reality of winemaking in the twenty-first century is frequently less *Little House on the Prairie* and more *Gattaca*. This is especially true for the industrial operations that pump out mega-volume commercial and masstige wines, as well as more premium bottles through the $40 range. Not all inexpensive wines have had extensive chemical intervention. But for wineries that want to keep prices low and production high, nature no longer gets the final say on flavor.

"Instead of letting the grapes decide where they want to go, you're manufacturing . . . you're—*constructing* a wine to meet the palate of the individual winemaker," explained a salesman at the United Symposiums American Tartaric Products booth. "And it's not really cheating," he volunteered, as if reading my mind. "It's creating a better product."

There is no fault that can't be corrected with one powder or another; no feature that can't be engineered from a bottle, box, or bag. Wine too tannic? Fine it with Ovo-Pure (powdered egg whites), isinglass (granulate from fish bladders), gelatin (often derived from cow bones and pigskins), or if it's a white, strip out pesky proteins that cause haziness with Puri-Bent (bentonite clay, the ingredient in kitty litter). Not tannic enough? Replace $1,000 barrels with a bag of oak chips (small wood nuggets toasted for flavor), "tank planks" (long oak staves), oak dust (what it sounds like), or a few drops of liquid oak tannin (pick between "mocha" and "vanilla"). Or simulate the texture of barrel-aged wines with powdered tannin, then double what you charge. ("Typically, the $8 to $12 bottle can be brought up to $15 to $20 per bottle because it gives you more of a barrel quality. . . . You're dressing it up," a sales rep explained.)

Wine too thin? Build fullness in the mouth with gum arabic (an ingredient also found in frosting and watercolor paint). Too frothy? Add a few drops of antifoaming agent (food-grade silicone oil). Cut acidity with potassium carbonate (a white salt) or calcium carbonate (chalk). Crank it up again with a bag of tartaric acid (aka cream of tartar). Increase alcohol by mixing the pressed grape must with sugary grape concentrate, or just add sugar. Decrease alcohol with ConeTech's spinning cone, or Vinovation's reverse-osmosis machine, or water. Fake an aged Bordeaux with Lesaffre's yeast and yeast derivative. Boost "fresh butter" and "honey" aromas by ordering the CY3079 designer yeast from a catalog, or go for "cherry-cola" with the Rhône 2226. Or just ask the "Yeast Whisperer," a man with thick sideburns at the Lallemand stand, for the best yeast to meet your "stylistic goals." (For a Sauvignon Blanc with citrus aromas, use the

Uvaferm SVG. For pear and melon, do Lalvin Ba11. For passion fruit, add Vitilevure Elixir.) Kill off microbes with Velcorin (just be careful, because it's toxic). And preserve the whole thing with sulfur dioxide.

When it's all over, if you still don't like the wine, just add that je ne sais quoi with a few drops of Mega Purple—thick grape-juice concentrate that's been called a "magical potion." It can plump up a wine, make it sweeter on the finish, add richer color, cover up greenness, mask the horsey stink of Brett, and make fruit flavors pop. No one will admit to using it, but it ends up in an estimated 25 million bottles of red each year. "Virtually everyone is using it," the president of a Monterey County winery confided to *Wines and Vines* magazine. "In just about every wine up to $20 a bottle anyway, but maybe not as much over that."

There are more than sixty additives that can legally go into wine. A salesperson manning the BSG booth, where liquid oak extracts were on display, cackled at the notion of bypassing chemical assistance in the winery. "Mother nature has odd tastes," she warned. "Sure, God will make wine. You just might not like it."

Scientific fiddling will also make wine, but you might not like that either. The end result can taste like what I drank with Lei: bottled root-beer float with a cork. Connoisseurs argue that such "controlled" winemaking, like some sort of auto-tune or Photoshop for the palate, yields squeaky-clean, soulless wines that are *too* perfect.

So can we say that bad wine is made with high-tech shortcuts, and good wine is manipulation-free? Bingo, advocates of natural wines would agree. Natural winemakers reject the machines, fining agents, designer yeasts, and enzymes that lead to "overripe, overmanipulated, and overblown" wines, so deemed by journalist Alice Feiring, patron saint of their cause. Processed wines are held up as the enological equivalent of processed foods, if not worse. Feiring blogged about a New Year's Eve "tragedy" in which she was forced to endure a bottle of industrially made Champagne: "It was cynical.

It was false. It was a traitor," she laments. Natural wines, which Feiring defines as "nothing added, nothing taken away," ostensibly offer fermented grape juice as God intended it: nuanced, honest, and gloriously imperfect. These wines are good. Even if sometimes, well, they're bad—"cloudy, algae-smelling weirdness that seems like it was made by unwashed French hobbits," in the words of *Food & Wine*'s wine editor Ray Isle.

You don't have to be one of Feiring's "militant vegans of the wine world" (her term) to concede that drinking a mixture of fermented grapes and yeast excrement treated with egg whites and sulfur dioxide doesn't sound like a treat. But that description, unappetizing as it sounds, could apply both to supermarket swill and to some of the world's most celebrated bottles. Château Margaux won't be as heavy-handed with the technological intervention as Treasury with a wine like Sledgehammer, it will use higher quality materials, and it will seek out different flavors. But unless you're in the militant vegan camp, a little chemical massaging of the wine isn't in and of itself what necessarily distinguishes good wine from bad. Winemaking has long fused art with science, even if that's not the story most drinkers are told. The Bordelaise have been fining wine with egg whites for centuries. They're also no strangers to sulfur dioxide, a preservative that was already going into the wines of antiquity to prevent them from spoiling. Even barrels, which today seem like the epitome of tradition, were once newfangled technology that the Romans adopted after several millennia storing wine in clay containers, called amphorae. Some producers pride themselves on using "preindustrial" methods that reject all additives—with little regard for the fact that the ancient Romans were doctoring their wines with pig's blood, marble dust, seawater, and even lead, a source of sweetness. And though the chemicals dosed into wine can sound alarming, keep in mind that, say, tartaric acid actually occurs naturally in grapes. When it comes to wines that have been "manipulated" through science, the distinction between good and bad can be one of degree, not kind.

Controlled winemaking has thrown a wrench in the quality conversation. Before, bad wines were easy to spot. They were categorically bad, in the technical sense of the word. Flawed, faulty, messed-up. They stank of horse stalls and used Band-Aids, thanks to Brettanomyces yeast in contaminated, unsterilized barrels. They reeked of vinegar from too much oxygen exposure, or smelled of sauerkraut and rotten eggs from too little. The pumps and powders have all but eradicated these flaws. "Fewer than 1 percent of all bottles available in the international marketplace exhibit a winemaking fault," writes wine critic Jancis Robinson in *How to Taste*. So in a sense, we've perhaps forgotten what *really* bad wine tastes like. The gap between "bad" wines and great bottles is also shrinking as winemakers use chemical shortcuts not only to avoid blatant mistakes, but also to copy the high-end producers—to replicate the effect of oak for a fraction of the price of real barrels, correct for inferior climates, and keep quality high in crummy vintages. "It is one of the ironies of the wine market today," writes Robinson, "that just as the price differential between cheapest and most expensive bottles is greater than ever before, the difference in quality between these two extremes is probably narrower than it has ever been." The industrial revolution in the winery has effectively democratized decent wine.

"A guy in the Central Coast"—the heartland of jug wine—"can make a Cab that tastes a lot like a Napa Valley Cab using these products," boasted one salesman at the trade show, leaning on a glass display case full of white, brown, and yellow powders. He stepped closer and lowered his voice. "The higher-end guys hate it."

I touched down back in New York feeling more sympathy for the sommeliers who'd stuttered unhelpful answers to me when I first approached them about what made a good wine. So maybe there wasn't a single right way to measure quality. But I was still missing a standard that I could embrace for myself. Price, chemistry, critics' "aesthetic system"—they all seemed too narrow, with obvious flaws and inconsistencies. And I wasn't ready to concede that how a wine was made defined its quality, any more than I could accept that every Beatles song was great just because it was by the Beatles. I was more inclined to believe that the answer involved the moment where wine hits our lips. I knew Lei's wines and the Yquem I'd tasted were in separate leagues. Even friends of mine who didn't know "Shiraz" and "Syrah" were one and the same could easily tell commercial from crafted. I brought two bottles of Australian Shiraz—a $7.99 Yellow Tail and a $39.99 organically grown Jauma—to a dinner party, where I decanted both, so no one would see the bottles. People took exactly one sip of the Yellow Tail before dumping it. "I think you've done permanent damage to my taste buds," Matt complained. I had no doubt there was a distinct difference. I just didn't know how to articulate it.

It was on a whim that I emailed Paul Grieco. Paul was the self-appointed "Riesling overlord" of New York and the co-creator of the Terroir chain of wine bars, which included the hole-in-the-wall where Morgan had first taken me for drinks. Despite a long, well-regarded career at some of Manhattan's most respected fine-dining institutions, Paul was widely regarded as nuts. People (affectionately, I think) called him a "madman" behind his back. He did wine by his own set of rules. Since the wine world's traditionalists hadn't been able to help me resolve the quality conundrum, I hoped maybe its rebel would.

Paul had strong opinions about wine, and he was not above tormenting his customers to be heard. At Terroir Murray Hill, he assaulted his guests with Black Sabbath and Motörhead on Heavy Metal Mondays, a weekly theme night honoring wines grown in metal-rich soils. He printed up wine-themed temporary tattoos and plastered them on anyone who'd sit still long enough. The Terroir wine list, or what Paul referred to as "the Book," ranted and raved for sixty-one convoluted pages, more manifesto than beverage index—and totally, deliberately impenetrable. It "gives the middle finger to the guest," he said once, proudly. He launched the Summer of Riesling to champion what he considered an unfairly maligned pariah of a grape, refusing for five summers straight to sell a single glass of white wine if it wasn't Riesling. You want a Sauvignon Blanc? Fuck you, here's a Riesling. Want Chardonnay? Fuck you, try this Riesling. Customers turned around and left. Paul's (now-ex) business partner threw a fit. But Paul thought it was well worth losing a few customers in order to spread the gospel of Riesling. I especially appreciated that, to the abject horror of wine snobs everywhere, Paul's list featured the supermarket schlock Blue Nun next to $1,900 Sassicaia. With some boxed wine thrown in for good measure. As someone who'd come around to seeing that there were no clear, objective criteria for what made a wine "good," I respected that Paul didn't thumb his nose at all "bad" wines. He didn't *like* Blue Nun. But he appreciated its historical significance, as the bottle that had introduced Americans to—and then alienated them from—the Riesling grape.

When I met Paul at Terroir Tribeca, a bar that resembles a very hip, very comfortable dungeon, Paul looked a little unhinged. A thin mustache trailed the contours of his upper lip, so skinny I could have traced it on with a Sharpie, and a scraggly black beard crawled toward his chest like Spanish moss.

Even when you're agreeing with him, Paul has a tendency to sound like he's arguing with you. We quickly established that neither of us cared much for the pretention that often gets served up with a glass of Sancerre. And he proceeded to scream at me anyway.

"It's fucking grape juice with alcohol! It's a beverage of pleasure! And ultimately, no more, no less!" he roared. "I think you should rip apart the entire sommelier wine industry and tell us all that we're full of *shit*! . . . For all of our talk, for all of our focus, for all of our studies, for all of this highfalutin posturing that we go about, we have not gotten people to drink! More! Wine!" We sat perched on tall metal stools and Paul slammed both hands down on the table after each word—Drink! *Slam.* More! *Slam.* Wine! *Slam.* "When Noah's Ark landed on Mount Everest eighty-five hundred years ago, what was the first thing Noah did? Planted the vine, grew grapes, made wine, got drunk, and passed out naked! So if we draw civilization back to that point—and why the fuck not!—from the beginning, wine has been with us! So"—he jabbed a finger at me—"why are we having such a *fucking* hard time getting people to drink more wine and get comfortable with it?"

Paul wanted to change the world, and to him that meant getting people to drink more wine and get comfortable with it. "Our wine world, as Thomas Friedman would say, should be flat. Flat and big as fucking shit," he yelled. Paul believed wine was "transportational." But he hated the people who "continue to elevate the preciousness of this little wine world": "I want you to be able to go to Oklahoma City or wherever the fuck it is and go to your local grocery store and there'll be a six-pack of Budweiser for—what does it cost? Seven bucks, let's say. And next to it there'll be a six-pack labeled 'Terroir Pinot Grigio.' And it'll be $8 or $9. A little upcharge, but not enough to dissuade you from going, 'Hmm which one . . . Hmm I'm having family over . . . BOOM!'"—*Slam!*—"Let's go with the Pinot Grigio.'"

Paul was interrupted by a distributor, who stopped in to pour him a sample of Greek wine. As Paul sipped the small taste, he deliberately steered the conversation away from the bottle and toward the general situation in Greece. Unlike Joe and Lara at L'Apicio, Paul didn't care to hear a story about the winery, or its vintner. He wanted to drink it for what it was—not what he imagined it to be, not for how dreamy the view was from the vineyard. Just how the wine hit him. He was known to go to tastings dressed like a fugitive—glasses, hat pulled down, no eye contact—to avoid having to make small talk that would distract him from the wines.

When the distributor left, I asked Paul what he looked for in a bottle.

"The wine must be yummy."

That was vague. "Are there any particular . . . criteria that goes into yummy?" I asked.

"One sip leads to a second sip," he said. "One glass leads to a second glass. One bottle leads to a second bottle."

Just then a leggy German wandered in searching for an aperitif, and while Paul tried to talk her into a glass of sherry, I mulled over what he'd said. *One sip leads to another.* That definition of quality, of what made a wine "good" seemed so obvious. So simple. So . . . true?

I liked that it allowed for bad wines to be great in the right moment. I thought back to a Fourth of July I'd spent on a beach in Massachusetts. The night had gone from fine to fantastic thanks to a bottle of bland, cheap bubblegum-water rosé from God-knows-where, undoubtedly made with a designer yeast strain plucked from a catalog and a whole laundry list of additives. And nothing would convince me that Morgan's precious Rousseau would have been better. It would have distracted from roasting marshmallows, from the people, from the lobsters we cracked open on paper plates covered with sand. In that situation, that great wine would have been a bad wine. There were times where the Rousseau, or any of the "greats," just weren't called for. Their grandeur, no matter how good, was excessive. One sip of the manipulated junk-booze rosé had led to another sip, and then another bottle, because in that moment, it was a perfect wine.

But Paul's definition also allowed—and hinted—that wine could be more. A sip that led to another sip because the wine was pleasing reflected just one of the many feelings that wine can produce. Great wines turn one glass into a second because the first sip elicits a sense of wonder and curiosity. Great wines keep us coming back for more sips—and more glasses—not because we're thirsty, but because there is something we didn't quite understand the first time around. It intrigues us. It is cryptic.

One sip leads to another simultaneously acknowledged that wine was a process. Good wine leads you on a journey to try something else. The first glass of one wine could lead to a second glass of something else. Perhaps better, perhaps worse, but at least a new experience, with new dimensions.

"So," I asked Paul when he returned, "did you think the Greek wine was yummy?"

He lifted his eyeglasses so the frames were balancing on his eyebrows, under his spiky dark hair, and gave me a long look through narrowed eyes. "I thought I already told you that for me, one sip led to a second sip. You saw me have a second sip."

I looked down. He'd finished the glass.

"Yeah. And there you have it: Yummy."

Maybe that's the thing about greatness. It defies formulaic expression. As Morgan argued, there is some mystery to it—just as no single chord elevates a piano riff from melodious to haunting, and no one color determines which paintings stop us in our tracks. If greatness could be given by a formula, it would become trivial. But we know it when we taste it. And in the way the memory of it lives on.

CHAPTER EIGHT

The Ten Commandments

IN THE COURSE OF MY STUDYING, TASTING, AND TIME ON THE FLOOR, my vocabulary was growing in unexpected ways—"evolving," as sommeliers would say of an older wine, whose "aroma" had turned into a "bouquet."

A "flight" was no longer something that required a boarding pass, but many glasses of wine in a row. "Extended skin contact" wasn't a pickup line; it meant soaking grape skins in their juice to add texture and color. A "pooled house" was a restaurant where the staff combined their tips, not a swanky place to visit in the Hamptons.

A "single" was one shift, a "double" was two, "Restaurant Week" was "like permanent brunch," and brunch was hell. That's when the "SOEs"—people with a sense of entitlement—came in for nice things they didn't want to pay full price for. A "full turn" was the life span of a table during service, from seating to resetting—"*mise*-ing." The dining room could do three full turns a night on the weekends, and sometimes even three and a half "in the season," the months between October and December, when New Yorkers binged like there was no tomorrow. At the start of each turn, the sommelier would "mark" the table with glasses, then "play the guest" in the hope he could "stretch them out" to a spendy bottle. "Necrophiliacs" liked ancient, vinegary wines that were close to dead. Drinking a great wine too soon made you guilty of "infanticide." A "Switzerland wine" was a neutral bottle that played nicely with all the dishes on the table. A "hand sell" was something weird that needed the sommelier to vouch for it, and if the guest picked it out herself it became a "trigger wine," prompting the somm to describe its flavors, just to be absolutely sure the table wanted an unsulfured orange wine from Slovenia aged in amphorae. A "call wine" was the boring thing that timid wine newbies ordered automatically: Sancerre, Prosecco, California Cabernet. It often overlapped with "cougar juice," aka "cougar crack," aka big, sweet Argentinian Malbecs, oaked Chardonnay, and ultra-green New Zealand Sauvignon Blanc. Cougars' ex-husbands went for the "BSD" wines, code for big-swinging-dick bottles with big labels, big price tags, big Parker scores, and big flavor. Real cork dorks thought that was tacky. They preferred "unicorn wines," rare, small-production gems that were somm status symbols and immediately posted on Instagram by anyone who'd ordered, tasted, or laid eyes on the bottle.

When I first started hanging around sommeliers, I had no clue what they were talking about half the time. My notebooks were dotted with question marks. "Morgan says wine is cooked???" (translation: heat damaged) or "wine aged under floor??" (translation: under *flor*, as in a layer of yeast). I scribbled jargon to look up later at home, or stopped to ask for definitions. The latter was always dicey with Morgan because it usually meant getting even more words to Google.

But over the past few months, the language of wine-speak had become second nature. Nowhere was the change more dramatic than in my arsenal of tasting notes, those verbal descriptions for a wine's aroma and feel. (Don't be fooled by the name: Tasting notes describe smell and flavor more than taste.) My repertoire of words had become big, full-bodied, rich, chewy, and yes, sometimes a little cloying. "Yummy" would suffice for Paul. Not me.

Sommeliers, the scientists in Dresden, and my perfumer-coach Jean Claude Delville all stressed that intelligent sensing requires fluency naming smells. Language helps us categorize and recall past experiences. (Some experts speculate that we forget events from our infancies because we can't form words at such a young age.) Attaching a name to an odor makes that aroma more intense, recognizable, and emotionally charged. "It nails down the memory," one researcher told me. If we don't have the vocabulary to describe an experience, our struggle to convey that encounter in words—and it *will* be a struggle—corrupts our impression of it, a phenomenon known as "verbal overshadowing." Asked to talk about something like a glass of wine, people who lack the terminology to do so later become far worse at recognizing the same wine again than individuals who weren't pressed for words. People who have jargon to rely on aren't as affected by verbal overshadowing.

Guided by this logic, I'd been greedily amassing a scent vocabulary through my routine of blind smelling aromatic essences, sniffing ingredients as I cooked, and calling out the odors that wafted by on my treks around the city. A rich glossary was crucial for my Court of Master Sommeliers exam, which loomed on the horizon, inevitable and intimidating, like an audit. A good stable of words would help me form a mental concept of the wines that I blind tasted, and ensure I could describe them without getting confused.

The official tasting grid from the Court of Master Sommeliers instructs somms to describe wines using a relatively mundane range of descriptors that fall into the broad categories of "fruit," "non-fruit," and "earth/mineral." Like the overachievers that they are, the sommeliers dream up tasting terminology that goes way beyond "apple" or "mushroom." Earthy? Try "sweet, soapy juice with decomposing wet log, truffles, compost aromas." At each blind tasting, be it at EMP, the Union Square offices, or with my old crew from Queens, I added to a running list of the esoteric things people came up with after sticking their noses in each glass. It sounded like they were reading recipes from a Wiccan book of love spells: "wild strawberry water," "dry *and* rehydrated black fruits," "apple blossom," "saffron lobster stock," "burnt hair," "decomposing log," "jalapeño skin," "old aspirin," "baby's breath," "sweat," "chocolate-covered mint," "spent ground coffee," "confected violet," "strawberry fruit leather," "pleather," "freshly molded dildo," "horse tack," "dusty road," "lemon rind," "nail-polish remover," "stale beer," "fresh-tilled earth," "red forest floor," "pear drops," "cowhide," "desiccated strawberry," and "Robitussin."

Whenever it was my turn at the glass, I felt pressure to invent equally obscure descriptors. There were things coming out of my mouth I swore I'd never say about a wine. A little dehydrated pomegranate seed? Don't mind if I do. If I smelled something like strawberries, who's to say it wasn't bottled strawberry water? If I got basil I'd throw in chervil too, though I wasn't 100 percent sure whether it was an herb or a species of rodent. I tried to stay grounded in reality. But four minutes can feel like an eternity when you're the only one talking, and I wanted to show that I was improving. So I kept reaching for words to impress my tasting partners. After all, I'm a writer. Thinking up bizarre descriptors is part of my job. If there was one place I could go toe-to-toe with the somms, it was generating an outlandish lexicon.

As I joined in the verbal arms race, I began to worry that tasting notes, which were supposed to help elucidate a wine's flavor and solidify its impression in the taster's mind, were actually obscuring the experience in some way, and even a bit dishonest. If I was making stuff up, how could I be so sure no one else was? To accurately process the experience, I needed to be sure I had the right words to contain it. I wasn't sure I did. I wasn't even sure how to judge what the "right" words were.

If there's one group not given to fluffy adjectives, it's economists. Knowing that the *Journal of Wine Economics* has been a consistent fact-checker of wine world traditions over the years, I went digging into back issues to see if I could find anything on tasting notes. Academics' diagnosis? Wine-speak is in crisis.

Tasting notes began as a way to guide drinkers toward bottles and tease what to expect after pulling the cork. They are now badly failing the very people they're meant to help. A 2007 study gave amateur wine drinkers two different wines, along with a professional critic's review of each, then tasked them with matching the tasting note to the correct glass. The volunteers sipped a pair of German Rieslings, and had to decide which the expert had called a "lively" wine with "a dose of rich mineral character," and which was "very refined with a driving slate imprint that intensifies the already seething soil/fruit battle." In theory, the task should have been a breeze, since those characterizations were composed to capture the flavor of each wine. And yet the subjects were stumped. They did no better than if they'd been told to pair the tasting notes and wines at random.

Who can blame them? "The pretense that we shall be able to discern all those tastes and aromas is pure bullshit and only a bullshit artist can claim to be able to do that," declared Richard Quandt, a Princeton University economist, in a different paper for the *Journal of Wine Economics*. Critics' tasting notes are neither consistent nor informative, he concluded. But we are "happy to read their evaluations, because we are largely ignorant of the quality of wines."

Even the experts are confused, in part because tasting notes often reference abstract concepts like "minerality," a buzzword that took off in the '90s and now peppers every issue of *Wine Enthusiast*. You can grab a grapefruit to understand the citrus notes in a wine said to have "layers of grapefruit and minerality." Figuring out where to turn for a whiff of "minerality" isn't so easy. Should you grab a rock? A wet piece of metal? As it turns out, there's no consensus over what it means. In another study featured at a conference hosted by the American Association of Wine Economists, French researchers polled winemakers and drinkers in Chablis, a region famous for lean Chardonnay most sommeliers would describe as "mineral," to see how the world's foremost experts in minerality define the term. The results were all over the map, from "gunflint" to "mineral water."

My crisis of confidence over whether there was any common understanding around the words we were using came to a head one Saturday morning when it was my turn to captain our blind tasting group. Along with a bottle of wine for each somm, I also brought in a blind smelling exercise: six plastic cups, which I'd filled with various herbs, then covered with aluminum foil poked with holes. One cup contained chervil, since it came up so frequently in everyone's tasting notes. If the somms could smell chervil in their wine, surely they could smell chervil in chervil. *Some sort of grass?*, people guessed when they sniffed the cup. *Mushroom? Celery?* "I have no idea," someone finally conceded. I realized with dismay that not even my guides, New York's finest sommeliers, necessarily knew what they were saying.

Abandoning tasting notes wasn't an option. Sommeliers rely on them to sell wines. Drinkers consult them to anticipate what flavors they'll find in a bottle. And I couldn't master blind tasting—or savvy sensing—without words. Yet I wondered whether "petrol" and "minerality" were the best we could do. If we're imprecise in our language, we're imprecise in our tasting, and imprecise in our memories. What I call imprecision—and others call bullshit—is abundant. The accuracy and potency of what I perceived was only as good as the words I had to articulate it. Could there be a better way?

On a crisp Wednesday morning, while I was still in California, I loaded a rental car with grocery bags containing all the ingredients you'd need to cater the country's most disgusting dinner party. I had caramels, a green bell pepper, dried apricots, Rose's lime juice, one can of asparagus, cassis syrup, strawberry jam, and two boxes of Franzia wine that thudded against the backseat as I careened up and down San Francisco's hills. The cement slopes gradually gave way to Staples stores, Denny's chains, and self-storage lots. As I neared my destination in Davis, the suburban strip malls flattened into dun-colored farms. Billboards advertised ANIMAL CLINIC FREE SURGERY

ESTIMATES and ITCHY SCALP? VISIT OUR LICE SALON. I drove past Cattlemens Steakhouse and the neon-sign vestiges of the Milk Farm Restaurant (former home of the all-you-can-drink milk contest) to Ann Noble's low, brown house at the corner of Eureka Street. The name was fitting, given Ann's track record for innovation. My search for the origins of the tasting note had brought me here, to a home surrounded by chicken sculptures and Buddhist prayer flags.

Talking about wine as a medley of spices, plants, fruits, and other specific smelly things is such a solidly ingrained practice that it's easy to imagine it always having been this way. That King Tutankhamun, Louis XIV, and Benjamin Franklin—all wine connoisseurs in their day—were also gargling their wines trying to decide if they picked up black, sour, or Maraschino cherry in their glass. In fact, this naturalistic, food-based lexicon is about as traditional as disco. It took root in the 1970s, and Ann created it.

The ancient Greeks and Romans, who extensively documented the culture and cultivation of the vine, gave only succinct "thumbs up" or "thumbs down" assessments of their wines, evidently finding little reason to delve into the nuance of flavor. In *The Learned Banqueters*, the Greek rhetorician Athenaeus pithily praises wine from the Setine grape as "first class" and Caecuban as "noble," while Horace, in *The Odes*, sums up Sabine wines as "humbly cheap." Their reviews focus on how wines affected their physical well-being, not their taste buds. Setine is "not so apt to make a man drunk," observes Athenaeus. Pompeii's wines are "productive of headache, which often lasts so long as the sixth hour of the next day," gripes Pliny the Elder. He endorses Sentinum as the favorite of many emperors, who "learnt from actual experience that there is no danger of indigestion and flatulence resulting from the use of this liquor." Imagine how much more useful wine reviews could be if they had continued in this tradition.

More than a thousand years later, wine snobs were still mostly mum when it came to the tastes and smells they savored in bottles. Samuel Pepys, a high-ranking officer in the British Royal Navy, needed only a paltry half sentence to describe a Château Haut-Brion he tried in 1663: It was, he wrote, "a good and most particular taste that I never met with." (Fast-forward three hundred years, and Robert Parker's review of a 1983 Haut-Brion would run on for six sentences.)

In the eighteenth and nineteenth centuries, better winemaking methods improved the quality of wine. This, plus the growing influence of restaurants and sommeliers, helped transform it from an ordinary beverage into a cultural touchstone with social cachet. Since appreciating a fine Burgundy or Bordeaux had become a marker of status, people naturally wanted to tell each other how much they relished this refined pastime, and they developed a new language with which to wax poetic about their Pinot Noirs and Merlots. Early critics initially described wines as though gossiping about friends, with broad pronouncements about each bottle's character, not its flavor. In his 1920 *Notes on a Cellar-Book*, George Saintsbury applauds a red Hermitage whose age "had softened and polished all that might have been rough in the manliness of its youth," declaring it the "manliest French wine I ever drank." For the next forty-odd years, critics continued in this vein, the writer Frank Schoonmaker, for example, cheering a French Muscat's "considerable distinction and real class." The qualities drinkers valued in wine were the same as those they prized in people: honesty, grace, charm, refinement.

In the 1970s, a group of scientists at the University of California, Davis, decided that such ambiguous language must be excised from their modernizing field. They were bringing scientific rigor into the winery, so they needed scientific terminology to discuss their results. In glossaries published at the time, Davis enology professors rail against the "fanciful terms . . . so often found in the popular press" and implore their colleagues to abandon words like "elegant."

But when Ann arrived at Davis in 1974 to teach a course on the sensory evaluation of wines, she was appalled by how little progress had been made in generating a tasting vocabulary. She sat in on a classroom of aspiring vintners, who were told to take turns listing what they smelled in a glass of wine. They couldn't. They were "grasping," Ann remembered, "trying to pull straws out of the sky."

After she took over as the class's professor, Ann combed through her cabinets for everyday odors like blackberry jam, vanilla extract, and dog fur, then placed them in glasses. She made her students blind sniff and memorize these "standards" in what became—and remains—a mandatory crash course in putting consistent labels to around 150 odors. (The course's final exam gives students a lineup of aromas and wines, which have been poured into black glasses to mask their color, and tasks them with identifying each one by smell alone. It's more challenging than it sounds: In forty years, no one's ever aced the test.) The process of building this olfactory dictionary was nicknamed the "kindergarten of the nose," and Ann eventually formalized the vocabulary into a circular chart of six dozen descriptors she called the Wine Aroma Wheel. She developed a shortlist of terms by surveying professionals and cataloging what her students came up with organically. Then she banned words that were "vague" (good-bye "fragrant") or "hedonic" (nix "elegant"), so all that remained were "specific and analytical." The aromas fell into broad categories like "spicy" (consisting of "licorice," "black pepper," and "clove") or "nutty" ("walnut," "hazelnut," "almond"). It was the first time that winemakers, wine drinkers, and wine critics had a standard way to speak to one another, and the Aroma Wheel became the lingua franca of the wine world, codifying the naturalistic references that we use today. "Few people reading about wine today can fully understand the extent to which virtually every significant wine writer or blogger now uses these descriptive terms," wrote Roger Boulton, an enology professor, in a report on Ann's contributions. A researcher at the Burgundy School of Business likened Ann to a modern Moses: The Aroma Wheel, he said, "is like the Ten Commandments."

Ann, who retired from Davis in 2002, answered the door in purple sweatpants. She had flushed cheeks and wild tufts of short gray hair that stuck out like a baby chick's fluff. As I stepped into her house, I congratulated myself on picking up the smell of dog just before meeting Ann's German shepherd mix. He was called Mosel, after the German wine region, and followed in the footsteps of pets Pinot Noir, Riesling, and Zinfandel. "Mosel, your breath stinks today," Ann announced. I sniffed a few times, hoping to pick up the trail.

The sommeliers in my blind tasting groups live in a lexical universe that Ann created, but few of them had ever heard of Ann or her work. "You're visiting who?" a Master Sommelier puzzled when I bragged about getting to meet Ann. This was a red flag. It suggested to me that the pros might not have stopped to think critically about their tasting notes. They too mirrored what they heard others doing and repeated the same bad habits. It was like the wine world was stuck in a giant game of telephone, and the message had become an indecipherable mess.

When we say we smell blackberries in a wine, we aren't smelling real blackberries. The wines we taste never contain any actual blackberries—or raspberries, pineapples, or petrol. (Austria had a scandal a few years back when antifreeze ended up in its wine, but that was illegal, and people certainly didn't go around extolling the aroma.) Saying "blackberry" is essentially our way of communicating that we've picked up a smell that we know *other* people have called blackberry in the past. There is a code and consistency to tasting notes. Although some Syrah really does smell distinctly of bacon and olives, and some Tempranillo of leather, there is also a standard set of terms we know to attach to these grape varieties. In Court exams or in competitions, judges want to be sure that if you are presented with a Syrah, or what you *think* is a Syrah, you will repeat those key words to show you understand. Morgan is nose-blind to rotundone, the chemical that gives Syrah its black-peppery scent. And yet that wouldn't stop him from *saying* he smells rotundone, if all other signs point to Syrah. Failing to do so would cost him points. Attempts to translate tasting notes into other languages make clear just how figurative the terms are. Morgan might say a red has notes of cooked meat, bacon, blackberry preserves, plum, and vanilla. In China, where each of those descriptors has been assigned a local equivalent, a sommelier would praise that same wine's aroma of Chinese sausage, salted pork, dried hawthorn, persimmon, and pine nuts.

Ann had agreed to take me through her "kindergarten of the nose." Who better to refine my wine vocabulary than the person who helped invent it? I wanted to audit my own tasting-note terminology to be sure that I could truly pick out the aromas I claimed to find in wines, plus I was keen to undergo the same olfactory training regimen that Ann taught to professional vintners.

Spend just a little time with Ann, and you'll find she names the aromas around her as though introducing new people who have joined the room. "Smell that—that's the vanilla you get from the cardboard," she said, opening up a box of wineglasses. She lined up a few dozen of them on her kitchen counter and began divvying up my groceries between them. She poured a few ounces of either red or white boxed wine into each of the glasses, then added individual ingredients like asparagus juice, soy sauce, or chopped bits of orange peel. She kept a running commentary on the contents of the glasses. "The thing about the craft caramels is they're vanilla-y and buttery . . . *Oooooh!* I just got an aroma *howling* out of it. . . . Except for the sulfur note, those apricots are much better than usual. . . . I'm going to keep the glass because the smell is *so* cool."

"I'm part of the smell-dominated world," Ann explained. "'Listen to Your Nose' is my mantra."

Ann's friend Hoby Wedler, a twenty-eight-year-old graduate student in the UC-Davis chemistry department, arrived shortly after lunch bearing the gift of an unusual scent. He passed around a small bag of Grains of Paradise—peppery, gingery kernels he'd bought from a spice seller in Chicago. "It's a trip, isn't it?" he hooted. Hoby, like Ann's husband, is blind, and he shares Ann's passion for scents.

"One of my favorite things to do is drive on some of these amazing roads we have in Napa or Sonoma Valley and just roll the windows down and leave them down for hours and do an aromatic exploration of the land," Hoby said. "You'll be blown away by what you smell." He recommended Highway 101. The I-5 was "olfactorily boring."

"No, no, no! You're forgetting the feedlots!" protested Ann. "The feedlots wake you up."

"They do," Hoby conceded.

"Used to be when they dried alfalfa in Dixon, the wind would come up howling from the south and it smelled like there was a marijuana bust."

As a child, Ann did what few of us ever do: She practiced labeling the aromas she inhaled. When she biked around her neighborhood, she'd point out olfactory landmarks, not visual markers. Clean laundry. A rose bush. She still gives directions by telling people to take a right at the smoky smell. Ann's "kindergarten of the nose" is so named in part because it corrects a gap in our education that should have been addressed back when we were sipping juice boxes and taking naps. While parents frequently encourage children to label visual and auditory cues, like the color blue or a dog's bark, olfactory objects rarely get much attention. As a result, most of us never learn a standardized aroma lexicon that would let us talk about and identify odors. (The French are a notable exception: Evidently viewing an astute palate as a critical life skill along with grammar and math, in 1990 the French government launched "taste education classes" throughout the country's primary schools. These included lessons on describing odors, smelling via retro-nasal olfaction, and savoring the distinctive character of French cheeses.)

"It's like when you're teaching a kid color: You show him red and say, 'This is red,'" Ann said. She handed me a glass of white wine mixed with canned asparagus juice to smell. "This is asparagus," she instructed. I inhaled and tried to follow her direction to go beyond sniffing and really *smell*. "By listening to your nose, it's my weird way of saying, try to get your brain to focus *just* on the smell," she explained. "It's sort of Zen Buddhist because it's all paying attention to the now. . . . The most important thing is to focus, and focus is coming back to being there." Focus. I closed my eyes. I tried to block out the sound of Ann's clock, which played a birdsong to mark every hour. *Ignore Mosel's breathing and his bad breath*, I told myself. I inhaled again, deeply like Jean Claude had taught me. I held the air for a moment in my lungs, and exhaled through my nose. I thought about Ann's suggestion to put words to the odor, so it would be lodged deeper in my brain. "If you don't store the information in some retrievable, specific way," she said, "it's just this amorphous thing that comes back amorphous." The asparagus was woody. A bit green, with a mustiness. The subtlest hint of garlic.

We deconstructed each of the smell standards one at a time, working our way through everything from anise and vanilla to butter and sliced pineapple. Hoby had trouble telling the canned asparagus from the canned green bean.

"You don't brutalize a green bean like this," Ann explained, holding up the asparagus. "And it doesn't have this canned, green, sulfur-related state."

Lychee, she pointed out, moving on, had citrus, vegetal, and floral notes. But even "floral" is vague. So-called fresh flowers, like rose and lavender, have a dry, clean scent that doesn't linger. By contrast, "white" flowers, like jasmine and gardenia, have a heavy, heady, sweet fragrance with a hint of something animal and rotten mixed in. Nature, the ultimate perfumer, doses their bewitching scents with trace amounts of indole, a chemical that, you'll recall, is also found in human feces and on pubic hair. There's something poetic about this: Timeless beauty arises from the complex intermingling of both the putrid and the divine.

People perform so poorly when it comes to naming smells that scientists have speculated that this skill is beyond human ability—the wiring of our brains makes it impossible. Show a dozen strangers a picture of grass and ask them to identify its color, and I'd bet you a lifetime of mowing they'd all use the same word: green. Now give them a whiff of freshly cut grass and ask them what the scent is. Even though they've smelled it a million times, they'd probably give it all kinds of different, vague labels, from "lemony" to "recess in fifth grade." In the journal *Cognition*, a linguist observed that if people struggled to name sights as much as they do to name smells, they'd be "sent for medical help." "It's almost like we have a neurological deficit for naming smells," remarked the neuroscientist Jay Gottfried.

Recent research suggests that we actually do have the right brain structure to put words to odors. Rather, in line with Ann's theory on childhood and smells, it's our social conditioning that's wrong. To investigate whether nature or nurture is to blame for our olfactory muteness, linguists in the Netherlands conducted a study involving English speakers and members of the Jahai, a Malaysian hunter-gatherer tribe that has a rich lexicon for scents. The participants were asked to identify a set of scratch-'n'-sniff odors. The tribespeople, who grow up learning to discuss smells the way most Americans do colors, labeled the aromas quickly, easily, and consistently. The Jahai needed around two seconds to name each odor. The English speakers each fumbled for an average of thirteen seconds, and even then, they never really got to an answer. Given (hardly exotic) cinnamon to sniff, one person babbled, "I don't know how to say that, sweet, yeah; I have tasted that gum like Big Red, or something tastes like, what do I want to say? I can't get the word. Jesus, it's like that gum smell like something like Big Red. Can I say that? Okay. Big Red. Big Red gum."

"The long-held assumption that people are bad at naming smells is not universally true," the researchers concluded. "Odors are expressible in language, as long as you speak the right language."

The Jahai seem to have an advantage because their language includes more than a dozen terms that apply exclusively to specific categories of odor. There is a word, *plʔeŋ*, for the "bloody smell which attracts tigers," which describes the scent of crushed head lice or squirrel blood. This is not to be confused with *pʔih*, the smell of blood from raw meat. *Sʔ̃iŋ* refers to the smell of "human urine," "village ground," and, worse yet, there's *haʔɛ̃t*, the stinking odor of "feces, rotten meat, prawn paste." English speakers, on the other hand, could probably brainstorm only a handful of terms that are unique to odors, such as "musty" and "fragrant." "Stinky" tends to be our go-to catchall for what the Jahai split into *plʔeŋ*, *pʔih*, *sʔ̃iŋ*, *haʔɛ̃t*, and other terms.

It's not true that we English speakers have no scent language to speak of, however. Ann had established a lexicon, and I was looking at it: thirty-one wineglasses, each with a splash of red or white wine mixed with fruits, vegetables, herbs, or spices. There was cinnamon, black olives, cloves, pear, dried apricot, blackberry jam, cassis, vanilla, clove, and anise—all of which were also now words in my arsenal. They weren't specific to smell—like "stinky." But they worked. Or at least they had for a while.

Tracing the evolution of tasting notes, I was surprised to learn how humdrum the lexicon used to be. Ann had largely limited the Aroma Wheel to items you could pick up at the supermarket. Our "kindergarten of the nose" had, appropriately, consisted of ingredients that kindergarteners would know. The most esoteric reference? Froot Loops, to mimic the aroma of Riesling, Muscat, and Gewürztraminer grapes.

If you've recently bought wine, you'll know that precious descriptors like "pain grillé" have lately wormed their way into the once-straightforward vocabulary. A diploma from Le Cordon Bleu would be helpful in deciphering a *Wine Spectator* Pick of the Year with flavors of "pâte de fruit, hoisin sauce, warm ganache, and well-roasted applewood." Some wines begin to sound vaguely painful, like the Provençal red that's "studded with dried anise and singed juniper notes" with "a bolt of iron . . . buried deeply on the finish." And it's hard to imagine that Robert Parker wasn't on some controlled substance when he celebrated a California Cabernet with "no hard edges" that nonetheless has a "skyscraper-like texture" *and* "comes across like a flawlessly constructed dress from an haute couture house in Paris."

Pushed to be entertaining and distinctive, wine pros have raided ethnic cuisine, botanical gardens, architecture, and drug cabinets for obscure and luxurious-sounding descriptors. Adrienne Lehrer, a linguist and the author of *Wine and Conversation*, told me about a wine critic who approached her after a book signing. The man confessed that in his reviews, he often extolled bottles' subtle aroma of quince—not because he'd smelled that fruit's apple-and-pear perfume, but because the word sounded fancy. "I figured no one could challenge me because no one knows what quince is," he admitted. "But I've never smelled a quince either." These elaborate tasting notes risk alienating would-be wine lovers, who read reviews promising "singed juniper notes," and when they fail to pick up the cornucopia themselves, assume either the wine is broken or their noses are.

Bias has also crept in. According to research presented at a meeting of the American Association of Wine Economists, reviewers save rarefied, evocative terms for more expensive wines—these "elegant," "smoky" bottles evoke "tobacco" and "chocolate"—and they slap simple two-cent words on cheaper plonk—care for a glass of something "good," "clean," and "juicy"? There's a certain logic to this: Flowery expressions can help justify coughing up big bucks for a bottle. Who wants to drop several hundred dollars on "Froot

Loops" or "canned asparagus"? A wine with "stylish plum," "smoky cassis," and *"framboise"* sounds like a much more lavish experience.

Academics, sommeliers, critics, and winemakers have proposed various ways to bring discipline and specificity back to tasting notes. Matt Kramer argues in his book *True Taste* that the key attributes of wine quality can be summed up in just six words: "harmony," "texture," "layers," "finesse," "surprise," and "nuance." Eric Asimov, the *New York Times* wine critic, does Kramer one better, proposing that with only two words—"savory" and "sweet"—you can "explain more about the essence of any bottle than the most florid, detailed analogies ever could." Kathy LaTour, a professor at Cornell's School of Hotel Administration, beats them both with her suggestion to trade tasting *notes* for tasting *sketches*. Her research shows that scrapping words and, instead, rendering a wine's flavor in colors, swirls, lines, and doodles may be the best way for novices to remember new wines and wrap their brains around different styles, without suffering the effects of verbal overshadowing.

But wine people tend to be a wordy breed, and they aren't quite ready to give up their rich vocabularies for a mere handful of words or a drawing. Instead, the latest solution for curing tasting notes has once again emerged from scientists' labs.

I'd timed my visit with Ann so that I could also meet with Alexandre Schmitt, who had made his annual pilgrimage to California from Bordeaux. Because Alexandre would surely tell you this within a few moments of meeting him, I will spare no time in letting you know that he is a former perfumer whose training in wine started when he began a close tutorship with the winemaker at Chateau Petrus, the famed Bordelaise estate that sells its bottles for approximately an arm and a leg. The two men set up a trade: Alexandre, graduate of the esteemed Institut Supérieur International du Parfum in Versailles, would teach Petrus's Jean-Claude Berrouet everything he knew about olfaction, in exchange for which Alexandre would learn everything Jean-Claude knew about wine. This is akin to Anna Wintour personally volunteering to mentor an up-and-coming fashion designer, and Alexandre's partnership had about the same effect on his career. Before long, the haute couture houses of the wine world—Petrus, Château Margaux, Château Cheval Blanc, Château d'Yquem, Opus One, Harlan, Screaming Eagle—were hiring Alexandre to coach their winemaking teams on how to smell and discuss what they smelled. "When I'm around, I kick their ass," Alexandre bragged. He boasts that he can identify 1,500 aromas. To put that in perspective, he estimates most trained wine tasters can label 80 to 100 distinct scents. Given a set of smells to identify, the average person can put names on a measly 20.

Alexandre offers two-day "olfaction seminars" for groups of up to twenty people that regularly sell out at $800 a seat, according to Alexandre. He was teaching one that week at the Wine Business Center in St. Helena, which is where I met him.

"When you are tasting a wine, it's easy to mention lots of flavors," he lectured his students, mostly local winemakers. "But if you don't know them for real, it is just a lyrical or poetic way. It's not really objective. It's not rational."

In lieu of the canned beans Ann had prepared for me, Alexandre's desk was covered with dozens of clear glass vials containing industrially prepared aromatic essences. He dipped narrow strips of white paper into each one, then passed them around the class. The smell menu for the morning included indole and β-Caryophyllene, a compound present in clove oil.

People like Alexandre want to see professionals trade the poetry of gastronomy for the precision of chemistry. Alexandre required us to associate the words we used with standardized, laboratory-grade aromas, so that we would all anchor our conception of "strawberry" to the same exact essence. By his measure, relying on a physical strawberry, as Ann had, was imprecise. Was the strawberry fresh, frozen, or in a jam? Organic or conventionally grown? Which species?

This is the first step in a larger movement that seeks to tether tasting notes to the chemical composition of a wine by having tasters name the specific compounds that are responsible for the odors in a glass. It's the difference between smells *like* and smells *of:* A wine made of Grüner Veltliner smells *like* grapefruit, but it smells *of* thiols, the chemical that contributes to its grapefruity aroma. According to this more scientific system, tasters should describe notes of "vanilla" and "hazelnut" as "lactones"; "strawberry" and "raspberry" aromas as "esters"; and scents of "beet" and "dirt" as "geosmin." Yet in many cases, the chemical lingo actually confirms the logic of comparing the scent of wines to certain foods. Under Ann's rubric, you'd say a Gewürztraminer smells like lychee and rose. The new approach would have you refer to it as "high in terpenes"—a class of compounds that are present in both lychee and rose, and lend them their signature perfumes.

Hoping to rein in whimsical and potentially confusing tasting notes, the Guild of Sommeliers has instructed somms to embrace the technical terms, at least when discussing wines with other experts. (I assumed this was why Morgan had fretted over his anosmia to "rotundone" and not "black pepper.") Calling tasting notes "useless and self-indulgent at best," Geoff Kruth, a Master Sommelier and the Guild's chief operating officer, said the new language was meant to "make a connection between understanding the intrinsic, objective factors that are in a wine and the ways to describe them."

The technical approach requires analyzing which chemicals give a wine its distinct aromatic character. As it happened, some of the technology that had made this new wine-speak possible—by shedding light on the chemistry of wine—was pumping away in a lab just downstairs from Alexandre's classroom.

After Alexandre ended class for the day—"Okay. I'm tired of you. I think it's time to stop"—a few of us went to the first floor to visit the offices of ETS Laboratories. We trailed behind one of their scientists, past rows of desks topped with bubbling beakers and scales. The white noise of beeps, fans, and humming motors made it sound like an ICU wing, and many of the machines were actually six-figure pieces of hospital equipment, which work as well on blood samples as they do on a Cabernet. Winemakers throughout California, Oregon, and Washington send samples of their wines in progress to ETS for enological checkups, just to be sure their grape juice is fermenting properly, or free of bacteria that could cause flaws. ETS will go so far as to lend a hand with copying a competitor's wine. By measuring the levels of tannins, oak lactones, and other compounds in the rival's bottle, ETS can give wineries a road map for how to ferment and age their own wine in order to mimic someone else's. "Some winemakers are pretty addicted to that actually," our guide said with a chuckle.

While I was taking deep breaths of fecal-scented indole in the hope of making myself into a trustworthy smelling apparatus, little did I know that ETS's machines already had me beat. We stopped by a gas chromatograph–mass spectrometer, or GC-MS that can separate out the chemicals in a complex mixture and identify them using each one's molecular weight. It looked like the love child of a Xerox machine and an air-conditioning unit. Since the late '80s, researchers have used these devices to analyze how the aromatic compounds in wine—perhaps several hundred in all—come together to create its bouquet. The machine has helped develop the new chemical lexicon by identifying which compounds contribute to the signature aromas of different wines.

Just recently, for example, our guide boasted that his team had used the device to demystify what it was that gave certain California wines a cool, herbal odor. Before, people who smelled the wines would say they had "some freshness," or "a little bit of a minty character," he explained. Thanks to the GC-MS, they'd never have to be so vague. They could label the exact chemical that created the scent: eucalyptol.

This Chemistry 101 language is supposed to make tasting notes more objective. But as I considered this new lexicon in the context of wine-speak's long history, what had seemed like a pioneering break with the "bullshit" language of the past began to look less exceptional: Tasting notes have always said as much about the people drinking the wine as the contents of the glass, and the newest iteration is no different. In describing wines, we like talking about our ideal selves. What we claim to smell in a wine reflects the values and biases of the day. In the early and mid-twentieth century, when class hierarchies were more circumscribed, a delicious Sauternes would be praised for its "great distinction and breed," while a disappointing Burgundy that tasted more like a Bordeaux did not " 'hold to the blood of its clan' quite firmly enough." Under the auspices of scientific rigor, Ann's folksy food lingo came about at a time when America obsessed over healthy living, and the natural bounty comprised in the Aroma Wheel made wine seem as nutritious as a salad. "Composed of nature's bounty drawn from the four seasons, wines enjoy irresistible appeal to aging boomers obsessed with their physical well-being," writes Sean Shesgreen in an essay on tasting notes for the *Chronicle of Higher Education*. A fitness-obsessed mind-set in the *Buns of Steel* era of the 1980s brought a rush of new words to describe wines' bodies, just as we were getting obsessed with our own. Bottles were "fleshy," "broad-shouldered," "sinewy," or "svelte." More recently, our 100-point favorites have become farmers' markets in a bottle, a cornucopia of exotic fruits and vegetables that panders to peoples' fantasy of an artisanal, back-to-basics lifestyle. The references to "wax bean" and "wild strawberry" mirror our current passion with small batch and organic everything. And the push for "rotundones"? Even that seemed to satisfy a more recent movement where nothing can be trusted unless quantified. We want data on our fitness, our lovers, our hedonism.

I had expected to embrace the accuracy of this scientific language. At last, here was the wine world turning a critical eye on its bad habits, and trying to bring itself back down to earth. But as I mulled over my visits with Ann and Alexandre during the drive back to San Francisco, I couldn't help but wonder whether it was such an improvement. "Pyrazine" might be the most accurate word for the characteristic smell of a Sauvignon Blanc. Yet it also fails to capture anything close to the full experience. Under the new tasting-note regime, what used to be a Cabernet Sauvignon with layers of bell pepper, black currant, freshly tilled earth, and black pepper would become a wine with notes of pyrazines, thiols, geosmin, and rotundone. Accurate? Yes. Enticing? Not really. And besides, we don't necessarily know how all these aromas come together to create this smell. Combine pyrazines, thiols, geosmin, and rotundone into a glass, and you're not going to be anywhere close to an Haut-Brion. To be fair, tossing together some diced bell pepper with black currants, black pepper, and a handful of dirt won't approach its perfume either. Yet at least Ann's system doesn't purport to have that level of specificity.

My favorite descriptors from my blind tastings with Morgan had always been the ones that allowed me to lose myself in a story. They were more scenes than metaphors—impossible, imagined fantasies that, for all their bizarreness (and subjectivity), were far more evocative than "vanilla" or "lactone." They were the tasting notes that you could never say to a guest, or mention in an exam, but reflected how sommeliers actually remembered the wines. Morgan came up with the best:

> "That 'Incredible Hulk just stepped out of the nuclear reactor' type thing": Australian Shiraz.
>
> "Male ballet dancer": Nebbiolo.
>
> "Central Park South," the avenue where horse-drawn carriages line up, known for its distinct aroma of horse shit: Bordeaux.
>
> "Municipal garbage": bad, hot-climate Chardonnay. (Morgan sent me a four-hundred-word email to unpack this. You don't need to know the details, but it mentioned something about "physiologically overripe fruit.")

> "My tongue getting the shit kicked out of it by stiletto heels and elsewhere getting a cashmere blanket thrown over it from the sugar": off-dry German Riesling.
>
> "A fucking razor blade": Austrian Riesling.

And, most memorable and offensive of all, the sommelier who explained how he nailed Pinotage in a blind tasting: "Our unofficial tell, because you can't really say this in public, is that it's like a Haitian necklace, where you get a tire, douse it in gasoline, stick it around someone's neck, and light it on fire."

I found it reassuring to know there was a push to fact-check tasting notes before they got even more unhinged. Yet, seeing that there existed a more objective way to plunge into the aromas of wine had, in a weird way, helped me make peace with outrageous wine-speak. The best approach was . . . all of them. I wanted it every way. I craved the analytical, objective language, which I could connect back with the actual chemistry in the glass. It kept me honest. It could stop critics from passing off flowery marketing jargon as objective descriptions. It linked wine back to the processes and decisions that had shaped it. It gave memories a more solid form. There was one night, just after a storm, when I'd stepped out onto the street with Morgan. "It smells like spring," I said. He sniffed and was silent a moment. "It smells like petrichor," he finally replied. Petrichor, that name for the perfume the earth gives off after a rain, from the Greek *petros*, meaning stone, and *ichor*, the ethereal fluid believed to flow through the veins of the gods. That specificity locked the moment—and the scent—in my mind.

I also wanted license to use more creative descriptors. With the language of science, and even with Ann's terminology, almost every glass of wine could sound the same. Red fruit, blue fruit, black fruit, stewed fruit. Morgan's wild expressions whet my appetite for wine. And while the evocative tasting notes were less precise, they could be more accurate. Taste and smell are subjective experiences, and reaching into metaphor and poetry often did more justice to my personal experience of the wines. Technically speaking, Chenin Blanc often smelled of baked apple, honeydew, ginger, and damp straw. Personally, I always recognized it because one whiff got me thinking of a wet sheep holding a pineapple. The scent of a sweaty French guy at the airport meant I probably had my nose in a Bordeaux. The aroma of my grandfather's cologne—sharp, slightly minty—was my tell for Cabernet Franc. My recess from childhood—autumn, wet leaves, dirt—was Pinot Noir.

The words mattered, but I thought about what Ann and Hoby had told me. That the most important thing is paying attention. I rolled down my windows and let the frigid air hit my face. My hair whipped at me from all sides.

On my way out of wine country, heading back to San Francisco, I passed the woody scent of cedar that reminded me of campfires my classmates and I had been forced to make on our (odious, wet) school camping trips to Oregon's mountains. Then hay. The area around Indian Valley was smoky. Cooking smells began to emerge as the farmland disappeared. San Rafael smelled like sweet-and-sour chicken; Larkspur like potatoes cooking with rosemary. The hulking shadows of Muir Woods provided a final blast of nature—resinous pine and bark, moss, with a hint of shoe polish. I smelled the salty brine of sea air mixed with a thick, soapy perfume of detergent and garlic even before I saw the signs for San Francisco. It was then that I realized I'd driven the whole way without turning on the radio. I'd had other things to pay attention to.

CHAPTER NINE

The Performance

SINCE I FINALLY HAD THE RIGHT WORDS TO TALK ABOUT WINE, I WAS eager to try my hand at recommending bottles to others. But if you think it's hard to get a reservation at one of New York's top spots, just wait until you try to get hired there. The best restaurants—which largely overlap with the ones that have sommeliers—hire according to a diabolical catch-22: You must have worked in New York City restaurants to be hired in New York City restaurants. "But have you served *in the city*?" is the inevitable follow-up question to anyone who may boast of her previous floor chops. Most aspiring service pros get around this impasse by lying. Morgan did for his first somm job. "This is like, kill or be killed," he rationalized. I had no moral compunctions about embellishing my résumé. Only, there was nothing to embellish.

My best chance at working the floor as a sommelier—okay, my only chance—came down to passing the Certified Sommelier Exam. Initially, I'd regarded preparing for the Certified exam as a way to adopt sommeliers' training regimens and gain credibility as I attempted to infiltrate their circle. And actually taking the test would help me gauge whether my training had elevated me beyond my original philistine status. But more and more, I pinned my hopes on a Court diploma as an essential stepping-stone to a higher level of understanding—a means to an end, rather than an end in and of itself. Morgan and his friends didn't obsess over the health of their tongue papillae and memorize the interior subzones of the Similkameen River Valley purely for their own edification; it was because these drills and deprivations helped them care for their guests' palates at a higher level. I'd come to think that the ultimate test of what I had learned about wine and the senses came down to whether I could apply that knowledge, and bring other people around to the kinds of experiences I'd discovered. And besides, after months of hearing about the stresses, pressures, and joys of their jobs, I was itching to give it a go.

In a few weeks, I would be taking the Court's Introductory Exam, a written test that is a mandatory prerequisite for attempting the Certified. Provided I passed the first level, I would tackle the Certified only a few weeks after that. (Because the slots fill up quickly, I, rather optimistically, had registered for both tests in one go.)

My immediate concern, when it came to the Certified, was service. Between my time at TopSomm, my trail at Marea, and my hours spent studying instructional videos about pouring procedure on the Guild of Sommeliers' website, I'd seen somms go through the steps of service enough times to think I had it down. All the same, my first time popping Champagne in front of a live audience couldn't be during the Certified Exam itself. Given that few restaurants were eager to trust some writer with their PXs, I needed another way to practice formal service on real, live guests. So I decided to prep for my exam the way sommeliers do: by entering a competition.

Since Morgan's Master Sommelier Exam was now two months out, he'd opted to squeeze in extra practice by entering the Young Sommeliers Competition, the longest-running somm competition in the United States. It is organized annually by the Chaîne des Rôtisseurs, an international brotherhood of gourmands that traces its roots to thirteenth-century France and the Royal Guild of Goose Roasters. This can perhaps explain why members show up to their events festooned with neck ribbons—color coded by rank—and weighed down by medals, then address one another with French titles like *confrère* and *bailli*. (Their flair for pomp and circumstance certainly doesn't make it likely that somms will drop their nickname for the Chaîne: the "old, rich, white-man fraternity.") For the Chaîne's members, who share a robust appetite for good meals and good service, the Young Sommelier Competition is a way to keep standards high at their favorite fine-dining haunts. For Morgan, it was another chance to run through his serving skills in the adrenaline-pumping format of a timed test, one that would hold him to the Court's most formal standards of service. That sounded exactly like what I needed to do.

As with TopSomm, Morgan had qualified for the Chaîne's semifinals by taking an online exam. The questions—mostly impossible, from my vantage point—had ranged from "What is a *muselet*?" (a miniature mussel, I guessed) to "Who is Champagne Charlie?" (the life of the party?). I'd missed the deadline to enter as an official competitor, but I sweet-talked the Grand Echanson, head of the Chaîne's wine activities, into letting me participate in the semifinals, which included blind tasting, theory, and service.

The semifinals were to be held at the University Club, a 150-year-old private social club in Midtown Manhattan housed in an intimidatingly elegant palazzo-style building. Cell phones are banned beyond the lobby. Women, who were finally allowed to join in 1987, are banned from the club's sole swimming pool. (The men like to swim naked.) On the day of the competition, I arrived dressed in the same blazer and pearls that Victoria had approved for my trail at Marea. I wasn't taking any chances: The Grand Echanson had warned me that the judging would begin with an inspection of my attire and my fingernails. "It's a bit like being an oyster in front of the walrus and carpenter," he wrote in an email. This concerned me more than a little because in the Lewis Carroll poem, the walrus and the carpenter end up devouring all the oysters.

The judges were waiting for me in a private room, still heavy with the smell of their postprandial cigars. The four of them wore beautifully tailored suits and ties. If they had thoughts about my outfit, they didn't share. The *confrères*, who would play the guests for my service exam, took seats around a table set with water glasses and scoring sheets. The Grand Echanson announced that I could proceed.

Even if I hadn't learned how to silently remove a Champagne cork, you might assume that I could, at a bare minimum, walk in a circle without spastically jerking in all different directions. You would, however, be incorrect. When I got a few feet away from the judges, I realized I was about to walk counterclockwise around the table, lurched to my right to change course, then tottered back to the left as it dawned on me that my original direction had been clockwise all along. I briefly halted next to one judge—No! Error! He's not the host!—then hopped a few steps sideways toward the Echanson—shit, counterclockwise again—as everyone's heads swiveled, trying to keep track of where I was *and* ask if I could recommend something to pair with the appetizer of Dungeness crab with baby shiitake mushrooms, fennel, red-frill mustard leaf, and lobster cream.

"Of course," I enthused. I tried to sound excited about a Spanish Cava, a sparkling wine from a producer called . . . called . . . what *was* his name? "I'll just have to consult our wine list," I said apologetically. Morgan had told me the Chaîne liked somms to focus on the sell. I should have said something about the delicate *pétillance*, the third-generation winemaker, blah-blah-blah. Instead I said, "It has a little bit of crispness, but also the autolytic flavors that you get from the brioche to go with the lobster."

"Autolytic—is that related to car repair?" one of the judges asked.

Yes, sir, I do sound like an asshole, I wanted to say. It was the perfect example of what technical language *not* to trot out in front of a guest. "Those are the flavors you get from the dead yeast," I explained.

The table made a face. I made a face. Dead yeast? Really, Bianca?

"Ughhh," said one of the men.

Ughhh, I thought to myself.

The questions wouldn't stop. *Do not make things up*, Morgan had warned me. I answered with a rotating selection of sound bites that meant "I have no fucking clue" in elegant somm-speak. "I don't want to perjure myself, but I believe the Monte Bello is a Bordeaux blend." And: "I'd be happy to check with our beverage manager." Or: "You know, that's a great question. If you give me just a minute to check our reference texts, I'd be happy to answer that for you." At a loss for actual knowledge about the wines they ordered, I kept inserting "umami," one of Morgan's favorite words, whenever I had no clue what to say. "That Pinot Noir from Burgundy will have an umami depth to complement the meatness quality, but with the risotto with pine nuts you're going to also have a nice umami quality to refine, so, Chardonnay?" I sounded unwell. I forgot to polish the glasses and present the cork. I spilled Champagne on the table. I talked over their toast. I gave blank stares to basic questions like "Was 1982 a good year for Bordeaux?" which is the wine equivalent of asking, "Was some guy elected president in 2008?"

"She's like, 'Ho-lee *shit*, what the hell did I just wander into?' " I heard one judge say when my back was turned. Apparently, they thought it was going just as well as I did.

For my final service task, I'd have to decant an old bottle of red wine for the table. At Morgan's suggestion, I'd memorized an imaginary wine list, so I would have bottles to recommend, along with scintillating factoids about each of the producers. I'd been short on time and there was only one red wine producer from France on my made-up list.

It was Château Gruaud-Larose, one of Bordeaux's sixty-one Classified Growths.

And what would the gentlemen like for their final bottle? The Grand Echanson requested a 1986 Château Gruaud-Larose.

I couldn't believe my luck. Finally, things were looking up.

I assembled all of the materials I would need to decant and wheeled them over on the gueridon, a small cart, which I stopped just to the right of the Grand Echanson's elbow. I had a candle, which I lit; the decanter; two serviettes, three coasters; and of course, the wine, which was resting on its side in a silver basket that I had very thoughtfully lined with a white napkin. Check, check, check.

"Where is the Gruaud-Larose from?" one judge asked, acting the inquisitive guest.

"Saint-Julien," I answered. No sweat. He looked surprised.

I began to weave factoids into a little story about the wine as I prepared to open it. I told them how it was a Second Growth, one of the best producers in Bordeaux. A beautiful winery, with the same owner as Château Haut-Bages-Libéral. One of the only properties in the region with a hail cannon! Everyone seemed to relax.

I pulled out my corkscrew and stood over the supine bottle. I flicked the knife blade once, twice, slick and quick around the crown. Beautiful. Joe Campanale would be proud. I put the corkscrew into the cork. Dead center. Gorgeous. I was feeling confident. Chatty. For the first time, it seemed like they might actually be enjoying themselves. Superb.

I stabilized the metal edge of the corkscrew's fulcrum against the bottle's lip to coax the cork up and out, cheerily chitchatting about the tannic grip of Cabernet Sauvignon blends. I didn't give much thought to the wet sucking coming from the cork. Then there was a moist snap.

My first thought was that I'd been shot. My second thought was: I wish I'd been shot.

Wine had exploded from the bottle, raining Cabernet over the judges. Wine dripped off the table, down my face, and down the sides of the glasses. The white tablecloths were stained red. The carpet underfoot, red. I'd been the Grand Echanson's human shield, and my white shirt was splattered red. I was drenched. It looked like blood was gushing from my chest.

There was no point in varnishing the truth, and the judges made no attempt to. One of the four, a Master of Wine, suggested that the critics' rating system for wine offered the most helpful metric for my performance.

"In the wine competition world, we have many definitions of quality," he said. "We give gold medals and silver medals and bronze medals. And slightly below no award, there is a category that is familiar to all wine competition judges. It's called DNPIM. Do you know what that stands for?" I shook my head. "It stands for 'do not put in mouth.' "

That is me, I realized. I am the human equivalent of "do not put in mouth."

While my tableside demeanor was likely to make people lose their appetites, my blind tasting skills were in a much higher league. The Chaîne judges had found my performance on that front to be deceptively advanced. "I was surprised you weren't as good, as polished, because I was impressed with what you did here with your blind tasting," a judge told me after it was all over.

I, on the other hand, was less surprised by these results. I'd been fascinated, first and foremost, by the sensory aspects of the sommeliers' craft, and my service skills reflected as much. I was having trouble motivating myself to master an elaborate set of rituals that seemed to exist for the sole purpose of having sommeliers master an elaborate set of rituals.

Still, I had a test to pass, so I dutifully followed sommeliers' advice to redouble my efforts at practicing the steps of service at home. Like the demented host of an adult tea party, I'd totter around the kitchen table holding a cutting board (closest thing I had to a tray), pouring cheap Prosecco and pretending to answer empty chairs' questions about cocktail ingredients or Champagne vintages. Round and round I'd go, polishing, presenting, filling, spilling, splashing onto the table, and gumming up the floor. "I'm terribly sorry," I'd apologize to the chair. "If I can handle your dry-cleaning bill, please let me know." When Matt came home, he'd step in as a pretend guest. I quickly realized that I preferred the chairs, who didn't give me attitude and asked only questions I could answer. "This wine has a great deal of nuttiness," I said to Matt, as I presented him a bottle. He rolled his eyes. "*You* have a great deal of nuttiness."

But this felt incomplete. I was developing some of the muscle memory for serving, without any of the emotional intelligence. Acting as a judge at TopSomm, where I'd seen top-notch service in action, and trailing at Marea, which opened my eyes to the real-life pressures of the floor, had revealed the "how" of service. The "why" was more elusive. Did anyone really care if I poured from their right instead of their left, as long as I got the wine into the glass? I wanted to understand the rationale behind the sacraments of formal restaurant service. As actors would say, what's my motivation? Why did these rituals matter?

When Morgan heard about the disaster with the Chaîne, he went out of his way to get me a *stage* with him at Aureole. He was cramming for his own service test—it was one of two sections of the Master Sommelier Exam that he still had to pass—and I think he figured he could squeeze in some extra reviewing by prepping me. Whatever it was, I was grateful. I was given one week to trail him on the floor during his lunch and dinner shifts. With talk of me actually opening bottles and pouring, the *stage* at Aureole promised to be more hands-on than my time at Marea. Plus, where Victoria could be all business, Morgan had a philosophical streak. If anyone could account for service traditions, I wagered it was him. As he'd told me in our first email exchange, he'd "done a lot of thinking and writing about this for myself, to work out why what I do is actually of cultural and social importance."

Morgan was in a tizzy when I met him for my first day. "I need to take care of this water situation," he announced. "The immediate emergency is that there is no water."

Someone hadn't put in the order for Pellegrino, and Morgan was appalled by the prospect they'd be eighty-six sparkling by dinner. I followed him up a steep staircase to Aureole's three-room wine cellar, which was kept at a chilly 55-ish degrees and doubled as the wine team's office. There was a grainy printout of a man's face hung beside one of the desks. I thought for a second it might be a Wanted poster. It was. "*New York Times* restaurant critic Pete Wells," read the caption. The staff was on high alert for reviewers. A dozen more headshots were posted two floors down at the entrance to the kitchen, complete with a laundry list of each person's culinary pet peeves. *Vogue*'s Jeffrey Steingarten: "Likes: French fries. Dislikes: anchovies, desserts in Indian restaurants, blue food (excluding blueberries), kimchi." I tried hard to imagine a scenario where Aureole, whose "progressive American" kitchen serves pheasant, steak, and Maine lobster, could possibly offend Mr. Steingarten by serving him dessert from an Indian restaurant. Vigilance is the best defense, I suppose.

Like humans of the same vintage, thirty-year-old Aureole was starting to care less about coolness or trends than stability and a solid income. Seven years before, it had moved from an Upper East Side townhouse into a cavernous space in Times Square. Now a theater district mainstay, it attracts lawyers with corporate cards from the firms in the office tower above, as well as out-of-town couples splurging on a big night in the Big Apple. The menus and chairs are leather, the tasting menu starts at $125 a head, and the smooth jazz is played at a tasteful volume. California, Burgundy, and Bordeaux occupy a sizable section of the wine list, and foie gras can be ordered year-round. The last *Times* review, published just after the restaurant's relocation, declared Aureole a "Las Vegas event restaurant airlifted into Manhattan."

Morgan and I scrambled upstairs to fetch bottles from the cellar so we could restock the bar. I picked one up by its neck. Morgan looked like he was in pain. "Handle the merchandise with respect on the floor," he pleaded. He laid the bottle in the crook of my arm, so I was cradling it like a baby.

Lunch service kicked off with a business luncheon in the private dining room. Morgan marched in to check on the party whose meal was just getting under way. I counted the seats to tally how many people didn't have wine.

"Don't point," Morgan hissed.

I crossed my arms over my chest.

"Don't cross your arms!"

I put my palms on the station behind me and leaned back.

"Don't lean!"

Morgan launched into the rationale of sommelier protocol as he let me carry, open, and serve the bottles we fetched. Some rituals still seemed arbitrary. I should never "backhand" guests—the back of my hand facing their cheek while I poured—but must always serve them with my open palm directed at their face. Why? "It's a biblical thing," Morgan insisted. "It's an act of trust. You're not showing the back of your hand because you're not hiding anything in your hand."

Other steps of service were actually quite logical. When we opened a bottle of Champagne, Morgan neatly cut and removed the foil, as with any wine, then laid a folded serviette over the top. He had me curl my left hand around both the serviette and the neck of the bottle, so that I was grasping it to my palm with my thumb pressing onto the top of the cork. With my right hand, he made me twist the metal wire on the cage covering the cork—so *that*'s what a *muselet* is!—exactly six times to undo it. From that moment, my left thumb could never, ever leave the *muselet*, he warned. In my Court exam, it would be an automatic fail. In real life, it would be a threat to the life and limb of everyone around me. It turns out that Champagne corks are a menace to society. They erupt from bottles at twenty-five miles per hour, and bystanders have been bruised, banged up, and even blinded by flying corks. (One research paper on these "bottle-cork eye injuries"—the official term for catching a cork with your eye socket—muses, without apparent irony, that they "seem to be more frequent at the turn of the year.") This official, Court-sanctioned routine has been developed to ensure that no one gets maimed over their Wagyu beef carpaccio. Like I said, logical. To safely remove the cork, I held the base of the bottle in my right hand, so it was at a slight angle, then twisted the bottom back and forth to loosen the cork I grasped in my left hand.

It was all starting to make more sense. Having everyone walk clockwise keeps the staff from colliding on the floor. Putting coasters on the table signals a bottle has been ordered. Putting bottles on the coasters keeps drips from staining the linens. Putting corks on the coasters keeps the table from being smeared by wet corks, which some guests like to inspect to see how the bottle has aged. (A brittle cork, or one that's damp all the way to the top, could mean oxygen has seeped in and spoiled the wine.) The glasses go to the right of the plate, since most people are right handed. Nothing but the stem should be touched, because doing so could leave fingerprints and warm the glass bowl that will hold the wine. Sommeliers wipe the lip of the bottle before *and* after they remove the cork, just to be sure no mold or debris on the bottle's exterior contaminates the wine. They wipe the bottom of a bottle that's been sitting in ice, so water doesn't drip on the guests. They put older wines in a decanting basket, which keeps the bottles in the same horizontal position in which they've been stored and avoids shaking up sediment that could end up in someone's glass. After decanting, they snuff the candle—instead of blowing it—so smoke doesn't taint the wine's fragrance.

But those practical considerations accounted for only a fraction of Morgan's efforts, and I noted new service rituals whose purpose I couldn't yet explain. Morgan was a stickler for protocol and our evening shift evolved into a continuous recitation of things he noticed that were "not to the standards of service." The Heineken deposited for the gentleman on Table 30 before his date received her wine. The lack of consistency regarding which glasses to use for Syrah. Servers asking "All done?" instead of "Can we take your plates?" or showcasing "specials" in lieu of "additional menu items." He was galled by Aureole's habit of leaving wineglasses on a table after guests ordered a cocktail—a tactic meant to remind people they might like to buy a bottle. He flinched at the asynchronous landing of entrées around a table. The number of tables pushed into the dining room. The entire orientation of the dining room, which forced him to turn his back to guests. Not for the first time, he mumbled something about how this never would have happened at Jean-Georges.

To Morgan, these were compromises in quality similar to bartering your eternal soul to damnation. "It's a Faustian situation," he protested after he was forced to backhand two of the six guests in a corner booth while clearing their plates. "I want to openhand him, but I have to reach in. I can't pass another plate to my left hand, but I have to clear the interior position first."

Looking past him, I saw his boss, Carrie, talking to a table of regulars. She had one knee propped up on the banquette and an arm draped over the top of the bench, and was leaning against the seat's leather back. I decided it was best not to call Morgan's attention to this.

At each table, Morgan placed his torso and his limbs with deliberate care. There was no stray movement. Whenever he reached an arm down to help someone, it was always in a graceful, confident arc. He walked with his chin up and shoulders thrown back, a holdover from Jean-Georges. Before service each evening, Morgan's captain would correct the staff's posture. Rolling back their shoulders and sticking out their chests was meant to convey an aura of confidence, one that managers thought would subconsciously convince guests to spend more. I suddenly became aware of how much I was fidgeting on my feet, fluttering my hands, touching my hair, rocking backward. I remembered that Morgan had instructed me to do yoga to bring a higher degree of "crispness and physical attention" to each motion. He promised it would help with "being present with someone and present in your body."

Some of the service slipups that irked Morgan ran afoul of Aureole's standards. Most of them were violations of Morgan's own personal code of conduct, which was deeply informed by the Court's guidelines, but hurtled way past them into even more exacting territory. For example, Morgan made a big deal out of answering a guest's polite "How are you?" with a full sentence: "I'm doing wonderfully this evening, thanks." He thought the extra care of giving a response that didn't sound canned could alert the diner to their shared humanity and help her be more engaged in the moment. "It makes you a real person and not a robot," he said. "When was the last time someone in their life was like, 'Oh, we're not just going to procedurally stumble through our lives'?"

Morgan had lofty ideas about using wine to bond with his fellow humans. At lineup before service the following night, it was clear this wasn't a priority Morgan and the rest of Aureole's staff shared equally.

Carrie, Aureole's wine director, launched the nightly pep talk with some reminders about basic service protocol. This was stuff Morgan wouldn't be caught dead doing. She implored the staff to always "hug" the guests and never backhand them. "We want to act as the guests' arms so they don't have to."

After a few words on remembering to *please* deliver plates of food to the correct seats, the focus of the remaining half hour was selling. Carrie quizzed the servers on the wines Aureole offered by the glass, and made them recite tasting notes as though speaking to a guest. She was satisfied with a simple descriptor or two, like "dried flowers" or "medium acidity." But Morgan interjected after each wine to expound on its nuances. The Massolino was "really led by that sort of savory floral perfume." The J. M. Boillot had "a little bit more high toast taste, this campfire, roasted hazelnut, roasted chestnut side. It's imported by the same people who own Vineyard Brands, which I think is always interesting to note," said Morgan. No one in the room appeared to share his definition of "interesting."

"Anyone know why I asked about those particular two wines?" Carrie asked, trying to steer everyone back to the conversation she wanted to have. "Because we don't *sell* them," she scolded.

Morgan cut in. He had thoughts on this too. "Guys, for anybody a $30 or $50 glass of wine is really expensive, so I think the question you need to answer for yourselves is, why would somebody do that?" he said. "This is an eleven-year-old glass of wine. There's a luxuriance, an opulence, an intensity to those wines that is not offered by any of the other wines that are on the list. And doesn't everyone want to have the luxuriant, opulent, intense experience? I know I do. I can't afford it all the time. . . . But when I'm treating myself, that's how I spend money."

Carrie picked up where she'd left off, as though she hadn't heard him. "And with dessert wines, even if they don't order dessert, say, 'Would you like to order a glass of wine instead of dessert?' "

She announced a staff-wide competition to see who could accumulate the greatest number of perfect checks. A perfect table would order a cocktail ("An aperitif," said Morgan), a bottle of wine, and a dessert wine. There was a magnum of Champagne in it for the winner. "It's your sales, it's your money. You push to get those sales, you'll get the money," said Carrie. I half expected her to break into the speech from *Glengarry Glen Ross*: "Second prize is a set of steak knives. Third prize is you're fired."

Diners have long suspected restaurant staff of precisely these sorts of machinations. The paranoia—and stereotype—that sommeliers, especially, are out to squeeze money from their marks has existed at least since the early days of indoor electricity, feeding fear and mistrust of people like Morgan. In an 1887 restaurant review, a

New York Times food critic huffed that while there were "many criticisms to be made" about a particular Parisian eatery, ranking "above all" was the need for a "limitation of the privilege which the sommelier enjoys of recommending certain wines on which, it is to be presumed, he gets a commission." In 1921, a journalist grew so agitated about the possible spread of sommeliers to the United States—even during Prohibition—that he took to the *Times* to rally his countrymen on an offensive against this dangerous breed:

> This article . . . is written in the deliberate and ruthless hope of putting out of business an entire class of wage earners. It is written in the firm belief that, unless they are driven out of their present walk of life and forced to seek other means of earning a livelihood, their pernicious example will spread from Europe to America and place new and formidable obstacles in the path of the vast mass of Americans playing the national game of trying to make both ends meet. The wage earners in question are those strange employes [*sic*], infesting the better class restaurants of Paris, who are known as "sommeliers."

The writer failed to stop the infestation. But he wasn't wrong, in the sense that Morgan does report to two bosses when he steps out on the floor each day: Aureole and Aureole's customers. Both hope the diners will go home happy. Yet as I'd seen at Marea, Aureole didn't mind separating their guests from as much cash as possible in the process, which is not generally someone's primary goal when she goes out to eat. For all of his talk of finding wines that could recontextualize peoples' places in the universe, Morgan also had to consider his duty to the restaurant—which made higher margins off drinks than food—and to its staff—whose tips were calculated off the check totals. Aureole's front waiters could expect to make between $62,000 and $66,000 a year, its runners $52,000 to $58,000, and its back waiters $32,000 to $36,000—all a combination of the minimum wage they were paid hourly, plus tips, which were higher than in most restaurants because of Aureole's prices. Morgan, who took a bigger chunk from the tip pool, earned around $70,000 a year, considerably less than the low six figures he'd made at Jean-Georges.

Morgan relied on service to bridge the gap between these two masters. He would never stretch a guest past her budget. But he couldn't shortchange Aureole either. To get the drinkers in the mood for a special beverage—and make them feel as though it really was something special—he went out of his way to treat each table in an exceptional way. If he dressed up the night with his polished demeanor, the civilians he served might decide to dress it up too. Maybe they'd get a bottle, instead of a glass. Or spring for the Chianti Classico Gran Selezione over a regular Chianti.

Thanks to our multisensory makeup, Morgan's extra care could even enhance the flavor of the wine. We know this to be true instinctively, but labs have measured its effects as well: A study at Oxford University coauthored by Charles Spence fed people either a tossed salad, neatly placed at the center of their plates, or an artistically arranged version of the same salad, styled to resemble a Kandinsky canvas, with mushrooms juxtaposed at right angles to shredded carrots and asymmetric dots of orange dressing. Diners rated the second dish as far more delicious, and were willing to pay more for it. Morgan had power over how a bottle would taste. He was perhaps more of a winemaker than he realized.

To an extent I hadn't fully registered the first night of my stage, Morgan scrutinized the guests' behavior as closely as he did his own and the rest of the staff's, and held them to equally high standards. He seemed pained by people who didn't embrace fine-dining decorum to the degree he considered appropriate. "That guy's got a big ol' wad of gum. That's a great way to start your meal," he said sarcastically. "Over at

Table 114 there," he whispered. "There's the classic example of using the charger as a bread plate." He groaned at someone else using the charger as a coaster, and puzzled at people who'd drink cocktails—"the wrong pairing!"—throughout an entire meal. He was agitated by people who waved in the air to summon their servers, and people who kept their coats with them in the dining room. He paraphrased Daniel Boulud on the importance of coat checks: "We have a coat check not because we want to steal your coats, but because maybe you shouldn't keep your coat in the dining room." He got exasperated by men who removed their blazers. "At Jean-Georges, they *will* ask you to put your suit jacket back on." He watched in horror as a six-top drank a heavy Syrah—a "funky, black, oaky, fuck-you wine"—with raw fish.

"That's Morgan's inferno," he said. "You have something that tastes like a black milkshake with beef jerky stuck in it. Oh my God, and they're drinking that with *tuna*. There's a seventh circle of Morgan Harris hell where people are doing that forever. PlumpJack Syrah and raw tuna."

In Morgan's mind, there is a right way to do things. A code of service for the sommelier, and a code of conduct for the guest. Principles trump personal whims. Likewise, customization and comfort shouldn't come at the expense of correctness. Especially at the table, everything should be done in a proper manner, according to the particular ethos of that dining room. A restaurant is its own kind of cultural institution. It is not merely a trough where people come for their feedings. So don't act like it.

"I have romantic ideas about restaurants," Morgan admitted. "I like that whole experience—the old-fashioned everything, where everything is just-so. It's luxury that we're not comfortable with." He lamented the rise of California casual, of sneakers replacing leather shoes. ("Please let me always have enough respect for myself that if I'm going to bother to dress up in a suit that I don't wear running shoes," I saw him tweet later.) Morgan might wear hoodies to our blind tastings, but on the floor he put extra care into his appearance.

That night, he was wearing polished brown leather shoes and a snug gray suit, with a polka-dotted pocket square that matched his polka-dotted socks and tie.

Morgan had a vision for what the ultimate dining experience could be, or *should* be, and felt like he was failing his guests when he didn't achieve it. Sometimes, they got in his way. He shook his head at people trying to clear their own plates, or lifting a charger to pass it to the server. He wanted the diners to let *him* serve *them*. "The *service* is designed to *serve* you."

Other times, the guests got in their own way. "I feel like one of those vending machine robots," he grumbled when people order-fired a wine, pointing at a name on a page without asking for his help. Some diners who did this may have just known exactly what they wanted. But others seemed to feel guilty or awkward about having someone wait on them. Ironically, it was the people who didn't rely on Morgan and didn't ask him questions who bothered him the most. "I'm built into the cost of your meal!" he protested to me, barely outside of earshot of a young couple who'd selected, without consulting him, what he considered to be a terrible bottle of Sauvignon Blanc. He could have offered a wine that was much cheaper and way more delicious.

I'd noticed from eating out with sommeliers that, no matter how encyclopedic their knowledge, they usually put themselves entirely in the hands of the restaurant's somm, if there is one. Unless they see a bottle they've been dying to try, they'll give just two pieces of information: (1) what they want to spend, and (2) what style of wine they want to drink. (That could be as broad as "Old World, unoaked, savory" or as nitpicky as "I had Schloss Gobelsburg's Grüner last week and loved it—what do you have like it?") They let the somm, who knows her restaurant's list more intimately than they ever could, steer them from there.

Morgan and I were standing in the dining room of a Michelin-started restaurant where dinner for two would run at least $200, not including wine, tax, or tip. Occupy Wall Street would have taken one look at the people in this place and thought, *Tax the fuckers*. Yet as Morgan saw it, the restaurant was the most democratic institution in the world. The finest service, attention, and care were available to anyone, as long as they could foot the bill, and when the service was anything but the best, he felt like he'd shortchanged his guests. They were cheated out of the top-notch treatment that was rightfully theirs. He'd missed an opportunity to elevate their experience, maybe even change how they see wine.

"There's something egalitarian about restaurants. It's just, can you pay your check. Everyone gets the same great service. Everyone is welcome. . . . Like this isn't a service just for rich people. You don't have to tip," Morgan said. "There's something to me sacred and powerful about someone putting that experience in your hands. It'll cost them $200 to dine here tonight, and they'll be treated just like the person who spent $4,000."

This sounded a bit idealistic. And given what I'd seen at Marea, it didn't quite ring true. All guests are equal—but in a system of wine PXs and PPXs, some guests are more equal than others. When a prospective investor came into Aureole for dinner one evening, I watched each course get delivered by Chef Charlie Palmer himself.

But reading up on the history of the restaurant, I was surprised to learn that Morgan was, in a way, right to tout the egalitarian nature of a Michelin-starred dinner, pricey and out of reach as it is.

The restaurant as we now know it is a relatively recent phenomenon. It first emerged in France in the two decades before the country's aristocrats started being marched to the guillotines. Before then, a *restaurant* (because of course the word is originally French) was made from beef marrow, some onion, and maybe some ham rinds or parsnip. It was a type of consommé, a "food or remedy that has the property of restoring lost strength to a sickly or tired individual," according to the 1708 *Dictionnaire Universel*. Parisians could visit restaurants to order their namesake specialty and little else besides broth. France's food sellers then belonged to one of some twenty-five guilds that restricted members to a single culinary specialty. For several hundred years, hungry gourmets had to visit the *restaurant* for soup, the *rôtisseur* for roasted game meats, the *charcutier* for pork products, the *poulailler* for chicken, and the *traiteur* for a hearty working-man's meal of whatever the cook decided to throw together that day. (For glimpses of what it was like to enjoy all these delicacies—and more—served together, people could obtain tickets to watch the royal family eat their meals before an audience of onlookers at the Palace of Versailles, part of a centuries-old tradition referred to as the *grand couvert*.) The strict separation between purveyors of soups, chicken carcasses, and full meals began to relax even before revolutionaries stormed the Bastille. But the fall of the ancien régime took the guilds down with it, releasing chefs from noblemen's private kitchens into the public market. By the dawn of the nineteenth century, culinary experiences that had once been the privilege of the upper crust were now available to anyone with a few francs to spare. Restaurants represented "a form of cultural democratization," recounts Paul Lukacs in *Inventing Wine*, noting this was especially true for wine because bottles formerly reserved for the aristocracy were now funneled into the cellars of restaurants. There, all could partake. In his 1825 *Physiology of Taste*, Jean-Anthelme Brillat-Savarin, one of France's most committed hedonists, gushes that the inventor of the restaurant was, in his humble estimation, nothing less than a "genius." "Whoever, having fifteen or twenty pistoles at his disposal, sits down to the table of a first-class restaurateur, that man eats as well as and even better than if he were at the table of a prince," he marvels. *This is what I've been trying to tell you people,* I could imagine Morgan saying. Brillat-Savarin would no doubt have applauded Morgan's egalitarian spirit. Today, provided you can get a reservation and pay for it, Morgan is there to serve you, with the same level of care regardless of your tax bracket. He takes pains to ensure the guy on 114, whoever he is, eats as well as and even better than if he were at the table of a prince.

Morgan's fastidious attention to language and manners could make him seem anachronistic, like someone who trained alongside Carson the butler in *Downton Abbey*. Most twenty-nine-year-olds do not go around bemoaning the "stunning number of ways 'foie gras' is mispronounced in this country" or the improper use of chargers. But he was on to something with his fixation on decorum: Service rituals *do* matter, and not only to ensure nothing drips on the linens. Historians and anthropologists who study the evolution of table etiquette have documented changes in service style that have had cultural repercussions that reverberate far beyond a meal.

At no point was this more dramatic than in the shift from *service à la française* to *service à la russe* in the mid-nineteenth century. Here, again, the French led the way. Classy feasts in France, Great Britain, and America had traditionally been served in the "French" style. Guests would sit down at the table to find it heaping with a bounty of communal dishes, which servers would replace—albeit with minimal interruption—in subsequent courses, leaving diners to pass the dishes among themselves. (If you've been out to eat recently, you should recognize a variation of this under the new name of "share plates.") An early kind of dinner theater, the meal would be presented as a breathtaking tableau of platters, tureens, soufflés, stacked gelées, carved fruits, chalices, candelabras, and vases. But the food was usually cold by the time people started eating. As one French chef griped in 1856, the dishes often "lost something of their essential qualities." Whatever it was that finally convinced the French they'd had it up to here with the tepid temperature of their roasted lamb, by the 1880s, *service à la française* was out and *service à la russe* was in. With the switch, flavor took precedence over flair. Servers would bring each course in pre-portioned, pre-plated individual servings offered one after the other in an order determined by the chef. Other countries soon followed suit. *Service à la russe* was the rhyme and reason behind everything flying out of the kitchen at Aureole.

With the Russian style of service, chefs exerted more control over menus, servers assumed greater prominence in the dining room, and diners lost easy socializing over please-pass-the-salad small talk. This seemingly minor change in service recast the structure and social function of meals: Historians argue it was a turning point from dining as social communion to dining as culinary showcase. Newly empowered to dictate the order, timing, and composition of dishes, the chef, rather than his guests, became the star of the meal.

As I worked my final shift with Morgan at Aureole, I felt like I was witnessing another style of service in action. *Service à la russe*, yes. But also something like *service à l'esprit*. Morgan, like Victoria at Marea, was keenly aware of delivering both physical and psychic gratification. That idea had come up in my conversations with Paul Grieco, when we'd discussed Terroir's wild way of treating its guests. Service is only part of the equation, Paul had argued: During his tenure working with Danny Meyer, New York's resident restaurant-whisperer, Paul had come to appreciate the need for both service *and* hospitality. These were different things. And they were both vital on the floor. "Service is the technical delivery of a product. Hospitality is how the delivery of that product makes its recipient *feel*," writes Meyer in his memoir, *Setting the Table*. "Hospitality is present when something happens *for* you. It is absent when something happens *to* you."

Hospitality was the right term for the thoughtfulness that imbued Morgan's actions. While the captains, busboys, food runners, and front waiters at Aureole seemed more focused on delivering meals, I sensed that Morgan sought to create a mental state, an atmosphere. Perhaps it was his previous life as an actor, or the rush of pre-theater customers crammed into Aureole. Whatever it was, Morgan appeared to be putting on a show for his guests. Good service—and hospitality—was a performance, a kind of theater that set the tone for the experience. With chefs hidden in the kitchen and servers pressed for time, the sommelier had the luxury of providing the human touch that elevated a meal.

Being fastidious about his wipes and pours was Morgan's way of showing respect for his guests. In certain ways, it evoked the highly choreographed steps of a Japanese tea ceremony, an art form that masters spend their lives perfecting. The point is not just to give someone a cup of tea to drink; it's a way of honoring a guest. As with wine service, each action has significance: After the tea has been made, the host turns the tea bowl in two careful clockwise motions, so that the front of the bowl—its most attractive side—faces the drinker. Even if someone doesn't know the significance of the bowl's orientation, or the alleged biblical roots of Morgan's openhanded pouring, it's impossible not to value the deliberate effort a person takes in each measured breath and twist of the wrist. The feeling of Morgan's service could, like a good piece of music, transcend explicit knowledge of service etiquette to give someone pleasure. A guest could sense the care he took to please her through his choice of words, his body language, the precision with which he placed a glass.

Morgan believed that in the sum of these actions, the feeling he could create for his audience at Aureole was no different from what he could have achieved onstage.

"The restaurant, like the theater, can be a place that people heal and become whole again and that they notice their place on the planet and that they are humans. And in being humans they are special and particular and exist in a way that no other individual does," he said.

"We come to restaurants because we like to be taken care of," he added. "Everyone needs to be taken care of. We are all so much more fragile and delicate than we think." The first restaurants advertised to Parisian passersby with the motto "I Shall Restore You." Morgan's promise to his tables was not so different.

Morgan had a flair for the poetic—this is a guy who called his mother "Apollonian" and his father "Dionysian"—and I doubted that all sommeliers imbued their role with the same gravitas that he did. Yet if you work the floor day in and day out, for fourteen hours at a stretch, you should have an idea of why it matters and what makes it important. The guests at Table 112 might not have considered that they could "become whole again" this evening, over their black cod. But it would certainly never happen unless Morgan believed that it could.

Now it was my turn to see if I could be a custodian for guests' senses and spirits. Or rather, whether I could convince the Court that I was capable.

CHAPTER TEN

The Trial

When friends would ask me about this sommelier test-or-whatever I was taking, I'd play it off as though it didn't matter whether I passed. Just by prepping for the Certified Sommelier Exam, I'd had an extremely rewarding experience, I assured them. "You know, it's the journey that matters," I'd say, sounding way calmer than I felt.

Actually though, I was dead set on passing. It had been nearly a year since I'd immersed myself in all aspects of the sommelier profession and lifestyle, short of actually doing the job on my own. I couldn't stop now. Besides, the somms' fanaticism had turned out to be contagious. My original obsession with making sense of their obsessive ways had morphed into an obsession with the things they obsessed over. High-acid Riesling, neti pots, chervil, elegantly placed coasters, properly chilled biodynamically grown Beaujolais. One by one, I had adopted them all. Especially after seeing Morgan in action and grasping the philosophy of service, I was determined to try my hand at working the floor.

I took the Introductory Exam, a seventy-question written test, shortly after my *stage* at Aureole. I passed, which meant I could proceed to the next level and attempt the Certified. This should have been encouraging. It wasn't.

I always knew it would be an uphill battle for me to pass a test geared toward professionals with at least three years in the wine or service industry, especially considering I'd had less than a year to prepare *and* had started out an oblivious civilian. But victory appeared more and more unlikely as the Certified test date neared. Not only had my performance at the Young Sommelier Competition been something of a disaster, but the feedback I got in the weeks before the exam was bleak. It seemed like everyone I talked to had needed at least two tries to nail the test. Several of my friends had just failed the Certified, one of them in spite of his solid tenure at a Danny Meyer restaurant, where wine classes were offered to employees—a nice leg up, given that there's no prep course you can take for the Certified. He hinted I was done for. "Your real handicap is you just don't have experience on the floor," he informed me when I dropped by his restaurant to see how his exam had gone. "I've spent enough time actually serving, so the muscle memory really took over. That's going to be your hardship." I went to Morgan in a panic. He assured me I'd probably do okay if I memorized 80 percent of the information in the Guild of Sommeliers' study guides. Okay, easy enough. Except to put that in perspective, the Guild has six different guides for France alone, most of them way longer than the U.S. Constitution. One of the more "obvious" facts to remember: RM stands for *récoltant manipulant*, meaning the Champagne was made by a winemaker who also grew the grapes, 95 percent of which must have originated in his vineyards. (Oh, and SR is *société de récoltants*, CM is *coopéerative manipulation*, ND is *négociant distributeur*, MA is *marque d'acheteur*, and NM is *négociant manipulant*. I was going to want to know all of those too.)

The theory part of the exam would be a straight-up test of wine facts. I was already up to one thousand flash cards, which I'd loaded onto my phone so no matter where I was, I could take some time out to memorize essential-but-arbitrary wine trivia. For instance: *Normale*-grade bottlings of Brunello di Montalcino can't be released until January first of the fifth year after harvest, *Riserva* Brunellos until the sixth year. Because, sure. I rehearsed the information whenever possible. "Actually, that Riesling is completely *trocken*, meaning dry," I corrected my mother-in-law over dinner, "because although it's a *Spätlese*—or late harvest—it has less than nine grams of residual sugar per liter, and at least seven grams of acid." Matt stared at me in horror. I was beginning to sound dangerously like Morgan.

For the service section, I would be required to open and serve wine while juggling questions about cocktails (What's in a Sidecar?), aperitifs (What's Lillet made with?), and digestifs (We're trying to pick between Scotch and Irish whiskey—what's the difference?). And, of course, I'd be asked which wines to pair with whatever dish my mock guests were eating for the purposes of the exam. I needed to have a wide range of specific wines to suggest at the ready, including their name, price, producer, grape variety, vintage, and style. So basically, I had to memorize an entire wine list of around fifty to seventy selections. The event was like some weird hybrid of Trivial Pursuit, a ballroom dancing competition, and a blind date. Even my personality would be on trial. Since somms, unlike chefs, interact personally with the people who are eating, I'd be required to show the Court I knew what I was doing *and* that I was a likable person who could win strangers' trust. A handout from the Court spelling out the correct "Demeanor of the Professional Sommelier" opened with instructions to be "quietly confident but not arrogant." *Am I quietly confident or am I arrogant?* I wondered with dread. I had a lot of questions. I had a lot of doubts. I worried I might need acting lessons.

Even blind tasting, where I thought I'd be strongest, now looked iffy. A few weeks before I was set to take the test, the Court unveiled a brand-new format for the exam's blind tasting grid, the worksheet that we would use to record our impressions of the wine and that would be used to score us. (Master candidates blind taste six wines out loud; Certified examinees do a written analysis of two wines.) The grid had separate sections for each aspect of the wine we were required to analyze—its aromas, structure, grape variety, and so on—and we were expected to fill out the grid while we blind tasted, then hand it in for the judges, all of them Master Sommeliers, to grade. All well and good, except that with the redesign, the Court had put in additional sections, revamped the ratings scale, thrown in fresh grape varieties, and come up with all kinds of new attributes to rate. Somms were having nervous breakdowns on social media. "I imagine you can understand my moment of panic on seeing something completely new," wrote a man from Baltimore who'd spent sixteen years working in restaurants. "My comfort with the testing process has been undone." I would have said the same, if I'd ever felt comfortable to begin with.

The taste training I'd done with Morgan and the other somms had been geared toward the more challenging format of the Master Sommelier blind tasting exam, meaning I had been tasting a far greater range of wines—and analyzing them in more depth—than would be required for the Certified. But I heard horror stories about exam-day nerves destroying the delicate harmony of peoples' palates, and I wasn't taking anything for granted. My morning workout now consisted not only of reviewing the fifty-odd essences in my kit from Le Nez du Vin, but also blind tasting, alone, in the kitchen, before breakfast. To be sure I was sensitive to tiny variations in alcohol, acid, and sugar levels—the secret to nailing a wine's structure—I plunged into a palate-refining regimen devised by UC Davis sensory scientists to train professional wine judges. Per their instructions, I ordered enough beakers, scientific scales, and powdered chemicals to land myself on an FBI watch list. Next, I made Matt blind test me on precise dilutions of citric acid, acetic acid, sucrose, and whiskey while I worked at pinpointing the concentrations of each solution—about four different concentrations per chemical, which I tasted at random in batches of thirty. I repeated this palate quiz a few dozen times (sorry, Matt) until I was sure I could tell medium acidity from medium-plus acidity, and 12 percent alcohol from 13 percent alcohol from 14 percent alcohol. In a desperate move to internalize the flavor of Chablis, a wine I almost always got wrong, I also convinced Matt to help me with the associative learning exercise proposed by Johan Lundström, the neuroscientist I met in Dresden. "One of the best pairings," Johan had advised, "is to do something while having sex." Word to the wise: Nothing kills the mood like coughing Chablis through your nose.

At least the sommeliers in my EMP tasting group shared my desperation. With their Master exam just around the corner, they were all on edge. Fights broke out. Yannick Benjamin, the somm who was taking the test for his ninth and final time, exploded at his partner after flubbing a flight in one of the final tastings before the test. "*Fuck*, man! You're so annoying! Give me feedback! I'm doing this thing in a week!" Yannick shouted. That same day, Morgan, normally unflappable, ran out of time during his flight. It was a rookie error and the first time I could recall seeing it happen. The anxiety was also bringing out Morgan's inner philosopher. His Twitter feed had become a string of motivational aphorisms, like "Results are for losers. Good process is for kings and gods."

Moving up a level in the Court could mean a hefty raise for Morgan and the other somms. According to a survey by the Guild of Sommeliers, Master Sommeliers make, on average, $150,000 a year, over twice as much as Certified somms ($60,000) and nearly three times as much as Intro candidates ($55,000). In New York City, experienced somms could earn anywhere from $60,000 to—at the extreme upper end—$140,000 a year, most of it in tips, which meant they were at the mercy of customers' generosity and their restaurants' popularity. Pay for Master Sommeliers who worked the floor would top out at around $150,000, though they could make more by ditching service to manage wine programs for large restaurant groups or to become distributors or consultants. Many of them do leave, worn down by the grind of a punishing nocturnal lifestyle with little in the way of flexibility, job security, or benefits. Some restaurants might throw in healthcare or a retirement plan. But most were stingy, spurred by thin margins to nickel-and-dime the staff, often by keeping people in the tip pool rather than moving them to a salaried role, which would require the restaurant to bear the burden for their pay. (This has led to lawsuits—as one somm observed, "There's just no good way to run a restaurant unless it's slightly illegal.") The sommeliers in Morgan's generation had come to their jobs at a younger age than their predecessors—in part, people told me, because more of them grew up around wine and in the midst of a food renaissance, in part because the economy was bad when they graduated in the late 2000s, and in part because of the industry's cheapness.

"Now the average age of a sommelier is closer to twenty-seven than forty-seven," said Levi Dalton, a former somm who hosts the podcast "I'll Drink to That." "The industry has been like, 'Oh, well, we want to encourage the youth.' But really what they're saying is, 'We'd like to encourage more cheap labor. . . . We would rather not have a middle class. We want to make this really accessible to younger people who will work eighty or ninety hours a week, not complain that they're not going to make a lot of money because they get to learn about wine, and when they're not happy with that anymore, then we'll get somebody else who wants to do that.' That's been pretty much the move. And it's really cycled out a whole generation of sommeliers."

Yet many Master Sommeliers insist they didn't seek their diploma for the money. "For the caliber of experience and knowledge that we have at this level, look at any other industry—banking, finance, law, medicine—we make a fraction of what the highest-paid employees make," Laura Williamson, a Master Sommelier, told me. "It's about personal process and path. One that's driven by inspiration." Not that money is frowned upon as a motivation. Ego is. I'd heard complaints from an older generation of sommeliers who suspected that too many of the up-and-comers, including people like

Morgan, were just out for fame and glory. That is *the* cardinal sin among service pros, who are supposed to deflect all focus away from themselves.

Whether it was for fame, fortune, or just the pursuit of knowledge and experience, the Court was swamped with people wanting to take its tests. In New York, seats for the Certified exam had filled up immediately, so I'd had to register in the closest city that offered the test in my time frame: Virginia Beach, Virginia, a stretch of artificial sand three hours south of Washington, D.C. A group of coastal scientists once picked it as their Beach of the Month for being "almost completely devoid of natural beach processes."

At first I'd been annoyed. The airplane's dryness would be murder on my nose and wreak havoc on my immune system—the last thing I needed was to catch a cold. Yet I'd gradually come around to the idea, and was now actually looking forward to visiting a community of sommeliers who worked outside one of the big oenophile meccas, like San Francisco or New York. Hoping to meet up with local somms, I posted a message on the Guild of Sommeliers site. Annie Truhlar, who'd spent almost two decades working in Virginia Beach restaurants and was also taking the Certified, told me to call her on Saturday the week before our exam. She hung up almost as soon as she answered the phone. She was studying. Had to call back in ten. No interruptions.

When we finally spoke, Annie volunteered to pick me up at the airport. And because getting into the car of a stranger you met over the Internet is always a good idea, I told her I'd see her next Monday afternoon, outside arrivals.

Annie waved at me from the driver's seat of a charcoal Yukon SUV with a cracked windshield.

"I haven't been on a plane since I was twelve," she announced as I hoisted myself into the car. Annie was thirty-five, had a round face that looked slightly sunburned, and spoke with the smallest hint of a

Southern drawl (even though her service skills were "on point," she hoped the Court wouldn't pull "daggone decantin' out of their ass"). She grew up just outside Winston-Salem, where her grandparents owned two farms, a few rental houses, and a trailer park. She'd never traveled farther north than Maryland, and that trip had been just a few months ago, when she took the Certified exam for her second time.

"This past time, in Baltimore, I studied for two weeks relentlessly and ate Adderall like it was candy. And I was *so* upset when I failed it," she said. She'd decided to go for it again. "I had some money in savings and I was like, 'Screw it, I'm taking the test.' . . . My third damn time. . . . I've paid a thousand bucks! On level two! Jesus."

The $325 exam fee was a hefty investment for someone who makes, in Annie's words, "shit money"—$4.50 an hour, plus tips, to be precise. Annie's husband, Chuck, a plumber, wasn't wild about her dipping into their savings, especially with four kids in the house. But Annie had explained to him that getting the Court's Certified diploma would mean a huge raise. Way more than the hospitality associate's degree she was getting from Tidewater Community College. Plus, more and more restaurants were hiring only people who'd passed the test.

"We have to live paycheck to paycheck sometimes," Annie said as we barreled onto the highway. "The sommelier certification is really about a level of income increase for me in the service industry. It really is substantial. You talk about going from a tipped employee to a $60,000 base salary."

The roar of jets occasionally drowned out the ends of her sentences. "OCEANA AIR BASE!" Annie hollered by way of explanation. The home of the navy's fighter-jet fleet was a fifteen-minute drive from Zoës, the local surf-'n'-turf restaurant where we'd be taking the test, and black planes crisscrossed the sky. "People call it 'the sound of freedom,'" Annie yelled. "You'll see bumper stickers: 'If You Don't Like the Sound, Go Back to Where You Came From.'"

Speaking of the military, Annie's seventeen-year-old son was up in Richmond right now swearing into the navy, which wasn't so different from her plan when she was his age. She rattled off her family history as we drove toward the Virginia Beach strip. Annie's stepdad had been in the U.S. Army Band, and Annie, who'd played brass in the marching band all through high school, had counted on joining too. That was until she got pregnant her senior year, when she was seventeen. She and Chuck moved into a trailer, and Annie went into food service like her mom, who waits tables at Olive Garden back in North Carolina. Annie gave birth a week after she turned eighteen. Since then, Annie's worked just about every front-of-house position, and a few back-of-the house too. As we cruised along Atlantic Avenue, the town's main drag, she pointed out a Best Western, where she'd manned the front desk. It shared a stretch of road with Nightmare Mansion, Top Gun Mini Golf, Oh Fudge, Forbes Salt Water Taffy, and Sunsations, which had crammed its big glass windows with boogie boards, sunscreen, a sign for hermit crabs, and neon tank tops that read JUST TWERK IT. A tattoo parlor next door advertised "all sterile body piercing."

Annie fell into wine for a very simple reason: "seeing how much money it could make you." Back when she was still working as a waitress at the Cavalier Golf & Yacht Club, a members-only spot created by and for old Virginia families, she served a table one evening that picked out a $550 bottle of Montrachet. "I didn't know what it was that made that bottle worth $550. I just knew that I sold that bottle, and added it to my check. All their food was already $300—now I have a $1,000 table. Now I have a $1,000 check! And that's two hundred bucks! And an hour and a half of my life? I don't mind a hundred-dollar-an-hour salary, you know? It doesn't happen all the time, but I was like, 'So what *is* it about that bottle that makes it $550?' And I just started asking questions and I became fascinated."

For Morgan and the other sommeliers I'd gotten to know, wine is a calling. They'd put neurobiology degrees and BAs in English lit aside for a life in the cellar because it was their passion. They spent weekends nerding out over great vintages of Austrian Riesling because they considered it "fulfilling," that state of being so coveted by—and the luxury of—the upper- and upper middle-classes. For Annie, a career in wine meant Chuck and her kids could breathe a little easier. This wasn't a more satisfying alternative to a desk job; it was pretty much Annie's only option. I had found the anti-Morgan. Where his oeno-fixation bordered on irrational, Annie's was practical, even pragmatic.

The Cavalier fired Annie just when she was about to take the Certified for the first time. Her boss claimed she charged a fraudulent credit card tip. "Didn't happen," said Annie. It took two months before she finally ended up as a server at Cypress Point Country Club, which she realized too late was the Franzia to Cavalier's Montrachet. Cypress Point served little besides wine from Canyon Road, which will set you back around $5.99 a bottle at your local liquor store and is likely to have a healthy dose of Mega Purple. "It was heartbreaking," Annie said. "I gained eighty-five pounds in two years." Cypress Point had no wine audience to speak of, which was depressing for Annie but seemed hardly unusual for Virginia Beach. The town had a quantity-over-quality vibe. We drove by all-you-can-eat seafood buffets, a Little Italy–themed complex called "Big Italy," and high-rise hotels so hulking that it was difficult to see the ocean from the beachfront road.

Annie decided she'd teach her customers to love wine. After her first boss left and before the new one started, she stopped ordering the Canyon Road and bought craft beers, new wines, and some bubbly. She came up with a punch menu, launched "Wine Down Wednesdays" featuring discounted bottles for $15 each, and came up with Sangria options and sparkling-wine packages for all the Cypress Point brides. She eventually talked her way into a sommelier title. "My boss didn't even know what it was," she said. "He had to go look it up and he was like, 'So you're essentially—yeah, you're a sommelier here.'"

That was a year ago. Now, Annie felt stuck in a rut. Thirty bucks for a bottle was pushing it for the country club's clientele. "I finally got Champagne in, two bottles, but no one wants to pay $50 for it," she griped as we completed our loop of the main strip. "I'm not being used to my full potential." She wasn't jiving with the rest of the Cypress Point staff. "They have that whole, 'Oh, Annie, she's a sommelier, she thinks her shit don't stink.'" That, at least, was one thing Virginia and New York had in common.

Annie pulled into the driveway of one of Virginia Beach's three Hilton Hotels so she could point out Salacia, a steakhouse under the hotel carport she considered among the nicest restaurants in town. It was really one of the only places around here that held itself to the Court's level of service, she told me. She stared at it, letting the SUV idle. "That's where I'm supposed to be. I feel it in my bones I could manage a restaurant like that very well."

I'd counted on eating dinner alone at my computer while reviewing Chilean wine laws, but Annie asked if I'd blind taste with her, so we ended up at the hotel bar of a different Hilton.

Annie and I quizzed each other and fussed over our palates. She was agitated because her nose was all stuffed up with a cold, or maybe allergies, so she'd ordered a plate of Buffalo chicken wings she hoped would burn out the congestion. My burger arrived with raw onions. *Raw* onions! Did no one grasp the magnitude of taste-bud contamination that could result from *raw onions*? I scooped them off with a knife, not willing to take the chance of touching them—my fingers might still stink the next morning.

Confidence leaked out of us with each passing hour. By this point, Annie had pretty much accepted she'd have to go to Raleigh in a few months to take the test again, for the fourth time. I was guessing I'd be joining her.

"I've been reading for three years," she wailed. "I've been studying for three years, and there's *still* stuff I don't have committed to memory. I see the question and I'm totally blank. I mean, I damn near forget my first name."

I'd had Morgan to act as my wine fairy godmother. Annie was mostly left to her own devices. There was a local tasting group she'd wanted to join, but it met Thursday afternoons, when she had to work. Getting access to the Guild's study guides was tricky because the study guides were online and Annie didn't have a computer, and even if she could find a computer, she didn't really know how to use one. Her old boss at the Cavalier had been a Certified Sommelier, but at Cypress Point, there was no one to offer advice. She'd essentially learned the proper technique for pouring, walking, talking, dressing, and folding during the exam itself. And the Court's formal system had nothing in common with Cypress Point's laid-back approach. The first time Annie took the Certified, she showed up in a white shirt, black tie, and black apron—her usual work uniform—oblivious to the fact that the Court mandated suits *only*.

It put into perspective the extent to which my training had been an embarrassment of riches. I'd been able to rely on sensory scientists, Master Sommeliers, soon-to-be Master Sommeliers, and even Master Perfumers to devise elaborate tasting routines and coach me on smelling. I had collectors who'd opened up their cellars so I could try bottles I never could have afforded on my own, plus all the free wine I could drink (and then some) from the hundreds of distributors who flock to New York, the most diverse wine market in the world. Annie had been doing it all by herself, and there was no plan B.

That night, as I struggled to get to sleep, I saw flash cards whenever I closed my eyes. Morgan had sent me an email: "Make sure you get sleep and are well hydrated the day beforehand! Failing to prepare is preparing to fail!" Easier said than done when the rumble of fighter jets made it sound like one was about to land in the hotel parking lot. *It's just a stupid test,* I repeated to myself to calm my nerves as I ransacked the bathroom for something that could be used as earplugs. I realized, though, that I wasn't just nervous for myself. I worried about Annie. If I failed, life would go on. I would take it again. I had no one depending on me. For Annie, though, passing the test was something that could fundamentally change her family's life. It was not just a stupid test at all.

We were both in bad shape when Annie picked me up the next morning. She felt self-conscious in her new suit. She hadn't been able to decide whether to brush her teeth, and now she regretted having gone ahead with the toothpaste. Coffee had also been an ordeal. Hot, iced, or nothing? She'd gone iced, but was that the right call?

I hadn't slept much thanks to the sound of freedom. I woke up at dawn to iron my blazer, review some more, and properly time my teeth brushing so I'd leave my tongue enough time to recover. Blind tasting would be the first section of the day, and I wanted to have an appetite and a neutral palate going in. Everything was going according to plan, right up until the second I scalded the front of my tongue. *Daggone tea.* I tried to find some wine to gargle with, just to get oriented to this horrible new normal, but the mini bar was useless and when I called room service to order a glass of Chardonnay, the woman on the phone paused for a very long time before saying it was a bit early for wine now wasn't it, so she'd have to check with her manager. I'd also had my corkscrew confiscated by airport security. My new one didn't have quite the same grip, which rattled me. I felt like I didn't know myself: Who was this person losing her cool over a *corkscrew*? As we drove to the test, Annie pointed out a brick apartment complex behind the Birdneck Food Mart, where one of the Oceana fighter jets had recently crashed. It seemed like a bad omen.

When we pulled into Zoës, a clapboard building behind an office park, it looked like we'd arrived at a convention of undertakers.

Somber men and women in black suits milled around the parking lot. Most of them seemed to be in their twenties. When I took the Court's Introductory exam, I'd sat next to a Pilates instructor and a medical devices engineer. Here, almost all the examinees worked in restaurants. Alex, a blond twenty-four-year-old, sold wine at a restaurant in the suburbs of New Jersey. Devin was a server at TAO, a mecca for models in New York. Sean, a superhip bartender wearing vintage Gucci loafers with no socks, had driven up from Richmond with his fiancée, a Miley Cyrus lookalike who managed three different restaurants. She referred to herself and Sean as a "restaurant power couple." A few women worked at Zoës. "I Flonased this morning," one of them bragged. The lone civilian was a woman named JJ, an amateur pastry chef in her forties who designed research satellites for NASA.

At eight o'clock, Annie and I took seats across from each other in one of Zoës maroon booths. I was instantly worried about the lighting (dark) and color of the upholstery (red). These were not ideal tasting conditions.

Stop, I told myself. *Nerves destroy your confidence, and you need total confidence to tune in to these tastes and smells.* I closed my eyes while I waited for everyone else to file into their seats. *Breeeeeathe. Go blank.*

Morgan had summoned the wisdom of martial-arts legend Bruce Lee to advise me on how to tackle blind tasting. "Empty your mind," Morgan's email began, quoting Lee. "Be formless, shapeless, like water. You put water into a cup, it becomes the cup. . . . Be water, my friend." Advanced martial-arts masters are said to enter a state of complete mental clarity, or "unconscious consciousness," called *mushin*, meaning "no mind." They shed their thoughts, emotions, fears, and ego so that they are able to receive the experience before them in a pure way, free of interference. In this state of "perfect unguardedness," they are fully aware, they witness, and they react. *Mushin* is often likened to the state *mizu no kokoro*, or "mind like water," in which the mind becomes still, like the surface of a pond, so it can reflect exactly what it's shown. Nerves and feelings create ripples. "Ultimately," Morgan riffed in his email, "tasting isn't about the wine. It's about you and how well you've honed your ability to detect its truth."

Even though I'd been bemused by (and, okay, skeptical of) the martial-arts analogy when Morgan first suggested it, I had to admit that there were parallels with blind tasting. As crazy as it sounds, thinking about it in terms of the Zen mind-set had helped. Blind tasting does require you to "empty your mind" so you can be totally aware and receptive. You have to let go of doubts, fears, and feelings so you can absorb the tiniest details of the present. You have to shut off the part of your head that is tempted to rely on shortcuts, like brands, or what you've messed up in the past, or whether you're likely to be poured two Viogniers in a row. Much of what's thrown at us in our everyday lives is meant to play to our cognitive biases. With tasting, you can succeed only by discarding them. You have to get to the true experience, unmediated by preconceptions or the filter of your own ego. I found it refreshing to consciously make an effort to contemplate the world as it is, not as I imagined it.

One of the four Master Sommeliers got up to make a very brief introduction. We had forty-five minutes for the first two parts of the exam: We'd have a pair of wines to blind taste, then forty questions on the written test. "Think long, think wrong," he said. And—begin.

I picked up my glass of white wine and inhaled deeply, without swirling, to capture the aromas that had gathered above the wine while it sat still. Its scent was subtle. Citrus, more savory than sweet. Briny. Like seawater with a dollop of sour cream. I began ticking through boxes in the printed-out grid we'd been given. Straw color. Grapefruit, lemon, pear, tarragon. I hesitated at the category marked "aromatic flowers." I circled "slight/none," then crossed that out and put down "dominant." I smelled the glass again. I crossed out "dominant" and put "slight/none" again. *Think long, think wrong. No. Do not doubt yourself. Experience and record. No mind.* Olfactory fatigue was setting in. I sniffed the red wine to try to shake my nose back into action, then went back to the white.

There was—I cringed even thinking it—a minerality to the wine. It couldn't be . . . could it? I sipped. Definitely dry. No new oak. Moderate-to-moderate-plus acid, moderate alcohol, little phenolic bitterness. More sour than ripe-fruity on the finish; a nudge for Old World over New World. I *tthup—tthup—tthupped* the wine along with the mouths around me. It sounded like one hundred sucking drains were being emptied at the same time.

Initial conclusion: cool or moderate climate (because of the lower alcohol, higher acidity), Chardonnay (because of the pear, citrus notes, and moderate-intensity aromatics), Old World (because of the mineral dominance, sour finish, and herbal, stone quality). I *ttthh-huuuupppped* again. Final conclusion—I couldn't believe what I was about to put down. But it had to be. Burgundy, I wrote. Chablis, one to three years in age. I said a silent thank-you to Johan Lundström and moved on.

I inhaled the aroma of the red wine and exhaled a deep sigh of relief. I had this. It couldn't be anything else. Ruby color. Ripe raspberry, strawberry, blackberry, plum, blueberry, cassis, with jammy characteristics. A hint of, yes, pyrazines. Vanilla, cinnamon, baking spices, and drying tannins between my lip and gum—definitely some new oak. I skipped over the category for "game, blood, cured meat, leather," which just sounded disgusting and didn't apply. Dry, with sweet tannins, moderate-to-moderate-plus alcohol, moderate acidity. Final conclusion: Cabernet Sauvignon, California, one to three years in age.

I traded my tasting grid for the theory exam and noticed Annie, pale and intent, already filling in her answer sheet. The test was partially multiple choice, mostly short answer, and anything but obvious. One question listed producers—Château Rayas, Giacomo Conterno, Dr. Loosen—and instructions to name the primary grape varietal used in their wines. Name two sub-regions of Chianti. Order these Californian American Viticultural Areas from north to south.

What is the main grape varietal of Switzerland? "Chasselas," I wrote down, grateful to Annie for making us review that the evening before. How many vineyards can you attach to the name of a Premier Cru Chablis? If you buy a wine for $20 and you get five pours per bottle, how much do you have to sell your glasses for if you want to get a 25 percent cost of goods sold? What river is next to Hermitage? Could I possibly pass?

Annie and I were the last two people to hand in our tests. We filed back out into the parking lot, where people were attempting to reverse-engineer what had been in each glass.

Our guesses were all over the place. People had called the red wine Aussie Shiraz, French Syrah, Nebbiolo, Tempranillo, Malbec, Cabernet Sauvignon. "A lot of people did Cabernet," said Devin, who'd finished early and taken a more comprehensive poll. For whites, he'd heard Pinot Grigio, Chenin Blanc, Sauvignon Blanc, Chardonnay. I found three others who'd gone Chardonnay from Chablis, including Alex, the guy from New Jersey. Annie had considered it before settling on Chenin.

Each of us had a specific time by which to return to Zoës for our service test, but we clung to one another and didn't budge from the restaurant's entrance. In part, we wanted to give moral support. Mostly, we hoped the people coming out of the exam would leak details about what went down inside.

It seemed ugly. Four at a time, the examinees went into Zoës. And four at a time, they staggered out like they'd warded off body blows.

"I-I thought I was going to cry," said Aaron, who worked at a hotel restaurant in D.C. He was ashen.

Annie told me later she'd seen JJ, the NASA satellite designer, run out while sniffling back tears. "Allergies," JJ insisted.

Between fees, books, travel, and practice wine, the test takers had generally invested about $3,000 each in prepping. They were pissed that all that money was on the line, and frustrated that a raise or new job was slipping away. "I really need this," Annie said at one point, more to herself than to me. She and the others spent almost every day of their lives on the floor. But the service exam was at a higher level than anything they'd ever encountered before.

"No one asks questions like that! No one *ever* asks questions like that. I had some weird-ass wine questions," one guy fumed. "That shit was set *up*."

The Miley Cyrus doppelgänger sympathized. The Champagne her judge had ordered was totally confusing.

Annie appeared alarmed. "I'm not very well versed in my Champagne producers, just because I don't have my hands on them all the time," she whispered to me.

She was right to be concerned. At our level, the judges were likely to test us on France's major Champagne houses, wine heavyweights who produce a great deal of the world's most coveted sparkling wine. More specifically, we'd need to know the names of each producer's *tête de cuvée* ("head of the vintage," roughly translated). These wines are the producers' premium, higher-priced bottlings, which are usually released only in years when the grape harvest is outstanding. You might buy a bottle of Moët & Chandon for someone you like. But you'd only buy a bottle of Moët's *tête de cuvée*, Dom Pérignon, for someone you love. A 1996 Dom Pérignon costs $650 at Marea, more than ten times the price of Cypress Point's most expensive bubbly.

Annie had never tasted, served, or been in the same room as these wines. It's not that she didn't know Champagne, it's just that Cypress Point wasn't in the Dom demographic. Just a few minutes before, Annie had been raving about a new sparkling wine, Blanc de Bleu, that had been a huge hit with the Cypress Point brides, ever since she added it to her list. If Veuve Clicquot's La Grande Dame is the Queen Elizabeth of Champagnes, then Blanc de Bleu is the Disney princess. The wine is turquoise, flavored with blueberry extract, and so cartoonish-looking that the company has to clarify on the label that fruit—"premium grape"—was involved in making the beverage. Annie had no practical reason, given her job, to know these *cuvées*. She had no sense memory to associate with their flavor, no idea what the French names meant, and no confidence in how to pronounce them. They were, for all intents and purposes, just sounds she had to memorize and repeat.

I immediately stopped reviewing cocktails and started quizzing Annie.

"What's Laurent-Perrier's *cuvée*?"

Silence. "I don't know. Let me see again? Grande—how do you say that? *Seek?*"

Grand Siècle. We tried a few more. Taittinger makes Comtes de Champagne. Moët & Chandon makes Dom Pérignon. Laurent-Perrier . . .

"Holy shit. Laurent-Perrier. Um. Seecle—"

"Grand Siècle," I filled in. "It means 'grand century.'" I asked if she knew any Laurens. Maybe she could make up a story to remember the wine?

"I do know a Lauren." Annie thought a moment. "Laurent-Perrier . . . Laurent-Perrier . . . Laurent-Perrier . . . My friend Lauren has a grand big ole butt." She laughed for the first time that day. "Okay, so, the grand ass of the century! Laurent-Perrier. Grand Siècle."

We stopped when it was my turn for service. Annie gave me a hug.

"Be one with the tray," she said gravely.

The exam proctor stopped me at the entrance to Zoës. I was to serve Master Keith, and I was to address him as Master Keith, the proctor informed me. Master Keith would be having a 2002 Sir Winston Churchill *cuvée*.

I felt my stomach tighten with nerves. Everything until now had led me to believe that I would have to open and pour a bottle of sparkling wine. And yet until now, there had been a chance—a small, barely perceptible chance, a chance that was really more of a hope—that the Court would ask me to do something else besides open a bottle of sparkling wine.

Sparkling-wine service was the standard Certified test, sure. But with all the changes in tasting grids and stricter standards and so on and so forth, I was hoping the Court might mix things up. My red-wine explosion at the Young Sommelier Competition may have been bad. But my track record for opening sparkling wine was even worse.

Weeks of practice had only revealed how many different things could go wrong between the moment when I loosened the cage and when I poured the bubbly into the glass. There was the cork that shot past my temple into the ceiling. The bottle that overflowed with Prosecco the second I opened it. The bottle that shot a cork past my temple into the ceiling *and* overflowed with Prosecco the second I opened it. The two bottles that wouldn't open at all. "You are not certified to serve people because you might kill them," Morgan's friend Mia, also a sommelier, finally mustered after she watched my technique.

With a brief prayer that Master Keith had a good insurance policy, I stepped into the dining room.

Master Keith was seated alone at a table set for four. Two of the plates were covered with white printouts that read LADY. Master Keith said that he and his brother were out with their wives.

"How are you?" Master Keith asked. He was thin, with slicked-back black hair, graying at the temples.

I answered in a squeaky voice so high-pitched I could barely hear it. "I'm doing wonderfully. How are you?" I followed Morgan's advice: Answer the question fully. I hoped Master Keith felt our common humanity radiating through.

Master Keith repeated his order for the 2002 Sir Winston Churchill *cuvée*. "Who makes that again?" Master Keith pretended to wonder.

"Pol Roger, sir." First hurdle cleared. I walked clockwise around the table, folded two serviettes at my station, marked the table with the glasses, brought over the ice bucket, and presented the wine, giving its year, *cuvée,* and producer. The bottle I held was a dummy, some inexpensive Cava meant to stand in for the good stuff, since the Court wasn't about to spring for a few dozen *tête de cuvées.* I tried to appear calm as I brought the loaded weapon to my chest. I curled one hand over the barrel, and another over the body of the bottle.

Master Keith watched. I twisted and I prayed. With a beautiful, quiet fart, the bottle surrendered its cork.

As I poured the wine—first for the women, then Master Keith's brother, and finally Master Keith—Master Keith prattled off questions. What were other good vintages for Champagne? Could I suggest some Irish whiskies? He was having the plank-grilled salmon. What might be nice with that? What else did I have from that part of California? Hmm. What about an Australian wine made with the same grape varietal?

Something strange and unexpected was happening: It was going well.

I was shooting the questions out of the air. I'd never felt such command over the material. I was standing firmly and moving with confidence. I was actually being charming. I gave him white wine recommendations from Santa Barbara, Sonoma, and Yarra Valley as he challenged me to see how deep my expertise would go. While I arranged the bottle on ice, we made small talk about where he should eat next time he visits New York. I suggested that since Master Keith obviously enjoyed quality Champagne, like this lovely Sir Winston Churchill, he might enjoy Marta, a sommelier hangout beloved for its reasonably priced Champagne. He was smiling. I was smiling.

Even though my floor experience was limited to trailing at Aureole and Marea—plus my kitchen table and the Chaîne's competition, if you could count that—something like muscle memory kicked in. It was like learning the steps of a dance. The first thirty-two times you rehearse, you have to think about where to put your feet. Then the thirty-third time, it just clicks. Your body moves. It hadn't happened to me before this moment. And just in time, everything flowed.

I fielded a few more questions about cocktail recipes and aperitif options. Then, just like a guest at a table in a restaurant, Master Keith thanked me. He said he'd think it all over.

While I waited for Annie to do her service round, I sat outside next to a man in his forties, a wine distributor who was so nervous about going in for service that his hands trembled.

The day had left a bad taste in my mouth, one that hadn't come from the morning's wines. I may have been feeling more confident in my performance, but I was less confident in the Court.

The Court of Master Sommeliers prides itself on maintaining high standards among wine professionals. It deliberately hews to formal service etiquette, assuming that once its examinees master the highest form, they can always tone it down. Fine. I had no qualms there. I love standards as much as, if not more than, the next person.

What troubled me was the total disconnect between the Court's vision of wine service and the real world. We were like members of a forgotten bacchanalian tribe preparing for a wine utopia, where only people with money to burn ate out, speeches about quartzite soil were a turn-on, and everyone got their own ice bucket. How many New York restaurants—save maybe Eleven Madison Park or places of that caliber—had given tables their own ice buckets since Nelson Rockefeller's days? Who wanted to banish the extra tables in favor of frozen water on a pedestal or make staff trip around them during service? Annie, Devin, Alex, me, even Morgan: We were all training ourselves to maintain a set of standards that were, for the most part, utterly unrealistic in today's dining rooms. And as Annie had discovered in the course of three years and at least a thousand dollars, there was no natural, organic way to learn these rules. What happened in the service exam didn't look anything like what most people encountered in their restaurants. Sure, maybe the restaurants should look more like the Court. But shouldn't the Court also look more like the restaurants?

For all the talk of raising the quality of service in the wine world, I also couldn't help but wonder if the Court was, in practice, rewarding people for the exact thing we were supposed to be fighting: lazy palates. To pass the test, Annie and I, along with everyone else in Virginia Beach, had been required to memorize *tête de cuvée* Champagnes that, we were instructed, ranked among the best wines in the world. We didn't necessarily need to know *why* these bottles—or others in the canon—were the best. We'd never tasted them, so we certainly couldn't decide for ourselves if they were any good. They were the best for the simple reason that we'd been told they were the best.

In other disciplines, be it art history or modern poetry, students are also required to learn the classics. But they actually get to experience the works for themselves. They analyze Picasso's brushstrokes against Botticelli's, or Eliot's rhythms against Yeats's, and develop their own theory of whether a piece is great and why.

We winos were merely repeating the party line. We continued to inflate the canon without firsthand knowledge of these supposedly miraculous bottles. Some people would go on to try the wines and form an opinion for themselves. But at those prices, most of us wouldn't. We'd recommend these wines because others recommended them to us. This wasn't the way to make sommeliers into true wine stewards. It was the way to make wine stereotypes and perpetuate the same old ideas.

I thought about what Paul Grieco had said the first time we met at Terroir. He'd railed that the wine world's current approach to service was a failure. More sommeliers, more books, more fancy titles. Yet not much more wine was being served. I wondered if it was time for a new approach.

Annie was a total mess when she came out of the exam.

"I wasn't good enough. I don't think it was good enough," she said. She needed to get out of there, and so we climbed back into her car to go for a drive. She took me to a spot on the beach where she and Chuck had gotten married. Her two youngest kids had been their ring bearer and flower girl. She called Chuck. "Damn, man. I just need to be faster with those wine recommendations," she said into her phone. He said something back and she looked even more upset after hanging up. "Louis *frickin* Jadot," she said, and slapped the steering wheel. She'd blanked on the name when she had to give a pairing. "It's fight or flight. And I went flight. It was like, '*Alllllllllll* of the information has left my brain.'" We passed by the brick shell of the Cavalier Hotel, a luxurious property that was being renovated. "I'd wanted to gun for an opening in the new place in April, when it opens," she said, already expecting the worst. "Louis *FRICKIN* Jadot." We got tacos at a smoky bar near the beach, then circled back to Zoës. "For the love of God and everything holy in Jesus's name I hope I pass," Annie said as she pulled into the parking lot. "Why couldn't I think of a wine? I wrote the freaking list. Côte de Beaune. Côte de Beaune! Louis. Freaking. Jadot. I should have just gone with Louis. Freaking. Jadot."

We all assembled in the rear of the Zoës dining room to hear the results. Someone from the restaurant was handing out sparkling wine, but we were all too nervous to drink it.

Master Keith took the floor. He gave it to us straight. "The statistics were born out." Many had not passed.

The tastings and theory had been pretty darn good. Service needed work. In short, we were too friendly, too cheap, too casual. Don't introduce yourself unless asked, he reminded us. Don't ignore your guests' tastes—if they like fancy wines and are willing to splurge, don't dump them with a pedestrian gimme wine. "When you have a guest who's drinking a *tête de cuvée* Champagne that would be $300, $200 on your wine list, why are you selling them a $20, $30, $40 bottle of wine? . . . It's like, 'Wow! They've got some money! Let's spend and have some fun with them!'" Don't be so vulgar as to mention price unless asked. "You would never talk about price in front of the queen. She'd be like, 'What? Do you know how much money I have? Off with your head.'"

They started to read off the names of the people who had passed. Alex from New Jersey had passed. The waitress who'd Flonased. Annie Truhlar.

"Me?" Annie looked stunned.

"Are you Annie?" asked Master Jared, checking the name on the piece of paper.

"Oh my goodness." She took her certificate. "Oh my God." She shook Master Keith's hand, then Master Cathy's, then Master Jared's. "This is my third time. Thank you so much. Oh my God." She hugged me. She had tears welling up. She stared at her certificate. "Oh my God. I can't believe it."

"Angelo Perez."

"Holy crap," said Annie, still examining the piece of paper.

"Sean Raposa."

"Oh. My. God," said Annie, rubbing her fingers over her name.

"Bianca Bosker."

"OH MY GOSH!" Annie looked up and threw her arms around me. "Yes! YES!"

Our Masters handed out purple pins emblazoned with the Court's symbol, which indicated our status as Certified Sommeliers. We attached them to our jackets. I texted Morgan a picture of my new accessory.

"Welcome to the club!" he immediately wrote back. "Slash the greatest profession on earth."

After calling Chuck and screaming into the phone with glee, Annie piled Alex, Devin, JJ, and me into her Yukon for a drink on the strip.

Neither Devin nor JJ had passed. Master Jared thought the pop of JJ's sparkling wine had been too loud. "It wasn't a Queen Elizabeth fart, it was a peasant woman's fart," grumbled JJ, who thought he failed her because she worked at NASA, not a restaurant. Alex's grader had written "*bare, bare pass*" at the top of his feedback sheet, but he was still ecstatic. He'd completely bombed his red wine, calling it Nebbiolo, and passed only because he'd nailed his white. He called it Chardonnay, from Chablis. The Court never reveals the exam wines, but by now I was sure as I could be without seeing the labels that my calls were spot-on.

The purple pins bestowed a certain air of authority, and Annie, Alex, and I flaunted our new status with confidence and just a little snobbery.

"I would only flush it half the time," Alex said when the subject of South African wine came up.

He ordered a wine made by a producer in Charlottesville and *tthupped* at the glass. "It's drinkable," he decided.

Annie corrected Alex when he confused "meritage" and "hermitage." "Hermitage is in the Rhône," she reminded him. Then she asked the waiter to check when the bartender had opened the by-the-glass Merlot Devin had ordered. It tasted oxidized, like it had been open awhile. It was opened three days before, our server confirmed. Annie glared with pleasure at this news. They peppered the server with questions about the kinds of Irish whiskey that were on the menu—virtually the same questions, verbatim, Master Keith had asked during my exam.

Annie was already giddy at the thought of leveraging her pass for a raise.

"They are going to pay me or I'm walking. They are going to *pay*," she informed us, toasting with a Mojito. She wouldn't let her new Certified status change her, though.

"I'm going to keep my good personality," she decided. "I'm not going to be a total bitch."

Alex shook his head. "Oh," he said. "I'm going to be a *total* bitch. You don't even know."

CHAPTER ELEVEN

The Floor

Paul Grieco didn't so much ask me to work for him as dare me to.

I'd been meeting with Terroir's mad genius creator every few weeks for more than six months. We'd sit in his underground lair, the office below Terroir Tribeca, debating everything from wine lists to the orgy that is La Paulée. I liked his uncensored take on wine. Some afternoons he'd go off on "esoteric juice." Another time he'd rant about Jesus's first miracle, turning water into wine, which Paul thought was a very unfortunate miracle as far as miracles go. "He made the whole thing seem fucking easy."

Now that I'd passed my Certified exam, I was planning to broach the idea of joining him at Terroir. He beat me to it. Paul wrote me an email to say that while passing the exam and writing about wine were great and all, didn't I want to "effect change on the ground in a very real and fundamental way"? "Didn't you want to change the world when you were young?" he asked.

This was El Grieco's way: Rev up the charm, lull you into a false sense of complacency, and then stun you into cooperation.

I'd watched him do it at Terroir. One Wednesday night, after one of our chats, he stepped out on the floor to help tend to customers. A table of twentysomethings nodded as Paul greeted them, smiled back while he smiled at them, and then they sat with jaws agape as he started to scream. "*That* is a whacked-out fucking journey!" he bellowed, stabbing at a wine on the list with his finger. "A whacked-out. Fucking. Journey. But!"—here he lowered his voice and leaned in, like he was offering them a special deal and didn't want anyone else to hear—"*I'll* take *you* on that journey. You wanna go on a journey that's a whacked-out fucking journey?"

Of course they did. So did the table next to them, who'd been listening the whole time. A perky blonde tapped me on the shoulder. "We just wanted to know—what's that wine?"

I wanted to go on a whacked-out fucking journey too. So naturally, I wanted to work for Paul.

Since embracing the world of wine, I'd plunged into tasting groups, competitions, distributor dinners, Master Sommelier boot camps, wine societies, wine clubs, wine auctions, and wine study groups. I'd dissected cadaver heads and lugged cases down ladders and eaten dirt and probably done irreparable damage to my tooth enamel. I'd been driven by a desire to understand what made cork dorks tick, what came with a more sensory-aware existence, what it was that made wine so endlessly fascinating, and which aspects of the bullshit-prone industry were meaningful. With all of these questions answered, the last challenge that remained was for me to take what I'd learned and set out on the restaurant floor.

When I first started out on this wine journey, I had aspirations of joining one of the high temples of wine—places like Eleven Madison Park, where sommeliers upheld the Court's code of conduct in crystal- and linen-bedecked dining rooms. I'd badgered Morgan and Victoria to let me shadow them at Aureole and Marea, in part so I could pass the Certified test, and in part because I was hoping they'd help me land a spot at one of the city's Michelin-starred gems. Such a path now seemed open, thanks to that work and the connections I'd made.

But as I considered my options when I returned from Virginia Beach, I realized that these restaurants had lost their original appeal. My experience with the Court and Annie and Paul had changed my outlook. I was frustrated with the Court's regimented answers and strict policies. They seemed to gloss over the complex realities of wine and its drinkers. Annie had found a multitude of ways, beyond the Court's formal playbook, to delight people with wine in a manner that worked in the real world. I also knew that the bacchanals of Paulée-goers and wine PXs would keep sloshing along just fine without me. In the rarefied dining rooms, I'd be preaching to the converted. I wanted to seek out the doubters, the oenophobes, the people who rolled their eyes when they heard "forest floor" used to praise a Pinot Noir, as I once would have.

From our multisensory makeup to the elusive nature of quality, everything I'd seen suggested that the formal Court-endorsed take on proper service was too narrow. The correct way wasn't necessarily the *right* way. Wine was already hugely intimidating. Placing it on a pedestal wasn't going to help. At Terroir, almost anything goes. Here was a place where I could marshal everything I'd discovered about people and wine to give others the kind of transformative experience I'd had.

Paul embraced an utterly outlaw, borderline-insane approach that he hoped would attract all comers to his beloved "grape juice with alcohol." If Marea was the wine shrine in the holy city where sommeliers, monklike, retreated to mull the mysteries of fine Burgundy, Paul was the feverish evangelical preacher speaking in tongues and performing outdoor baptisms. Quite literally, as it turns out. On a cross-country road trip a few summers ago, Paul put on a priest's robes, installed a baptismal font outside a church in North Carolina, and, bottle in hand, baptized people into his Church of Riesling (after cleansing them of the sins of Chardonnay). Part maniac, part prophet, Paul treated his Terroir wine bars as though they were, in the apt words of *New York* magazine, his "padded cell and laboratory."

Missionaries aren't rare in the wine world. At L'Apicio, Joe Campanale had also espoused a philosophy with his list: He wanted to introduce New Yorkers to organic and handcrafted wines from artisanal producers. But Joe, like most people, had run the restaurant like a rational person. Paul was willing to piss off his business partner, alienate his guests, and face down mutiny by his staff just to push the world toward the wines he believed in. He closed restaurants rather than compromise. He refused to carry wines that didn't move him, even if "cougar juice" would sell. He banned rosé until one of his somms begged him to reconsider, warning Tribeca moms would get out their pitchforks if it wasn't on the list by May. Around the time I met Paul, he had recently split with his partner, and the chain of Terroir wine bars had shrunk from five to two.

Never mind that. Because Paul was always concocting new schemes to expand the flock. Teaming up with Amazon for Terroir-curated wines, or why not Starbucks. Writing a book—sixteen actually, with sixteen chapters each, released one a year for sixteen years that in the end "all fit together to create some sort of art piece." Six-packs of Terroir-brand wine in a can. T-shirts with winemakers' portraits. Fuck Madeira night, let's do Madeira *month*. Bring in the German wine queen to guest somm!

And you cannot ignore El Grieco. He rallies his entire being to be sure that people pay attention. He will yell at you the moment you step through the door at Terroir—HOW ARE YOU DOING WELCOME!—and before you leave—HAVE A GREAT NIGHT THANK YOU CHEERS! Years ago, he stalked the floor of Danny Meyer's Gramercy Tavern in a checked suit that, though I haven't seen it myself, I've been assured was "fucking hideous." (Paul's fashion philosophy: "If, upon first reflection, you look at it and say it clashes, then I've accomplished my goal.") The Terroir Employee Manual prohibits "profane language." Paul doesn't give a fuck. Instead of "thank you," he says "rock 'n' roll." "Yes" is "rock 'n' fucking roll." A consulting company rented out Terroir's back room to celebrate replacing the *i* in their name with an exclamat!on po!nt, and the organizer made the mistake of asking Paul if he would tone down the obscenities. "Well, that should be fucking easy," Paul snapped when the guy was out of earshot. He radiates charisma, is tirelessly social, and manages, perplexingly, to be handsome, even with the weird beard.

The traditionalists who've devoted their lives to upholding wine's rules impugn Paul's motives. They call him an attention whore. In the gossipy way of the wine world, they whisper that he doesn't *really* love wine. "He just wants to use it as a vessel to communicate," a sommelier cattily complained.

So what if he does? Paul communicates well. He wants people to drink wine, not fetishize it. And Paul's wine list, the Book, makes readers thirsty for his bottles. A young somm told me the Book was what convinced him to work in wine. And for what it's worth, it's the only wine list that's ever made me laugh. The only wine list I've ever kept reading beyond what was strictly necessary and actually *wanted* to keep reading. There are shirtless pictures of Putin, screeds about street fairs, inside jokes, homages to winemakers, salutes to Lou Reed, guest contributors, rants about Trump, Nietzsche quotes, facts about sherry, and lines like "Pinot Noir is the Lindsay Lohan of grapes," all cut up to look like an issue of *i-D* magazine circa 1984. Some choice excerpts:

> If Jesus and Satan had a son (I guess the first question should be: in which state would Jesus and Satan get married?), he would be called Serge Hochar. . . . He is my savior and my tormentor. . . . He crafts heavenly grape juice that is sometimes not appropriate for human consumption. An hour in the company of Serge is like a walk in Nirvana or a weekly communal shower at Rikers Island. Suffice it to say, I am in love with Serge Hochar.

> To say Riesling is great is as obvious as saying Vladimir Putin is the Michael Corleone of Russia. . . . Balance . . . even Philippe Petit wonders in amazement. . . . Longevity . . . even Moses would be considered a young'un next to these wines. Sexiness . . . well, let's just say Eve would have dropped the Apple if there were a bottle of Riesling nearby.
>
> Barack Obama needs a glass of Riesling. Why? . . . Because Riesling will provide clarity, which you need in spades. . . . Because emotion is not what we want. We want leadership. And leadership demands risks. And risks demand a firm backbone. And now you seem to have the spine of a California Chardonnay—hollow, lifeless, character-less.
>
> The entire frickin' country of Greece needs a glass of Riesling. Why? . . . Because a complete turnabout is required to bring your country into the modern era of sound economic policy and only a glass of Riesling will snap you out of your Mediterranean slumber induced by too much suntan lotion and remembrances of past greatnesses. . . . Because the E.U. is spanking you for hitting a deficit of 10.7% of GDP in 2009 . . . and nothing soothes the pain like a cool glass of Riesling nectar. . . . Because paying back the E.U. and the I.M.F. 110 billion euros is going to require saving quite a few drachmae and there is no better bang for the buck than a glass of Riesling.

The Book ranges from Bordeaux classics to weird Lebanese rosé. Paul's wine philosophy cannot be so easily summed up as to call him a champion of natural wines, or small wineries, or hip alt producers. The Gospel according to Paul: Blessed are the bottles that are humble. ("I happened to grow up in a world where I loved the pariahs. I loved the outcasts. I loved things that were not the norm," he told me.) Blessed are those that are true, for they will be poured. ("Every time that I have a wine that meets that definition of yumminess—is true to place, is true to grape, is true to man—it brings me back to a very, very soulful place.") Blessed are those that transcend and enlighten, for they will make a Terroirist, as Paul's acolytes are known. ("We want to hold an object out there for our guests to reach toward, so when they leave here . . . they've learned something.") Blessed are the meek and undiscovered—the underdog grape from Croatia, the offbeat Greek thing that needs to be explained. ("I want to be a storyteller, not a cork puller.")

Terroir, the Book, Paul's tastes, his attitude—all of it has been a hit. Besides Paul's James Beard Award for Outstanding Wine Service, Terroir was named World's Best Wine Bar by *The World of Fine Wine*, the oeno-version of the *New York Review of Books*. A constant rotation of sommeliers, distributors, critics, and wine writers pass through Terroir's metal doors for a dose of Paul and whatever he's pouring. It's the training ground for ambitious somms who believe in a different kind of service: more human, less robotic. I met a sommelier who said seeing Paul with a big RIESLING (temporary) tattoo slapped on his arm had changed everything. "I was like, 'That guy is awesome as fuck,'" he said. "And that was the first time I realized, 'Wow, you can be punk *and* wine.'" Paul's staff has come from New York's most celebrated restaurants—Per Se, Gramercy Tavern, Union Square Cafe—to follow the True Path at El Grieco's "elitist wine bar for everyone." And now I was one of them.

You wouldn't know it from Paul's punk-rock aesthetic, but he grew up in the oldest of old-school restaurants, where waiters flambéd tableside and suits were a must. His earliest memories are of polishing glassware and forks at La Scala, Toronto's first formal Italian joint and the brainchild of the senior-most Grieco patriarch, Paul's grandfather. (He might have lent Paul his outlaw spirit: Rumor has it Paul's grandfather ran liquor over the U.S. border during Prohibition.)

Paul had zero interest in working in the family business. He wanted to be a professional soccer player, preferably playing for an Italian team as center midfielder—"I have to be in control"—and made it as far as the tryouts for the U.S. Olympic team until he was told that he was disqualified, obviously, because he is Canadian and this was, you know, *the Olympics.* He went to St. Michael's, a Catholic college at the University of Toronto, where he focused on hospitality—practicing it, not studying it. He was one half of a kilt-wearing duo called the Torments, who spent every Monday through Thursday planning an epic British New Wave dance fest. Fridays they executed, Saturdays they returned props, and Sundays were the day of rest. Perhaps not surprisingly, Paul was eventually asked to leave. He managed to accumulate so few credits in four years that if he went back to college now, he'd need two full years to get a degree. "Yeah, I was a massive fuck-up," he said. "But I had a blast."

After getting kicked out of school, Paul had no choice but to work in the family business, interest or no. He spent a summer at La Scala, then Paul's father shipped him off to Italy to learn about wine by bunking up with the first families of Italian *vino.* Paul left home an ignoramus, with a take-it-or-leave-it attitude toward wine. He returned a "relative genius." He'd found his thing: Wine combined art, history, religion, the culture of the table. "I'm like, 'Here it is. In studying wine, I get to do all the other stuff that I love.'" After a short stint at La Scala, he moved to New York. He's never left. He learned the rites of wine at the city's culinary landmarks—Remi, Gotham, Gramercy Tavern, and, briefly, Bouley. At Bouley, Chef David

Bouley's gilded French outpost, he survived twenty-eight days and one panic attack thanks to "an absolutely horse's ass" of a general manager, who took it upon himself to humble a supremely cocky Paul. It remains, Paul said, "the worst fucking experience in my life."

In 2004, he went back to throwing his own parties. With Paul in charge of wine and Chef Marco Canora in the kitchen, the pair launched Hearth, a cozy Tuscan restaurant. Then came Terroir E.ViL (aka East Village) and four more wine bars. After twelve years, they split. Now, every weekday, between nine in the morning and around midnight each evening, you can find fifty-one-year-old Paul in a closet disguised as an office in the basement of Terroir Tribeca, next to a sock monkey, several corked bottles of wine awaiting return to distributors, and a shelf stocked with Band-Aids colored bright blue so they'll be seen if they fall into the food. He remains a man on a mission. Possessed. In the words of El Grieco: "This is not a fucking hobby."

I was given a Terroir T-shirt to wear during my shift. Gone were the pencil skirts and blazers of Aureole and Marea. The first thing I needed to do was familiarize myself with Terroir's by-the-glass offerings. Paul sat me down at the bar counter one evening and made me try all seventy-seven wines in one go. And then he set me loose.

Most nights there were three of us on the floor, plus a runner to water people, *mise* tables, and drop food. Terroir Tribeca seats around seventy-five, and with our slim front-of-house staff we all did more than one thing. In any other restaurant, we'd have been sommeliers. Here, we were somms, servers, bussers, hosts, and runners all at once, though our main job was serving wine. Our by-the-glass section ran longer than many restaurants' full wine lists, so every time people ordered a glass of wine, it was like helping them pick out a bottle.

Each of us had been attracted by Paul's fervor and his disdain for convention. Justine, who'd worked with Morgan at one of his first somm jobs in the city, loved that she could talk to people like her—young, hip, into food—on their level, with real words, and without pretention. Jason, a mechanical aerospace engineer turned architect turned photographer turned aspiring programmer, raved that Paul was the "real deal." The other wine pros "are just full of shit," we lectured Sabrina, who was our runner most nights. She had helped with Terroir's marketing efforts, but after a few years of knowing Paul felt the tug of getting her hands on wine.

Terroir might have been unorthodox, but as long as Paul was breathing it would not be unorganized. The tone of my conversations with Paul changed dramatically as soon as I started working for him. He'd ascend from the basement on chaotic nights to pitch in with service and scream at us about whatever we were doing wrong. He made the Terroir hierarchy abundantly clear: We were the sea dogs, he was the pirate captain, and it was get in line or go overboard. Some of the strict rules of service were still in play. I got a twenty-minute lesson on serviette placement and clearing plates. "RESPECT THE CHEESE!" he bellowed at us before service one night, gesturing at a mangled wedge of curd. When Jason picked up two forks and went to place them beside a guest's plate, Paul grabbed Jason's wrists with both hands and held them in a vise grip. "We do *not* freehand the silverware," he hissed. Jason had made the critical error of carrying the forks with his hands, instead of placing them on a plate. Paul would stomp around the floor asking us questions to which the only satisfactory answer was "Because I'm an incompetent fucking idiot, sir." "Why is it taking so long to get Table Twenty's wine?" "How could you miss the napkins on the floor of your station?" There was a monthlong period where he only spoke to me in a yell.

Calm, simmering Paul was worse. I still get knots in my stomach thinking about the night I told him the tongue map he was drawing for two women at the bar was based on outdated science. He confronted me in his office at the end of my shift, when I learned that "quivering with rage" is a very literal description, not a metaphor. He spoke slowly to be sure there would be no mis-tak-ing his command. "Do . . . *not* . . . *EV-ER* contradict me in front of a guest," he said, with what I detected to be an almost undercurrent of evil glee thinking about how hard he would crush me if I disobeyed his orders. "If you do that again, you and I will *never.* Speak. To. Each. Other. Again."

It was stressful out there on the floor. Now, it was all on me. There was no Morgan or Victoria to help me get a crumbling cork out of a wine while a table got huffy, or advise on which glasses to use for white Burgundy. I was juggling many tables, tongues, and egos simultaneously, balancing service, hospitality, and sanity.

I did not always succeed. One of my first nights, Justine reamed me out for spending an unforgivable seven minutes indulging two guys at Table 70, who knew nothing about wine but were eager to learn. Thinking I'd steer them toward the classics and send them home with a story, I delivered a whole spiel about Bordeaux. The Classification of 1855, left bank versus right bank, the horsey taste, the blending of grapes. I left them licking their lips to try the bottle I'd sold them and bumped into Justine as I went to grab it. She was standing with her hands on her hips blocking my path to the bar, where we kept the wines. "What do you think you're doing?" she demanded. "There's no way you can spend that much time with a table! You can't give them so much information! They can't even *process* that much information! You're standing there using words they don't understand and they won't even admit they don't understand. And meanwhile all your other tables are going down in *flames*! In *FLAMES*. You have to be in and out."

I knew from watching Morgan order and take orders for bottles that to do my job, I needed to extract only two facts: your budget and your tastes. From there I could play matchmaker, like Amazon or Netflix suggesting books or movies. If you like Sauvignon Blanc from the Loire, you'll *love* Pallavicini's Frascati from Lazio. "What are you in the mood for tonight?" I'd ask the guest. The question could be intimidating to someone who didn't speak wine. If she hesitated, I'd make the question multiple choice: New World or Old World? Fruity or earthy? Blackberry or cow shit? And if she still had trouble answering, I'd go with: So, what's your favorite band?

I picked that up from Paul. He believed in pairing wines off of anything, because he knew we could talk you into enjoying almost any bottle. "Listen, we're dealing with the most fickle thing of all: taste," Paul lectured during one of our meetings. If you like Depeche Mode, you'll *love* our Depeche Mode wine. He mimed talking to a customer: "'Oh, I got the perfect Depeche Mode wine for you.' And you're left going, 'What the fuck is he talking about?' Then I'm going to bring you a fucking wine—what it is depends on my mood—but it all fits fucking Depeche Mode," he said. "I can make *any* wine on the fucking list fit Depeche Mode."

I got a crash course in the importance of molding guests' taste buds during an especially disastrous service one evening. A party of six guys in suits and collared shirts came in on Table 25. The host, a guy in his forties, wanted a California Cabernet for under a hundred bucks. Something like Jordan Cabernet. In other words, cougar juice.

"I want powerful. Big and powerful," said the short, bald man.

His shock bordering on outrage at seeing $300 bottles on our list told me the guy probably didn't know too much about wine. He knew just enough to know California Cabernet implied opulence and tasted opulent.

We didn't have a California Cabernet in his budget. We didn't have much that tasted like classic California Cabernet either. Paul tended to stock red wines as lean and mean as he is, and for that price I could count only one wine as unctuous as the guy wanted. What I had to offer him: the Tzora, from (cringe) Israel. It didn't quite have the ring of "Napa Valley."

I brought it over and poured him a taste along with two wines I knew he'd hate—a trick Justine had taught me to "make people pick the wine they need to pick." I poured him the Merino, a Syrah from Argentina.

He made a face. "Not powerful enough."

I poured the Tzora, the Cabernet Sauvignon blend, from Israel.

"That's oh-*kayyyy*."

And the Fronsac, a Merlot-heavy wine from Bordeaux.

He grimaced. "Oh, I hate this. This is terrible. Definitely not the last one."

He decided he didn't want any of them. I didn't have anything else to give him. After several more awkward conversations and a very long time waiting to see if Paul would have suggestions, the man, fed up and justifiably annoyed, finally said *fuck it*. He asked for the Israeli wine. Whatever. He'd been waiting fifteen minutes for something to drink.

Paul was even more pissed than the table. He held me back for detention after my shift.

"*You* drive the car. Not the guest. The guest *thinks* they drive the car. But *you* drive the car," he fumed. "If I'm with a group of people and I say I like California Cabs, that's a profound statement. I'm showing off in front of my guests. And all of a sudden, you show up with an Israeli wine? It's like, 'What the fuck? Like, what is this? I don't want this!' Of *course* they're going to say no. . . . I think the Tzora was a great pick. . . . I would have brought over the Tzora and said, 'Sir, we're *not* in California. We *are* in Israel. Jordan is medium-bodied, very unctuous, flavorful. Big-fruited, soft tannin. This is going to have *exactly* what you fucking want.' And you talk him into it.

"And there is an element of bullshit," Paul conceded. "I'd have manipulated the gentleman's mind to say, Okay, it's not California Cab. But it's going to be close. You have to make them feel good about their choice."

I thought back to La Paulée and the power of priming. Of course. We believe what we're told, *especially* with taste. Especially with wine. Make it nice, and it will be nice. The words we spoke summoned flavors on your tongue.

The point wasn't to trick people. We wanted to gently coax them into setting aside whatever biases prevented them from taking pleasure in fresh flavors. I'll concede an Israeli wine doesn't have the same automatic star power as a California Cabernet. If you were Mr. Big and Powerful, it could feel like getting doner kebab when you ordered a dry-aged rib-eye. But man, the Tzora was delicious, if you gave it a chance to win you over, and the Napa fans who tasted it usually ended up converts, toasting *"L'chaim!"* to the vines of the Holy Land. It took an open mind, plus some cunning on our part, for those epiphanies to happen. Since civilians assumed all Rieslings were sweet and sweet wines were tacky, I might put a palm over a Riesling label when I poured, or purposefully forget to mention the variety, just so a table would have a taste.

I understood why even wine-savvy sommeliers put themselves fully in the hands of other somms when they went out to drink. My fellow Terroirists and I knew each of the bottles on our list like they were people—which were the gimmes, the duds, the brainteasers, the tongue twisters, the inspirations. It was thrilling to match someone with a wine whose flavor made their eyes bug out. And though sometimes we did nudge people toward something more expensive, it wasn't just to finagle an extra three bucks on the check, but to give them a far superior bottle. I'd thought Morgan and Victoria might have been putting me off when they said they sometimes prized pleasure over profits. Not anymore.

Wine had so thoroughly soaked all parts of my everyday life that I didn't fully register how much I'd changed until I started working at Terroir, almost a year after my initial meeting with Morgan. The first time he and I spoke, it had been at Terroir. Now I was serving wine to people who sat at virtually those same seats.

As I answered questions about the list and guided people around the Book, I realized that my whole way of seeing wine—and food—had evolved. I cared what I drank, but I also cared what *you* drank.

I saw the potential for a glass of liquid to be the gateway for an experience that took you somewhere and revealed something without you ever needing to leave your seat. Merely liking a wine was a necessary but insufficient condition for being satisfied with it. A knockout wine took some doing to figure out. You couldn't make sense of it all at once. It would plant a question in your mind, or transport you to another place. *This is from where? Is that . . . pine needles I'm tasting? How did this get made? Why am I suddenly filled with nostalgia for my college girlfriend and our hikes through the Pine Barrens?* A glass reached its full potential when it left you with a story. It could be a story about the wine itself and the hippie in Germany who made it using his great-great-grandfather's methods. Or it could be a story about the night you drank that wine, the sweet smell of the Riesling instantly lifting your spirits so you stayed out later than you'd planned, and laughed so hard that the bar's owner—that guy with the weird beard—came over to see what was up. Or it could be a story about yourself, since you were shocked to discover the intellectual dimensions unlocked by senses you thought you used only for basic survival. Food could elicit such feelings too. But that experience of being nudged into a place where you're wondering about the world, and your place in it, could come more easily, more affordably, more reliably from wine.

We Terroirists were crushed when people order-fired whatever familiar thing they recognized in the Book. "That's such a shame. There are so many better wines on the list," whispered one of my colleagues on the floor when he saw me grabbing a Chardonnay for a deuce in the front. Not so long ago, I would have assumed this was snobbishness speaking. But really, we were disappointed that we couldn't rock you back on your heels a little. Maybe open up a new perspective, or at least make you question what you thought you knew about flavor. Paul required the civilians in his wine classes to pledge they'd never drink the same wine twice. I'd drop that fact at my tables to see if I could coax people into uncharted territory.

Don't get me wrong—of course I'd bring you the Chardonnay or Doc's cider and I'd be happy if you were happy. However, in the back of my mind I'd be thinking that in the grand scheme of what I *could* give you, the Doc's is boring. Watery! The Cornouaille is a mind-altering mess of blue cheese, cider vinegar, and Shetland pony that stinks and is *phenomenal* and utterly perplexing. The Château Belá Riesling is like Schubert had a baby with Grace Kelly and every bit as mind-boggling as that description implies. Wait till you get a hold of the Tempranillo that's like sucking on an old saddle, in a totally wonderful way. Instead of another jaunt through California wine country, you could be inhaling the smells of Lebanon, Austria, Greece, Israel, Slovenia. It's only a splash of wine we're talking about here and you don't have to keep it, or even pay for it. We merely want you to try it.

And yet so many people wouldn't even do that. There were times when guests just weren't in the mood. They'd had a bad day at work, and all they needed, as Paul would say, was a glass of fucking grape juice. In those instances, I was content to back off and bring them the alcohol.

Yet there were many, *many* more people who wouldn't let us take them to the next level because they were scared—of wine, of looking dumb, of being wrong, of not knowing the difference, of asking stupid questions, of getting long-winded answers with jargon like "aldehydic," and of putting an unknown thing in their mouths. I would watch fully grown adults recoil from glasses of wine and scrunch up their faces like toddlers being asked to eat broccoli. It's true that taste and smell are the most invasive and intimate senses. We're letting things into ourselves. Still, these people acted like I was trying to poison them, as if it were physically painful or dangerous to sip these wines. "What *is* this?" a middle-aged woman shrieked. Some seemed to take it personally. "You guys have weird stuff," another guest said accusingly. "This wine is weird. Why is it so weird?" When it comes to tastes and smells, if they're unfamiliar, unknown, and untested, the instinct is to reject them. Put that in my body? No thank you and no way.

I'd been on a sensory adventure. And each night at Terroir, it was my chance to take people on a journey of their own. The trick was convincing them to come along.

Let's say you were to come visit us at Terroir. You'd open the door and think it looks like a very casual, relaxed place. We're all in jeans and T-shirts. It's got wood tables, metal stools, a bar with a banged-up countertop, and a tiny, open kitchen. There's a chalkboard out front that says GET WEIRD WITH US! There are no leather-bound menus, no tablecloths, no hostess barring your way, no suits, no elaborate bouquets. Old movies are playing on a screen in back: *Pumping Iron*, *Top Gun*, *The Sound of Music*. Forget smooth jazz. There's Bowie or Chuck Berry cranked up a little too loud.

One of us yells hello when you walk in—probably Paul, who is somehow always the first to see a guest, even if I'm at the front—WELCOME TO TERROIR IT'S ALL GOOD. The wine list we drop off for you comes in a black three-ring binder plastered with stickers and doodles ("if you love manzanilla so much why dont you marry it??"). It says, We're not insulated from the world. We live in your world too. It's wine, but you don't have to take it so seriously. Rock 'n' roll.

And then you see the wines. You do *not* know what is going on. What's Epanomi? Malagou-huh? Why all the "TA, RS" numbers next to the Rieslings? Why does the "by the glass" section go on for *six* pages?! Where's the Malbec? No Sancerre? Seriously?

Rock 'n' fucking *roll.*

Paul wants to induce these kinds of crises because crises force conversation. He wants you to give up and close the Book. In fact, his dream is for there to be no Book. "But here in New York, in a city full of control fucking freaks, not everyone wants to give up control." Least of all Paul. Hopefully, not knowing where to go, you'll permit us to step in and be your guide.

Just as you're beginning to eye the room with a wild look of panic, or as I see you flipping through the pages for a third time, searching for a foothold, I'll sidle up to the table. Depending on where you're sitting, I might squeeze myself in next to the banquette on 26 so I can monitor the dining room while we talk—does 21 or 23 need water? How's 25 doing on their bottle? If you're on 27, I'm going to be squished into the corner so I can still—"WELCOME TO TERROIR GRAB A SEAT"—watch the door.

I'll have been eyeing you even before I get to you, trying to figure out who you are and what you will want. Victoria's lessons in smart stereotyping are paying off. We're near Wall Street, so you might be a finance bro. Guys in collared shirts and dress shoes are probably quantity over quality until happy hour ends at six. The financettes—power women with A-line skirts and nice bags—treat themselves well. I've got a delicious Oregon Pinot for you, eighteen bucks a glass. You could be a Tribeca artist, one of the few left in the neighborhood, and if you are you've probably been in before. I'll highlight whatever's new. You could be a fellow cork dork, in which case I'll point you to something special. If you're on a first date—and you probably are, we have lots of those—you'll be cheap and you'll look to me to be the night's entertainment. (Morgan was on to something. Let the show begin!) You'll be awkward with your love interest and want a wine with a story that's a conversation starter. I'll offer the Chateau Musar from virtuoso Serge Hochar, who used his wine cellar as a bomb shelter during Lebanon's fifteen-year civil war—and hey, when was the last time you tried a Lebanese wine? The third dates—couples who are comfortable but not *too* comfortable—will blow it out, angling to get laid. If you're the regular who brings a new girl in every week—always pretending it's your first time here, always paying with your corporate card, always getting her drunk on an empty stomach so you can make out against the bar—I'm going to push the cheese plate, hard, so the girl can soak up her Syrah. Be forewarned: You are not anonymous and we are very good at reading you.

I'll come over to your table and feed you a pickup line to get you talking. No dead-end yes/no questions. "What's happening?" I'll ask, or "What's on your mind?" I stole the openers from Twitter and Facebook, because if anyone knows how to get people to spill their guts, it's those two. The more I learn about you, the better I can persuade you and steer you to a wine destination.

I'll gauge which version of me you want. Do you want my spiel? Do you just need a glass of wine? Do you want me to admire you? To teach you? I'm a different me at every table.

Whoever you are, whatever you answer, I'm going to try to make you like me so you'll trust me to bring you something new. Man or woman, regular or newbie, this seduction has to happen fast. Maybe thirty seconds, tops. You're there to be with your friend or girlfriend or coworkers. And I've got to *mise* two tables, offer someone more wine, drop a check, polish glasses, refill 21, run to the cellar, and dodge Paul, who's seething in the corner.

Once I've got a sense for what you want, I have to sell you on the wine I know will take you someplace fun. And that's where things get interesting.

My pitch changes every time. I improvise at every table, playing to the scene. Morgan and Victoria had little freedom to stray from the sommelier script—*a good year . . . drinking very well right now . . .* At Terroir, we have total artistic liberty.

I'll draw on everything I've learned to convince you to come with me on tonight's journey. The art of tasting notes, the influence of expectations, the way to blind taste, the science of smell. Even the facts about Tuscan wine laws or Champagne methods.

If you're a cork dork, I'll give you the classic lingo. I want to show you I know your language so you'll trust me. The Jurtschitsch is classic Austrian Grüner, a citrusy, high-acid zinger with notes of radish and white pepper. If you're a curious amateur, I'll tack on a story to inspire your imagination. The Quenard comes from an area of France right across the border from Switzerland that combines the romance of the French with the exacting precision of *zee Sviss.* If you want to flirt with me, I'll teach you how to feel for high acid and high alcohol on your tongue. If you don't know a thing about anything, I'll scrap the wine-speak altogether and try to intrigue you with poetry and pop-culture free association—the kind of stuff Morgan would babble as we stalked the tables at distributor tastings. This Viognier is a total Gwyneth Paltrow—flowery, fresh, a little unctuous. This sweet, peachy Riesling is the Beatles circa "Love Me Do"; this other one is *Sgt. Pepper's Lonely Hearts Club Band*—funky and sky-high in acid. I'll sell you wines that are big, bold Kim Kardashian numbers, or lean and Hemingway-esque, or a suave playboy in a velvet housecoat. Sometimes, I'll take it too far: "This wine is like the girl you knew in high school who was a total goody two-shoes and got straight A's even though everyone knew she secretly smoked pot in the bathroom," I said to one customer. "I have no idea what you're talking about," he answered fairly. But usually, you're into it. "I'll take whatever you described as the T. S. Eliot wine," you might say, more charmed by that comparison than the fact it's from the Northern Rhône.

I won't abandon my Court conduct entirely. I will poke fun at wine traditions even as I make it clear I know them. I'll present your bottle, reciting the full label while holding it out for you to see, just as I did for Master Keith. Then I'll joke, "Looks just like a wine, doesn't it?" a crack at the conventions that I take scrupulous care to follow. I carry a *serviette*, pour openhand from the right, and wipe the lip with care because I know, even if you don't, that I'm showing you respect by doing things the right way. Morgan would be proud.

The best moments of the night come when people get it: They taste something, a switch flips, and they realize *This is what I've been missing.* A flavor makes them curious. They want more. They are suddenly dissatisfied with "just okay."

We try to share the tools to make that happen. Give a man a tasting note and he's satisfied for an hour; teach him to taste and, well, life changes. If you say: "Bring a glass of whatever because I really can't taste the difference," I'll return with two polar opposite wines—one, from Burgundy, that's a mud puddle mixed with cranberry juice; another, from Argentina, that's brownie-batter-cum-piña-colada. "Do you taste the difference?" I'll ask, explaining Old World versus New World, cool climate versus warm. You realize you can. You realize this is the first of many stories your food and drink will tell.

If things slow down, I'll pause a little longer at your table, bring out a few dissimilar wines, and quiz you about how much saliva you have in your mouth after each sip. A lot? That's from the acid. Breathe out like you're checking your breath. How far back does it burn? That's how you gauge the alcohol. I'll watch Paul draw diagrams of the tongue as he coaches people on assessing structure. "Okay, now, does the tip of your tongue tingle?" he'll ask. "Perks things right up, doesn't it? Rock 'n' fucking roll."

At Terroir, I always tried to take a guest somewhere with that glass or bottle of wine, with varying degrees of success.

Sometimes, she (or he) would give me subtle clues that she'd felt that extra oomph. She might call me over to say she hated to bother me, but what was the name of that bottle again? And could she maybe photograph the label?

Sometimes, she'd happily drain the first glass and then ask me to recommend another, different wine. She'd put herself in my hands a second time, and let me spin the globe again. I took two bros on a tour that started with relatively safe, full-bodied Shiraz, then skipped off to Pinot Noir from Oregon, then France, then all the way over to off-dry German Riesling.

Sometimes, a customer would straight-up tell me how much she loved the wine. Every time I came back to her table, she had a new observation. She'd get into my game of dreaming up wild tasting notes, which is when I knew she'd really thought about the glass. One table ordered a flight of three Cabernet Francs. They declared one a Taylor Swift, the other an Alanis Morissette, and the final one a Sean Connery.

Often, it was harder to tell whether I'd accomplished my goal. I thought I'd been successful in the moments when I glimpsed someone take a drink of a wine and then disappear into himself. He would break eye contact. His face would go blank. He would stop conversing with those around him, engaged in an internal dialogue promoted by the cloud of aromatic molecules he'd just inhaled. He'd look distracted, like he'd stumbled into some other place. Or he might cock his head, pausing for a moment as if straining to answer some question that had been raised, or to catch another clue.

And I didn't mind that I often couldn't tell whether I'd paired guests with a gateway wine. What happens between them and the glass is all theirs. It's their own adventure.

A sip of wine is not like a song or painting, which speak to many people at once, with a message locked for eternity in a chord or the sweep of a brush. The wine changes in the bottle, slowly evolving until its inevitable end, and it changes even more dramatically starting from the instant its cork is pulled. The liquid that forms our first sip is not the same liquid we drain from the bottle for our last. And the wine you drink is not the same as the wine I drink. It is altered by the chemistry of our bodies, the architecture of our DNA, or the backdrop of our memories. Wine exists only for you, or me, and it exists only in that instant. It is a private epiphany in the pleasure of good company. So don't let it slip by. Savor it.

EPILOGUE

The Blindest Tasting

THERE WAS ONE FINAL BLIND TASTING TEST I NEEDED TO TAKE. IT was the blindest blind tasting I'd ever attempted or heard of. I had to close my eyes, plug my ears, and place my head in a plastic frame so I couldn't move even a centimeter. Then I had to stuff myself into a narrow, dark space the size of a coffin. So, emphasis on the blind—and also emphasis on the tasting: I couldn't smell the wine. I could only bite down on a thin plastic tube and wait for someonc to squirt red wine, white wine, or watcr into my mouth.

For around twenty minutes, I lay on my back while a man standing near my feet injected the wine (or water) and shouted commands.

"Swish!" I'd hear his muffled voice call out as something wet trickled onto my tongue.

Then: "Swallow!"

"Swish!"

"Swallow!"

This setup, strange as it is, might sound familiar: It was borrowed from two pioneering experiments—mentioned in chapter four—that used fMRI scans to probe the nature of wine expertise. The first, published in 2005, was led by an Italian team, and the second, modeled after the original, was conducted by French researchers in

2014. Both studies recruited sommeliers and amateur drinkers to sip, swish, and swallow wine while inside fMRI machines so scientists could see what regions of their brains were activated by the flavors. The subjects weren't required to identify whether it was, say, an Argentine Malbec or a California Merlot they were drinking. But to be sure the study participants thought critically about the flavors, the experimenters posed three questions: (1) How much do you like the wine? (2) What kind of wine is it—red or white? and (3) Do you think you've tasted the same wine more than once? The two teams of researchers each separately discovered that when experts taste and analyze wine, their brains light up in a distinct pattern that looks nothing like the activity in novices' heads.

I was at the tail end of more than a year of intensive wine training and taste exploration. I'd demonstrated that I could perform like a sommelier—on the floor, in the Court's exams, and when faced with a flight of wines. My blind tasting was good, even "excellent," according to the president of the American Sommelier Association, Andrew Bell, who, as my former blind tasting instructor, had been surprised by the speed of my progress. If you handed me a glass of something made out of a classic grape varietal, I could consistently tell you what I was drinking.

Yet I'd also discovered that wine expertise is a slippery matter. I'd seen expectations play tricks on perception, and witnessed over and over again that the mind is the ultimate force that fine-tunes our senses. Though I'd initially wondered about super-noses and über-tongues, I no longer had any doubt: Advanced flavor-fanatic sommeliers don't possess better physical equipment, like ten times as many taste buds or thousands of extra olfactory receptor genes. Rather, it's their manner of thinking that is unique. They perceive and interpret the flavors they encounter in a more developed way, and that filter changes everything.

The brain was the final frontier in my quest for expertise. Scientists had mapped out the distinctive features of a cork dork's brain. Now I just needed to know how mine stacked up.

Getting pictures of your brain is not as easy as you might think, and I was surprised to learn that I needed permission to look inside my own head. After petitioning scientists from Stockholm to Chicago, I finally managed to get into an fMRI machine under the auspices of a study on taste that was already under way. It was being run by professor Yong-An Chung at Incheon St. Mary's Hospital in, of all places, South Korea. Seung-Schik Yoo, an assistant professor of radiology at Harvard Medical School and frequent collaborator with the St. Mary's team, had carefully reviewed the protocols from the previous sommelier experiments, and he and Yong-An agreed to replicate their format as closely as possible to assist me with this blind tasting to end all blind tastings. I flew to South Korea to meet the cheerful and indefatigably curious Seung-Schik, whose research ranges from 3D-printing skin to connecting rat and human brains so we can control the animal with our thoughts. Seung-Schik told me he'd had a passion for biomedicine ever since glimpsing an artificial heart on the cover of *Time* as a kid. "Something about it really excited my limbic system," he said. (A part of the brain involved with emotion and motivation, I clarified later.) His way of asking me to lunch was "Let's feed some glucose to our brain." So he was the perfect person to help.

Seung-Schik led me through the St. Mary's Hospital parking lot, where pajama-clad patients leashed to IV drips shuffled around the cars. I followed him into a basement room and lay down on a narrow plastic stretcher so he could load me into the fMRI. I must have looked nervous because Seung-Schik told me not to be put off by the low rumble of the machine's magnets. He knew graduate students who'd remixed the sound into songs.

I *was* nervous, but it had nothing to do with the bone-rattling grind of the fMRI. I was, for starters, concerned about being concerned. A group of men in white coats were about to look into my head, and I worried about them getting a full view of my anxiety, which is off the charts on a good day. But more than that, I was terrified that after more than a year of effort, energy, training, and dedication, my brain would betray me as a dud, a dunce, and a philistine.

I closed my eyes and tried to clear my head as I clamped my front teeth around a tube. Seung-Schik and his colleagues scanned me while I swished and swallowed a series of wines, then they scanned a matched control—an amateur wine drinker my same age and gender—while she too swished and swallowed. Like the earlier subjects, we both answered a few questions about the wines we tasted. And like the earlier researchers, the St. Mary's scientists promised they'd process our data, then compare the activity in my brain with the control's.

A few weeks later, Seung-Schik emailed me to say the results were ready, and I drove to his office in Boston to dig through the scans by his side. As soon as I arrived, he sat me down next to him and eagerly tapped a few keys on his laptop to bring up my files. I was treated to a terrifying vision of my own bald, decapitated head spinning over a gray background—a gratuitous little nightmare, courtesy of the fMRI machine. *Whatever he's found, it could be worse: At least your head is still attached*, I told myself.

Seung-Schik pulled up a grid of black-and-white brain scans that mapped out more than ninety different views of the brain. Many of those individual scans were, in places, dotted with orange, yellow, and red, and Seung-Schik quickly explained what I was looking at. As the other researchers had done, he and his colleagues had subtracted the activity in the amateur's brain from the activity in my brain, and the splotches of color indicated regions where my brain had been more engaged. He highlighted a small patch of red: It appeared that I'd been wiggling my tongue around a whole lot more than the control. This felt like more information than I wanted someone to know about me, and I suddenly felt very exposed.

The original fMRI study from 2005 had concluded that three

key regions of the brain show more activity in sommeliers than in amateurs while tasting wine. Two of those areas—the left orbitofrontal cortex and the left insula—are thought to collaborate in processing odors, tastes, and other sensory information, then turning them into an impression of flavor. Both of these regions also tackle complex tasks, like decision making and deductive reasoning, as well as ascribing value and pleasure to tastes. The insula is particularly remarkable when it comes to the latter. Scientists believe this long-neglected area of the brain helps distinguish humans from animals. It attaches emotional and cultural importance to sensory experiences—a bad smell turns into disgust, a caress ignites feelings of desire for a lover, the sound of a high C leads to wonder at a soprano's aria, and the sight of someone slicing open her finger elicits empathy. Damage to the insula can prevent us from grasping the emotion conveyed by a jazz riff or a violin's wail. It is the site where body and mind converge and we render felt experience into conscious thought. In short, the insula plays a pivotal role in how the world around us acquires meaning.

How did my brain compare to the experts'? Seung-Schik tapped a few more keys. Both the left orbitofrontal cortex and the left insula were lit up in orange. Seung-Schik smiled at me. I gave him a blank stare back. This was great news, he explained: Like the seven sommeliers in the original study, my brain had been much more engaged in those areas than the control's.

The third part of the brain that, according to the 2005 study, shows greater activity in sommeliers is the dorsolateral prefrontal cortex, or DLPFC. An intriguing part of our anatomy that continues developing well into adulthood, the DLPFC helps with abstract reasoning, memory, planning, attention, and integrating inputs from multiple different senses, among other functions. When the researchers observed its elevated activation in experts but not amateur drinkers, they came to a fascinating conclusion: "The analytic approach of sommeliers to wine tasting seems to replace the more emotional global experience of naïve subjects." Training not only makes sommeliers more sensitive to smells and tastes, but also ensures they analyze those stimuli instead of just reacting emotionally. We looked at the images on Seung-Schik's screen. The scans of my brain's activity showed this area was bright orange too.

Final diagnosis? I talked like a cork dork, walked like a cork dork, and, the fMRI scans had confirmed, I processed the world like a cork dork. All that practice and training had actually changed my brain.

Scientists are usually good at maintaining a sober poker face about their findings. But Seung-Schik verged on giddy.

"That's actually really cool!" he said, breaking into a grin. "So maybe, you could indeed be the true One," he joked. "Maybe I've watched too many Matrix movies. You're the One!"

But Seung-Schik wasn't finished. He directed me back toward his computer and ticked off a series of orange and yellow dots in the middle of my brain—the thalamic and striatal areas. The earlier study hadn't highlighted these regions in its findings, but they had been more engaged in my head than in the control's, and Seung-Schik thought this was too important not to point out. He was excited to see that my "deep brain" had kicked into gear while I was tasting. That row of dots, combined with the other three areas we'd just discussed, suggested engagement of my cortical–striatal–thalamic–cortical circuit, a pathway of the brain that can light up when we tap into executive functions. So what does that mean exactly? Seung-Schik began to tick things off. Complex problem solving. "Trying to figure out Pinot Noir and then what's in the wine, that was really complex problem solving. Don't you think?" said Seung-Schik. Response selection—"Ahh, I like that." Error detection—"Oh, *yeah*." Novelty detection. Recalling distant memories. Processing new memories. Given that this region controls so many advanced brain functions, seeing it light up while I drank wine, Seung-Schik said, "kind of makes the perfect story."

Oh, and there was one more thing. Seung-Schik hadn't instructed me to deduce what sort of wines he'd fed me during the scan. But my blind tasting brain had kicked in automatically. After getting pulled out of the fMRI, I'd told Seung-Schik that I thought I'd been drinking a Chardonnay from Burgundy—probably 2013—and a California Pinot Noir, same vintage. Seung-Schik showed me the bottles. I'd called the wines exactly right.

I started my journey keen to uncover whether any of us could enhance our senses in order to experience life in a more vivid and informed way. The scans from Seoul and from the earlier studies indicate that training does change us, even more quickly and profoundly than we realize. Yet these results not only show that we can evolve, but, importantly, why this transformation matters.

In response to the exact same tastes and smells, novices' brains stay relatively dark, while we, the trained tasters, summon the more critical, analytical, and higher-order parts of our brains—we demonstrate what the researchers call "higher cognitive processing modulated by expertise." In short, our engagement with flavor is more thoughtful and advanced. The setup of the experiment—which relied on pure flavor inputs, free of brands, labels, or prices—ensures that this was no placebo effect brought on by an obscenely expensive Château Cheval Blanc or a rare glass from Chateau Musar. Rather, the results suggest that honing the senses is a prerequisite to fuller, deeper experience. Sensations no longer waft by unnoticed and unrecorded. Instead, they are grasped, explored, and analyzed. They evoke curiosity, critique, associations, appreciation, and feelings of repulsion or ecstasy or sadness or astonishment. They enlighten and they inspire. They become a memory, and they slot into the library of experience that makes up our understanding of the world. Far from smell and taste being primal, animalistic senses, it turns out that learning to cultivate them engages, in a literal way, the very part of us that elevates our reactions, endows our lives with meaning, and makes us human.

Seung-Schik's pictures allowed me to see changes that until then I'd only felt in an abstract fashion. The most obvious transformation had taken place at the table. Wine had gone from something like a condiment—just some edible accessory that could enhance a meal—to the main event. A Viognier could set off a string of associations, ranging from people and places to philosophies and moments in history. A wine could be, in Paul's words, "a whacked-out fucking journey." It could also be a fast-food journey to the tank planks and liquid tannins I'd seen in Sacramento. Or it could be a fancy fucking journey to the imposing castles of Bordeaux, by way of a childhood memory of hiking trails in the Columbia Gorge. But it was always a journey. Before I realized what was happening, I heard myself talking about wines as though they were canvases someone had to see or books they had to read because, as Morgan promised, their life would be "recontextualized" by doing so. I never came right out and told someone that the bottle I was about to serve was a "way your humanity will be changed," as Morgan might have. But the thought crossed my mind.

I was eating and savoring differently. At times, this was visible to everyone around me. I'm not sure what Emily Post has to say about sniffing each and every forkful of food before you eat it, but that's what I was doing. I found it added an extra note of pleasure to the meal. It helped me tease out ingredients so I could copy a dish at home. I became one of *those* people who sipped wine and then, instead of swallowing it like a respectable human being, gnashed at the liquid, inhaled it, and even in public, produced a wet, hollow gurgling, as if drowning on dry land. Other times, my knowledge was less of a liability and more of an asset. I was at dinner one night with a friend who stared at me like I was psychic when I mused that the Crianza version of two identical wines was probably going to be rougher and a bit less polished than the Reserva. "How did you know that?" he marveled. Because, I explained to him, I spent approximately *five hundred hours* of my life memorizing flash cards.

More frequently, the differences were perceptible only to me. I'd take a bite of something and feel like I'd finally gotten the punch line to a joke I'd been hearing for years: *The salt plays off the sour, and the fat plays off Sangiovese's acid—my God, that's genius!* I had become more attuned to the power of names, colors, and prices to season our food for us, and I began to question my commitment to certain indulgences, like small-batch chocolate truffles, while rekindling my love affair with culinary pariahs, like American cheese. I know, I know: It's made with chemicals, and "cheese" is more a euphemism. But the mouthfeel is fantastic, it's the perfect smidge of saltiness to complement eggs, and it adds just the right amount of moisture to bagels.

Just because I'd found new value in the everyday doesn't mean I was immune to feeling the pleasures of an expensive meal or bottle of wine (FYI, if you're planning on opening some treasures, you can reach me at bianca.bosker@me.com). We can acknowledge the singular joy that comes from drinking a precious bottle and still be discriminating and thoughtful tasters. Maybe other people wouldn't get a rush from opening a bottle, like the 1893 Château Montrose I tasted, that pre-dates airplanes, women's suffrage, two world wars, and television. I did. I relished the sense that I was, through each sip, intimately connected to the past, physically consuming history in a way I never had before and, in an almost illicit fashion, seizing this invitation to destroy an heirloom. No bottle from the 2015 vintage, no matter how good, could mimic that. I could appreciate that the charm of a rare wine came not only from its flavor but also its reputation, history, age, scarcity, and price. But that didn't necessarily mean the big-name bottles were better. They came with the added burden of having to live up to their own hype (or cost). The best wines, regardless of pedigree, came with a story, and though it was harder to settle for wines I didn't love, those stories now revealed themselves more readily, and it was much easier to find wines I did adore.

While I would say that I had become a more thoughtful drinker, my friends would have phrased it differently. "Pain in the ass" is probably what they'd settle on. When we went out to eat at restaurants, I got stuck in long conversations with the sommelier. I was spending more on bottles than before—I'd developed a bank-account-draining weakness for old Champagne—and I dragged friends out of our way to visit wine stores that stocked unusual selections. When people came over to my apartment for dinner, they had panic attacks over what wines to bring. Some showed up with six-packs of Bud Light in protest. "Oh, it really doesn't matter, I'll drink anything," I'd reassure them, remembering how stressed I'd been just trying to buy cheese for Morgan and Dana. I *would* drink anything—at least one sip of it. But possibly no more. Paul's "one sip leads to another" quality rule was serving me well.

As I was preparing for the Certified Sommelier Exam, and even after I started working at Terroir, my friends and family made a lot of cracks about how tough it must be having to drink wine all day, and how they wish *they'd* thought of quitting their job to "research" booze. Many of the same people would corner me later, bring their faces close to mine, and confess, in hushed tones, that they knew nothing about wine. So, they'd ask, where do you start if you want to get your brain fired up like a sommelier's?

I gave them the same advice that had worked for me: Start by stocking your sense memory. Smell everything and attach words to it. Raid your fridge, pantry, medicine cabinet, and spice rack, then quiz yourself on pepper, cardamom, honey, ketchup, pickles, and lavender hand cream. Repeat. Again. Keep going. Sniff flowers and lick rocks. Be like Ann, and introduce odors as you notice them, as you would people entering a room. Also be like Morgan, and look for patterns as you taste, so you can, as he does, "organize small differentiating units into systems." Master the basics of structure—gauge acid by how you drool, alcohol by its heat, tannin by its dryness, finish by its length, sweetness by its thick softness, body by its weight—and apply it to the wines you try. Actually, apply it to *everything* you try. Be systematic: Order only Chardonnay for a week and get a feel for its personality, then do the same with Pinot Noir, and Sauvignon Blanc, and Cabernet Franc (the Wine Folly website offers handy

CliffsNotes on each one's flavor profile). Take a moment as you drink to reflect on whether you like it, then think about why. Like Paul Grieco, try to taste the wine for what it is, not what you imagine it should be. Like the Paulée-goers, splurge occasionally. Mix up the everyday bottles with something that's supposed to be better, and see if you agree. Like Annie, break the rules, do what feels right, and don't be afraid to experiment. I'd usually end this pep talk to my friends with some advice from the great enologist and flavor philosopher Émile Peynaud: "The taster also needs to have a particular reason for tasting if he is to do so effectively." Drink for thirst, but taste with purpose.

I'm biased, but on balance, I consider my wine-snob tendencies a minor and tolerable side effect of what has been a more significant and more positive evolution.

Blind tasting ranks alongside aerial yoga and pure mathematics as one of the things that's most guaranteed to make you feel like a total idiot. Facing down six anonymous wines is a lonely exercise where you can rely on no one but yourself. You have to trust senses that you are not used to trusting, and name things you are not used to naming. And after all that, you have to stake a claim, and be prepared for a group of ten or so people to tell you how moronic you are for thinking there's been new oak on this wine that was so obviously aged in stainless-steel tanks. You can mess up in spectacular ways, always in front of an audience.

And yet, perhaps counterintuitively, I found that I'd come away from my training in blind tasting with a new assuredness that infused other areas of life. Tuning in to my sense of taste—especially in situations of such uncertainty—had brought me greater confidence in my tastes in all things. I experienced firsthand what M. F. K. Fisher had intuited was true: "The ability to choose what food you must eat, and knowingly, will make you able to choose other less transitory things with courage and finesse."

With that confidence also came a new kind of awareness. I latched on to this Zen idea of *mushin*, or "no mind"—not because I thought my palate practice had made me into some hybrid martial arts/cork-pulling master of Buddhist philosophy, but because it was the closest analogue I'd found to describe what I was experiencing.

My time with Morgan and the other sommeliers had illuminated the value in striving for this no-mind state, where you empty your head of thoughts and distractions so you can fully, clearly absorb the present moment. I would reach for some version of that mind-set during blind tasting. Trying to shed my preconceptions and emotions in the minutes when I faced down a flight made me more cognizant of how they added a filter to other situations as well. And I sought to set that filter aside.

By practicing with this new perspective, I found a great deal changed. Beauty revealed itself in unlikely places. Even the monotony of commuting around New York acquired an unforeseen richness. I no longer smelled "street" or "city." I sought out Central Park when the stinky-sweet black locust bloomed, infusing the air with its overripe, honeyed perfume, and just after dawn, when the dewy fragrance of the park's lawns washed over me like a cold shower. There was the comforting aroma of laundry, cloying and dense, that enveloped me on Sunday walks around the Upper West Side. That corner in Midtown that always smelled inexplicably of vanilla, and the strip of the West Side Highway that glittered with the tang of cold metal and brine. I looked forward to quiet weekends in July, when New York cleared itself of some of its people and car exhaust, and the perfume of the city's routines asserted itself: Cement, hosed down at dawn by doormen, unleashed its petrichor; the heavy scent of grease and prickle of spice clouded the air around sidewalk vendors; a hair-spray aroma wafted from nail salons; and, as the sun beat down through the afternoon, baking trash released its essence of bubblegum and cadaverine—disgusting, to some, maybe. But I couldn't help relishing these odors, which revealed the heartbeat of the place in which I lived.

Lying in the fMRI machine, with my head wedged into a plastic brace and my eyes closed, a thought had occurred to me: This was as pure as tastings get. Not even the protocols devised by wine critics or Master Sommeliers could beat the blindness of this blind tasting. This was the most neutral tasting environment that existed.

It was also the worst way to enjoy a wine. It was not only sterile, but it robbed the wine of so much of the information that I'd come to appreciate. The radiant gold of an aged white. The horse-blanket musk of a Bordeaux. There was no soul in the liquid that ran from a syringe into a plastic tube and onto my tongue.

That soul comes from people. Just then, the enormous scanner was watching as my brain turned the mixture of amino acids and carotenoids into a story, one that might have the potential to make people think twice, and maybe even make them feel small, like a sack of water and organs.

Every person has the capacity to find and savor the soul that lives in wine—and in other sensory experiences, if you know to look for it. You don't need a trust fund or access to free wine. You don't need super senses. You don't even have to give up coffee or drink unreasonable amounts of alcohol at ten a.m. on Tuesday mornings. Feeling something for wine and unleashing your senses begins by just paying attention. And applying yourself with gusto.

ACKNOWLEDGMENTS

I AM GRATEFUL TO THE MANY MASTER SOMMELIERS, ASSISTANT sommeliers, perfumers, distributors, collectors, economists, radiologists, sensory scientists, synesthetes, explorers, auctioneers, and hedonists who shared their passion and expertise with me. Though they are not all mentioned by name, they have each played a role in giving shape to this book, and I remember every conversation with gratitude. In some cases, the chronology of these conversations and of certain events has been altered for the sake of explanatory clarity, but not in a way that undermines the accuracy of this text or its faithfulness in depicting my experiences over the course of a year and a half in the wine world.

My sincere thanks to Joe Campanale and Lara Lowenhar, for entrusting me with their bottles and patiently answering my endless questions (often more than once); to Geoff Kruth, for never oversimplifying anything and for letting me partake in adventures with the Guild of Sommeliers; to Annie Truhlar, for her comradery and honesty; to Victoria James, for her superb wisdom and wit (and excellent amaro); and to Paul Grieco, for rock 'n' fucking rolling, always, and letting me join in. David D'Alessandro was supremely generous in admitting a mere "taster" into his supertaster clan. Thomas Hummel and his colleagues kindly opened up their lab—and in so doing opened my eyes to the wonders of the nose, mouth, and brain. Likewise, I am deeply grateful to Seung-Schik Yoo, Yong-An Chung, and their teams at Incheon St. Mary's Hospital and the Harvard Medical School for their curiosity, support, and confidence that they could turn me into a mini-neuroscientist. Morgan Harris—I could fill another chapter with my thanks for Morgan, who so graciously shared his world, his knowledge, his tasting notes, his Chablis, his unflagging support, and his excitement for wine. He was the wine-whisperer I didn't know I needed, and has given me the invaluable gift of good taste.

None of those experiences would have been possible without the support of Lindsey Schwoeri, my incredible editor and champion, who, together with Emily Hartley and the entire Penguin team, has stewarded this book with the utmost patience, care, and enthusiasm. Everyone should be so lucky as to have a Richard Pine in her life, and I am eternally thankful to him for being my advocate, for knowing how to keep a secret, and for leveraging the support of Inkwell Management (especially Eliza Rothstein) to make this book happen. To Karen Brooks, Roger Cohen, Peter Goodman, Arianna Huffington, Susan Orlean, John McPhee, and Clive Thompson—thank you for being inspirations and guides.

This book was not something that lived apart from me, by which I mean it took over my life. And to that end, I sincerely appreciate the many friends and colleagues who stuck by me as I whined through hangovers, recruited them for taste experiments, and solicited their sharp eyes to review whatever I happened to stick in front of them—in particular, Kathryn Andersen, Christopher Berger, Dado Derviskadic, Anna Harman, Christine Miranda, Daphne Oz, and Alexandra Sutherland-Brown. I am indebted to Zung Nguyen and Cathy Germain for their moral support and snacks, and to Tanya Supina for joyfully sharing her love of wine and kindling my own. A

Nebuchadnezzar-sized thank-you to my parents, Lena Lenček and Gideon Bosker, for their faith, for their example, and for their advice. I've read every email. Almost every email.

And to Matt, my editor, chef, reader, muse, researcher, explorer, voice of reason, maintainer of sanity, love, and ally. Thank you. The best in me—and in this—is all thanks to you.

SELECTED BIBLIOGRAPHY

Ackerman, Diane. *A Natural History of the Senses.* New York: Random House, 1990.

Amerine, Maynard A., and Edward B. Roessler. *Wines: Their Sensory Evaluation.* San Francisco: W. H. Freeman, 1976.

Arakawa, Takahiro, Kenta Iitani, Xin Wang, Takumi Kajiro, Koji Toma, Kazuyoshi Yano, and Kohji Mitsubayashi. "A Sniffer-Camera for Imaging of Ethanol Vaporization from Wine: The Effect of Wine Glass Shape." *Analyst* 140, no. 8 (2015): 2881–886.

Bartoshuk, Linda M., Valerie B. Duffy, and Inglis J. Miller. "PTC/PROP Tasting: Anatomy, Psychophysics, and Sex Effects." *Physiology & Behavior* 56, no. 6 (December 1994): 1165–171.

Bourdieu, Pierre. *Distinction: A Social Critique of the Judgement of Taste.* Translated by Richard Nice. Cambridge, MA: Harvard University Press, 1984.

Brillat-Savarin, Jean-Anthelme. *The Physiology of Taste.* Translated by Anne Drayton. New York: Penguin Classics, 1994.

Bushdid, C., M. O. Magnasco, L. B. Vosshall, and A. Keller. "Humans Can Discriminate More Than 1 Trillion Olfactory Stimuli." *Science* 343, no. 6177 (March 21, 2014): 1370–372.

Castriota-Scanderbeg, Alessandro, Gisela E. Hagberg, Antonio Cerasa, Giorgia Committeri, Gaspare Galati, Fabiana Patria, Sabrina Pitzalis, Carlo Caltagirone, and Richard Frackowiak. "The Appreciation of Wine by Sommeliers: A Functional Magnetic Resonance Study of Sensory Integration." *NeuroImage* 25, no. 2 (April 2005): 570–78.

Clarke, Oz, and Margaret Rand. *Grapes & Wines: A Comprehensive Guide to Varieties and Flavours.* New York: Sterling Epicure, 2010.

Collings, Virginia B. "Human Taste Response as a Function of Locus of Stimulation on the Tongue and Soft Palate." *Perception & Psychophysics* 16, no. 1 (1974): 169–74.

Croy, Ilona, Selda Olgun, Laura Mueller, Anna Schmidt, Marcus Muench, Cornelia Hummel, Guenter Gisselmann, Hanns Hatt, and Thomas Hummel. "Peripheral Adaptive Filtering in Human Olfaction? Three Studies on Prevalence and Effects of Olfactory Training in Specific Anosmia in More Than 1600 Participants." *Cortex* 73 (2015): 180–87.

Delwiche, J. F., and M. L. Pelchat. "Influence of Glass Shape on Wine Aroma." *Journal of Sensory Studies* 17 (2002): 19–28.

Gigante, Denise, ed. *Gusto: Essential Writings in Nineteenth-Century Gastronomy.* New York: Routledge, 2005.

Goode, Jamie. *The Science of Wine: From Vine to Glass.* Berkeley: University of California Press, 2006.

Harrington, Anne, and Vernon Rosario. "Olfaction and the Primitive: Nineteenth-Century Medical Thinking on Olfaction." In *Science of Olfaction*, edited by Michael J. Serby and Karen L. Chobor, 3–27. New York: Springer-Verlag, 1992.

Hayes, John E., and Gary J. Pickering. "Wine Expertise Predicts Taste Phenotype." *American Journal of Enology and Viticulture* 63, no. 1 (March 2012): 80–84.

Hodgson, Robert T. "An Examination of Judge Reliability at a Major U.S. Wine Competition." *Journal of Wine Economics* 3, no. 2 (2008): 105–13.

Hopfer, Helene, Jenny Nelson, Susan E. Ebeler, and Hildegarde Heymann. "Correlating Wine Quality Indicators to Chemical and Sensory Measurements." *Molecules* 20, no. 5 (May 12, 2015): 8453–483.

Hummel, Thomas, Karo Rissom, Jens Reden, Aantje Hähner, Mark Weidenbecher, and Karl-Bernd Hüttenbrink. "Effects of Olfactory Training in Patients with Olfactory Loss." *Laryngoscope* 119, no. 3 (March 2009): 496–99.

Jurafsky, Dan. *The Language of Food: A Linguist Reads the Menu*. New York: W. W. Norton, 2014.

Kaufman, Cathy K. "Structuring the Meal: The Revolution of *Service à la Russe*." In *The Meal: Proceedings of the Oxford Symposium on Food and Cookery, 2001*, edited by Harlan Walker, 123–33. Devon, England: Prospect Books, 2002.

Korsmeyer, Carolyn. *Making Sense of Taste: Food and Philosophy*. Ithaca, NY: Cornell University Press, 1999.

Kramer, Matt. *True Taste: The Seven Essential Wine Words*. Kennebunkport, ME: Cider Mill Press, 2015.

Krumme, Coco. "Graphite, Currant, Camphor: Wine Descriptors Tell Us More About a Bottle's Price Than Its Flavor." *Slate*. February 23, 2011. Accessed September 06, 2016. http://www.slate.com/articles/life/drink/2011/02/velvety_chocolate_with_a_silky_ruby_finish_pair_with_shellfish.html.

Laska, Matthias. "The Human Sense of Smell: Our Noses Are Much Better Than We Think." In *Senses and the City: An Interdisciplinary Approach to Urban Sensescapes*, edited by M˘ad˘alina Diaconu, Eva Heuberger, Ruth Mateus-Berr, and Lukas Marcel Vosicky. 145–54. Berlin: LIT Verlag, 2011.

Lehrer, Adrienne. *Wine & Conversation*. New York: Oxford University Press, 2009.

Lukacs, Paul. *Inventing Wine: A New History of One of the World's Most Ancient Pleasures*. New York: W. W. Norton, 2012.

Lundström, Johan N., and Marilyn Jones-Gotman. "Romantic Love Modulates Women's Identification of Men's Body Odors." *Hormones and Behavior* 55 (2009): 280–84.

Majid, A., and N. Burenhult. "Odors Are Expressible in Language, as Long as You Speak the Right Language." *Cognition* 130, no. 2 (2014): 266–70.

McQuaid, John. *Tasty: The Art and Science of What We Eat*. New York: Scribner, 2015.

Mitro, Susanna, Amy R. Gordon, Mats J. Olsson, and Johan N. Lundström. "The Smell of Age: Perception and Discrimination of Body Odors of Different Ages." *PLoS ONE* 7, no. 5 (May 2012).

Morrot, Gil, Frédéric Brochet, and Denis Dubourdieu. "The Color of Odors." *Brain and Language* 79, no. 2 (November 2001): 309–20.

Noble, A. C., R. A. Arnold, J. Buechsenstein, E. J. Leach, J. O. Schmidt, and P. M. Stern. "Modification of a Standardized System of Wine Aroma Terminology." *American Journal of Enology and Viticulture* 38 (January 1987): 143–46.

Olsson, Mats J., Johan N. Lundström, Bruce A. Kimball, Amy R. Gordon, Bianka Karshikoff, Nishteman Hosseini, Kimmo Sorjonen, Caroline Olgart Hoglund, Carmen Solares, Anne Soop, John Axelsson, and Mats Lekander. "The Scent of Disease: Human Body Odor Contains an Early Chemosensory Cue of Sickness." *Psychological Science* 25, no. 3 (2014): 817–23.

Parr, Rajat, and Jordan Mackay. *Secrets of the Sommeliers: How to Think and Drink Like the World's Top Wine Professionals*. Berkeley, CA: Ten Speed Press, 2010.

Pazart, Lionel, Alexandre Comte, Eloi Magnin, Jean-Louis Millot, and Thierry Moulin. "An fMRI Study on the Influence of Sommeliers' Expertise on the Integration of Flavor." *Frontiers in Behavioral Neuroscience* 8 (October 16, 2014): 358.

Peynaud, Emile. *The Taste of Wine: The Art and Science of Wine Appreciation*. Translated by Michael Schuster. San Francisco: Wine Appreciation Guild, 1987.

Plassmann, Hilke, John O'Doherty, Baba Shiv, and Antonio Rangel. "Marketing Actions Can Modulate Neural Representations of Experienced Pleasantness." *Proceedings of the National Academy of Sciences* 105, no. 3 (January 22, 2008): 1050–54.

Porter, Jess, Brent Craven, Rehan M. Khan, Shao-Ju Chang, Irene Kang, Benjamin Judkewitz, Jason Volpe, Gary Settles, and Noam Sobel. "Mechanisms of Scent-Tracking in Humans." *Nature Neuroscience* 10, no. 1 (January 1, 2007): 27–29.

Pozzi, Samuel. *Paul Broca: Biographie—Bibliographie*. Paris: G. Masson, 1880.

Quandt, Richard E. "On Wine Bullshit: Some New Software?" *Journal of Wine Economics* 2, no. 2 (Fall 2007): 129–35.

Ranhofer, Charles. *The Epicurean: A Complete Treatise of Analytical and Practical Studies on the Culinary Art*. New York: R. Ranhofer, 1916.

Robinson, Jancis. *How to Taste: A Guide to Enjoying Wine*. New York: Simon & Schuster, 2008.

———, ed. *The Oxford Companion to Wine*. Third ed. New York: Oxford University Press, 2006.

Rosenblum, Lawrence D. *See What I'm Saying: The Extraordinary Powers of Our Five Senses*. New York: W. W. Norton, 2010.

Royet, Jean-Pierre, Jane Plailly, Anne-Lise Saive, Alexandra Veyrac, and Chantal Delon-Martin. "The Impact of Expertise in Olfaction." *Frontiers in Psychology* 4, no. 928 (December 13, 2013): 1–11.

Shepherd, Gordon M. *Neurogastronomy: How the Brain Creates Flavor and Why It Matters*. New York: Columbia University Press, 2012.

———. "The Human Sense of Smell: Are We Better Than We Think?" *PLoS Biology* 2, no. 5 (May 2004): 572–75.

Shesgreen, Sean. "Wet Dogs and Gushing Oranges: Winespeak for a New Millennium." *The Chronicle of Higher Education*, March 7, 2003. http://chronicle.com/article/Wet-DogsGushing-Oranges-/20985.

Smith, Barry C., ed. *Questions of Taste: The Philosophy of Wine*. Oxford, UK: Oxford University Press, 2007.

Spang, Rebecca L. *The Invention of the Restaurant: Paris and Modern Gastronomic Culture*. Cambridge, MA: Harvard University Press, 2000.

Spence, Charles, and Betina Piqueras-Fiszman. *The Perfect Meal: The Multisensory Science of Food and Dining*. Oxford, UK: Wiley-Blackwell, 2014.

Stuckey, Barb. *Taste What You're Missing: The Passionate Eater's Guide to Why Good Food Tastes Good*. New York: Free Press, 2012.

Suzuki, Daisetz T. *Zen and Japanese Culture*. Princeton, NJ: Princeton University Press, 2010.

Weil, Roman L. "Debunking Critics' Wine Words: Can Amateurs Distinguish the Smell of Asphalt from the Taste of Cherries?" *Journal of Wine Economics* 2, no. 2 (2007): 136–44.

INDEX